THE RELIEF OF KUMASI

THE LAST CONVOY OF THE CAMPAIGN ENTERING KUMASI

THE
RELIEF OF KUMASI

BY

CAPT. HAROLD C. J. BISS

WEST AFRICAN FRONTIER FORCE

WITH SIXTEEN ILLUSTRATIONS AND PLANS AND A MAP

METHUEN & CO.
36 ESSEX STREET W.C.
LONDON
1901

"FADE FAR AWAY, DISSOLVE, AND QUITE FORGET

.   .   .   .   .   .

THE WEARINESS, THE FEVER, AND THE FRET

.   .   .   .   .

WHERE YOUTH GROWS PALE, AND SPECTRE-THIN, AND DIES;

.   .   .   .   .   .

WHERE BEAUTY CANNOT KEEP HER LUSTROUS EYES."

KEATS.

PREFACE

THE closing year of the nineteenth century, one of the most eventful in British history, has afforded much to the chronicler. The all-absorbing war in South Africa, the Ashanti rising, and then the campaign in China, have combined to make an unprecedented call upon the attention of the public. Presumably from the difficulty of obtaining suitable representatives, not one of the newspapers had a professional war correspondent in the expedition of which the following pages furnish an account. For this reason, there seemed to be a danger lest this chapter in Her Majesty's long reign[1] should be inadequately recorded in proportion to its historical importance; and the author has therefore endeavoured to tell, as an eye-witness for the most part, the story of what has happened. The book has necessarily been written from a personal point of view; consequently, should there appear to be too much egotistic detail, he trusts it will be charitably remembered that he has written according to the impressions made upon his own mind, and also that this is his first attempt in literature. No man can write with complete accuracy about that in

[1] The reader will kindly understand that this book was completed before Her late Majesty's lamented death.

which he did not participate, nor convey the same kind
of interest to the reader. The number of the con-
temporary operations which have taken place in the
suppression of this rebellion, has made it impossible
for any single individual to take part in them all, even
had he served from the beginning to the end, and if
more space has been devoted to what the author
actually saw, that is due to the fact that the book is
primarily a record of personal impressions.

No attempt at criticism has been made: this would
have been not only an unbecoming liberty, but even an
impossibility, without a fuller knowledge of all that was
occurring than was then available. Doubtless, a Blue-book
upon this subject will, in due course, be issued for the
information of all who take an interest in West African
affairs. Accordingly, political and commercial details
have only been superficially touched upon, and that
only when absolutely necessary ; the writer's object
having been mainly to furnish a diary of occurrences.
From unavoidable causes, this book has had to be
written at great speed, and nobody is more conscious
than its author that it bears the marks of haste, though
he trusts exactitude has been secured in all points. On
this account, he craves the leniency of the reader, and
begs that it may not be forgotten that the story presented is one of plain fact, without any colouring of
romance. Until a standard history of this war be
written by some more competent hand, he hopes that
his little volume may be of use and interest in furnish-
ing a less worthy but not less reliable narrative.

He gladly acknowledges, with sincere gratitude, the
help afforded him by many friends, who, having been
present at other points in the field of operations, were
able to give him information regarding many things

which might otherwise have escaped him. As far as possible he has taken advantage of all published printed matter so as to secure correctness in details.

It is due to the kind permission of the Intelligence Department of the War Office that he is able to publish a copy of their map, which is the best obtainable. As, however, much of it has been compiled from the necessarily rapid work of officers moving about this little known country, it must be borne in mind that complete accuracy cannot be expected : for example, the alternative road from Fumsu to Bekwai *viâ* Obuasi does not appear. He is also indebted to the courtesy of Baron de Reuter for news derived from the reports of his Agency, and to the Editor of the *Standard* for permission to extract facts from that paper's Ashanti correspondence.

H. C. J. B.

WELLINGTON CLUB, LONDON, S.W.
January, 1901

CONTENTS

xi

CONTENTS

LIST OF ILLUSTRATIONS

LIST OF ILLUSTRATIONS

LIST OF ABBREVIATIONS

W.A.F.F.	West African Frontier Force.
W.A.R.	West Africa Regiment.
C.A.R.	Central Africa Regiment.
S.L.F.P.	Sierra Leone Frontier Police.
W.I.R.	West India Regiment.
I.S.C.	Indian Staff Corps.
R.A.	Royal Artillery.
R.E.	Royal Engineers.
A.S.C.	Army Service Corps.
R.A.M.C.	Royal Army Medical Corps.
75 m/m	75-millimètre gun.
pr.	Pounder.
C.O.	Commanding Officer.
C.R.A.	Commandant Royal Artillery.
P.M.O.	Principal Medical Officer.
C.T.O.	Chief Transport Officer.
N.C.O.	Non-commissioned Officer.
A.D.C.	Aide-de-camp.
Bn.	Battalion.
H.E.	His Excellency.
H.B.M.	Her Britannic Majesty's.
D.S.O.	Companion of the Distinguished Service Order.

THE RELIEF OF KUMASI

INTRODUCTION

PRELIMINARY CONSIDERATIONS

TO save people unnecessary trouble is a sound maxim to follow, and specially advisable on such an occasion as this. Life is nowadays too short to learn all one could wish : consequently, I may be forgiven, by those who know West Africa, if I state a few of the geographical and historical facts which, I venture to think, are necessary to enable the reader to intelligently follow the course of events in this Ashanti War of 1900. At the same time, I hope these particulars will help to interest him the more in the narrative of what occurred, as given in the subsequent chapters.

The West African colonies, with which we are now concerned, extend from French Senegambia down to the German Cameroons. The first one touched at, on the outward-bound voyage, is Sierra Leone, between which and the Gold Coast are Liberia and the French Ivory Coast. Liberia is the republic which was formed by the freed slaves from the United States, and the Yankee accent is very noticeable there to-day.

After leaving the Gold Coast, German Togoland and

French Dahomey have to be passed before sighting our next possession—Lagos. The course then is due east, and in the Gulf of Guinea. Southern Nigeria lies south-east of Lagos, no foreign possession dividing them. Finally Northern Nigeria (formerly known as the Niger Territories) extends from the northern boundaries of the Hinterlands of Lagos and Southern Nigeria (recently called the Niger Coast Protectorate) northwards and eastwards as far as Lake Chad, up to the southern frontier of the French Hinterland, and the north-western one of the German Cameroons, which all converge at this lake.

Each of these colonies of ours has its own Governor, staff of civilian officials, and troops, but they are none the less intimately connected with one another. In fact, I should never be surprised to hear in the future of their becoming united under one government. Northern Nigeria, for example, the most recent addition, is not at present self-supporting, and, therefore, Lagos and Southern Nigeria each contribute annually a large sum towards its expenses. Again, the troops, as has just been done in Ashanti, are moved from one colony to another as reinforcements, whenever emergency requires.

Sierra Leone is perhaps the most important colony of all this group, inasmuch as it is one of our first-class coaling stations. For this reason it has most troops. Freetown, the port and capital, is strongly fortified, and has a permanent garrison of one battalion of the W.I.R., together with some fortress batteries of artillery. There is also one more unit in this command, the W.A.R., which is immediately under the War Office, and has only recently come into being. The W.I.R., which has also some light field guns on its strength, has so long been part of our army that little need be said about it.

The men are West Indian negroes, the officers Europeans, and there is one British non-commissioned officer to each company. The regiment is armed and treated exactly like any line regiment.

The W.A.R., however, is somewhat different. There is the proportion, usual in African regiments, of British officers and non-commissioned officers, but its soldiers are recruited in the colony, and are chiefly Mendis and Temanis. They are little, agile men, and, being natives of the forest, are of the greatest use in such country; owing to this, they have rendered specially valuable service as scouts in this campaign, a kind of work the other troops were not very successful at, owing to their homes being in much less densely timbered lands. This regiment wears the red fez and blue uniform common to every West African force. This, however, will probably soon be altered to khaki, as was done in the case of the W.A.F.F. immediately prior to its going on service in this expedition, and the same change is likely to become universal along the coast. The men are armed with the ˙303 Martini-Metford carbine, and small swords; which latter are almost useless, for they are apt to trip up the men when moving, do not fix on to the rifle like a bayonet, and are too short to use as a sabre; which, after all, an infantryman does not want.

This ˙303 carbine, which is used by all our West African troops, is a most excellent little weapon for them, especially as the West African native is invariably weak in the arms. The wisdom of the authorities in this selection has been abundantly proved to any observant person, and one cannot be too thankful that the magazine rifle was not issued instead. In "bush" fighting the critical moment, when intensely rapid fire is required, does not seem to occur at all frequently and, when it does, the Maxims, which are liberally supplied to all West African infantry, would do ample execution.   On the other hand, the risk of men wasting their ammunition is greatly reduced.   Good fire discipline has always been regarded as the highest test of efficiency, but when one's company, usually about one hundred and fifty men in single file, is firing, it is practically impossible to control their expenditure in the effective way one would like.   When it is remembered that every box of ammunition has often to be carried hundreds of miles, that eight hundred rounds of small-arm cartridges is the maximum weight one carrier can manage for any length of time, one realises the enormous difficulty of its transport, and the care which ought to be taken regarding the way in which it is used.   To run out of ammunition might mean annihilation in impenetrable forests, and retirement would always be of the extremest difficulty and danger.   Nothing seems to please the black man more than to let off firearms.   No doubt, he imagines the noise of the explosion has a great moral effect, and the subject of ammunition supply and porterage is a detail which does not readily appeal to the inconsequent savage brain.

The Gold Coast has only its Constabulary (as it is at present miscalled), consisting of a battalion and a few 7-pr. guns.   These men speak Hausa, and are, therefore, commonly supposed to have been recruited from that race.   However, a glance at the map shows one that distance alone would prohibit such a thing, although, no doubt, there are Hausas amongst them.   The uniform and armament of these soldiers are really the same as those of the W.A.R., but they carry, as do all the troops in these colonies with the before-mentioned exception, the short bayonet instead of the cutlass-like sword.

Lagos, the best developed colony of all, has, to all intents and purposes, the same garrison as the Gold Coast, though rather less numerous; it is also similarly equipped and clad. The rank and file are a mixture of Hausas and Yorubas, the latter being the inhabitants of the Hinterland of this colony, but it is known as the Lagos Hausa Force.

The Southern Nigerian Regiment, again, resembles the Lagos force in all respects, and its men are of the same two races. During this year it has been called the 3rd Bn. W.A.F.F.

Northern Nigeria is somewhat differently situated to the other colonies as to its troops, which are more numerous, better armed, and more liberally supplied with British officers and non-commissioned officers than any except those of Sierra Leone. This force was raised in 1897 by Brigadier-General Sir Frederick Lugard, K.C.M.G., C.B., D.S.O., and Colonel Sir James Willcocks, K.C.M.G., D.S.O., with two objects. Firstly, because owing to the disputes with the French as to our territorial boundaries, which were then most vaguely fixed, it was necessary to have a considerable number of soldiers in that portion of our Empire, which had up to that time been but weakly held in military occupation by the Constabulary of the Royal Niger Company; secondly, because this enormous tract of new country would shortly have to be opened up for governmental and trade purposes, which necessitated a very considerable increase in our West African fencibles. The position at that time was one of grave emergency, consequently, the raising of these two battalions and three batteries, together with some Engineers and a Medical Department, was carried out with great expedition. The authorities at home were most liberal in their grants of every kind, and the armament was of the best. The uniform was originally blue. The infantry, each battalion with eight companies one hundred and fifty strong, was armed with the Martini-Metford carbine, and each company was supplied with a Vickers-Maxim ·303 gun. The batteries had the powerful 75-m/m guns, which throw a 12-lb. shell, and have done good service in the recent war. The artillery had also 7-pounders (which have again proved themselves insufficient for the work demanded of them), along with some rockets and Maxims. It must be remembered that all these guns are portable, the two heavy kinds being mounted on wheeled carriages, whilst the Maxims, for convenience in this country, are adjusted to tripod stands. Each battalion had its band—indeed the way in which the native soldiers played was quite wonderful. The tunes and bugle-calls were whistled to them by the European band-master, and they picked them up with surprising rapidity. The men were all Hausas and Yorubas with the exception of one company of Nupés, which was raised as an experiment, and did excellent work in the war. Northern Nigeria is peculiarly fortunate in having these fine races to recruit from, inasmuch as they are practically all natives of the colony. The vast stretch of country to the east and north-east is Hausa-land; the Nupé territory extends along the immediate left bank of the Middle Niger, and, as has been stated, the Yorubas inhabit the Lagos Hinterland, which adjoins this Protectorate on the south-west. These soldiers were able to be outfitted, immediately prior to their departure for Ashanti, with new uniforms of khaki, in place of their former blue ones, which in many cases bore the marks of hard wear and overtime almost to the verge of indecency. Owing to their new costume, the common

name given to them at first by the other soldiers in the
expedition was "The Khaki Soldiers"; but none the
less, the Northern Nigerian contingent looked not only
workmanlike, but very smart when they were inspected
prior to their going to the front. But the part of the
soldier's kit which suffers the most in this damp climate
of West Africa is the leather pouches and braces;
and these were invariably issued, in the first instance,
more than half worn out. One must admit one would
like to see this portion of the equipment replaced by a
bandolier cartridge-belt, which has three great advantages over the old pattern : firstly, the weight is removed
from the waist to the shoulders—no inconsiderable item
when each round of ammunition weighs an ounce;
secondly, cartridges would no longer be able to drop out
of pouches; and thirdly, the counting of a soldier's
number of rounds would be greatly facilitated.

The only other troops employed in this way, and the
only ones which do not come from the west, but from
the east coast was a weak battalion of the C.A.R., with
a small detachment of Sikhs, who were as new to the
dense bush as the majority of the Ashanti Field Force.
The principal races from which these soldiers are
recruited are the Yaos, Atongas, and Angonis, and excellent fighting men they make. The officers are British,
and this force is fortunate in having a large number of
its N.C.O.'s Sikhs. These grand soldiers of the Indian
Army and their intrepid bravery are too well known to
require further description. They had, of course, their
own uniforms and turbans, whilst the men of the
regiment also wore khaki and a rather elongated black
fez, which looked very well. They were armed with the
Martini rifle, with its well-remembered long bayonet.
They are small, wiry men, and formed a most noticeable

contrast to their gigantic N.C.O.'s. They have a peculiar habit, when starting, of chanting a savage pæan of their own, which sounds like a sort of question and answer appeal in music, the former part being solo, and the latter a general chorus.

Finally, a detachment of West India gunners, with their 7-pounders, completed the list of units which constituted the Ashanti Field Force.

So it came to pass that all the troops employed were young regiments, mostly composed of recruits, few of the men having seen any previous war service ; and this was the material our Commandant had to work with. Even their own officers were surprised at the splendid service the men have rendered ; they cannot be given more credit than their pluck and soldierly qualities merit. This is the first time in British history that a force composed entirely of native troops has ever successfully undertaken such a large task. My own part of the force, from Northern Nigeria, which was raised little more than two years ago, and therefore the newest unit of all, and which Colonel Sir James Willcocks himself previously commanded, was certainly never surpassed by any of the others. Owing to this circumstance, and to the peculiar interest one took in the men, I feel compelled to record my own satisfaction, which, no doubt, will be considered pardonable. It is also a comforting reflection that Her Majesty's West African troops have proved themselves practically able to cope, unaided, with all future native troubles on that coast. Owing to this fact, this campaign is probably the cheapest on record, despite the enormous cost of transport when only human carriage is available ; nor could a larger expenditure of money have enabled the work to be more satisfactorily finished.

It is known that when Colonel Sir James Willcocks arrived in the Gold Coast and thoroughly grasped the situation, the seriousness of which could not have been previously appreciated, he asked for troops from India, which were, one understood, to have been sent later on, had not the subsequent outbreak of hostilities in China made it impossible. Then a Soudanese regiment was hoped for, but it also never came, and a similar disappointment followed the offer of their services from the Jamaica Militia. British soldiers were at this time out of the question on account of the war in South Africa.

There is an unsupported rumour that all the West African forces will in time be amalgamated into one large body, like the Indian Staff Corps, and some more advanced conjectures even go so far as to hint at an African native army.

Even without reference to the political situation of the British nation, and the hostilities in South Africa and China, the Ashanti rising was most inopportune in so far as the West African section of our Empire was concerned at that time, for not one of these colonies could then with due caution be denuded of its troops, which are, naturally, not more numerous than circumstances require. In barbarous lands like these, the forces are usually split up into detachments, which garrison districts and preserve order. These small units are often separated by considerable distances. For this reason alone, it is far from easy to collect a regiment for service anywhere, and, under the most auspicious conditions, it must always take much time, progress being probably about a dozen miles a day as an all-round estimate. It would probably be as expeditious to entrain a concentrated unit at Aldershot for the sea, and ship them out to the seat of war, as to get a similar force of native West African soldiers from their own colony to another one on that coast.

Sierra Leone, not to speak of its being a most important coaling station, wanted its troops, because further inland, in the Gambia district, matters were unsettled, and have now gone so far as to necessitate punitive operations.

The Gold Coast force was quite unable by itself to wage war with such a powerful nation ; it was also widely dispersed both in the part of the colony south of Ashanti and the northern territories beyond it.

Lagos, the most peaceful of any, was not quite happy at the attitude displayed by the Abbeokuta people.

Southern Nigeria was known to be only waiting for the rains to cease before commencing hostilities with the inhabitants of the Cross River District, who had absolutely put a stop to trade, and refused all intercourse with the white men.

In Northern Nigeria it was even more inconvenient, because active measures were actually in progress, and the despatch of its complement of soldiers to the Ashanti Field Force will probably retard the development of this colony in a more marked degree than will be the case in any of the others. It was only on January 1, 1900, that this colony was formed definitely into a Protectorate, under Brigadier-General Sir Frederick Lugard as its first High Commissioner. He is too well known as an African explorer, pioneer of our Empire, sportsman and author, to require any introduction, but one would like to bring to remembrance here, that it was largely due to him, backed by Lord Salisbury's foresight and diplomacy, that we now, instead of the French, possess so much of the hinterland of Western Equatorial Africa. His adventurous and lonely journey, some years ago, through what now constitutes the south-western portion of his administration, was the cause of our now owning the large province known as Borgu. The French had actually gone to the extent of subduing its warlike inhabitants, but the prior treaties made by Sir Frederick Lugard with the native chiefs decided matters in our favour when disputes actually arose. Until the advent, in December, 1899, of the newly appointed High Commissioner, with the nucleus of his civil staff, the country had been held by the military; the control of affairs on the spot, at a very anxious time, from an international point of view, and the training of the recently organised force, being vested in the hands of Colonel Sir James Willcocks, to whose soldierly qualities, ability as an organiser, and tact, the success of both is due. A man of action, such as Sir Frederick Lugard, does not let the grass grow under his feet very long, though he had indeed a gigantic task before him, with between three and four hundred thousand square miles of scarcely known country to break in and develop. The charter, originally granted to the Niger Company, had hampered the action of the Imperial officers very much, and, until all legislative powers were taken from it at the commencement of last year, the administration of this barely explored region was practically impossible. Missionary enterprise and trade always find work for the soldier, so the early spring brought severe fighting up the river Benue. At the same time, owing to its unhealthiness, and the alarming death-rate amongst the Europeans, it was decided to abandon Jebba, at first selected as the capital. The two bases in this colony

had been Lokoja and Jebba : the former was situated at
the confluence of the Benue and the Niger, the spot
where the latter river turns westward to the sea; the
latter, an island, was about three hundred miles further
up the Niger, and north of Lokoja. Arrangements
were in consequence made for surveying parties to
penetrate into this untraversed tract of territory on the
left bank of the Niger, and select a site for a new headquarters. Each party had necessarily to be escorted by
a strong column of troops ; one was to go from Jebba in
the charge of Major (local Lieutenant-Colonel) Morland,
who commanded the first battalion, and one from Lokoja,
under the orders of Major (local Lieutenant-Colonel)
Lowry-Cole, to whom had been entrusted the second
battalion. These two forces were to work their way
inland from the river, and concentrate in the neighbourhood of Zaria, a large and powerful Hausa city.
As was rather anticipated, the kindly civilising influence
of the white man was not acceptable ; indeed, opposition
and fighting were met with. It was then that Colonel
Willcocks set out from Jebba to take command of these
amalgamated units ; however, just before he reached his
destination, a telegram offering him the command of the
Ashanti campaign overtook him, and altered his plans.

Before proceeding from these introductory remarks
to the commencement of the actual history of the
campaign, it seems imperative to add a few words about
the Gold Coast Colony and Ashanti, so as to enable the
reader to start with a comprehensive view of the general
position of affairs.

The Gold Coast has been known to the European for
centuries, and is probably one of our richest possessions
in West Africa ; this naturally explains our preference
for having full control over it and declining to allow the

Ashanti to have any right of veto, even where his own country is concerned. It is only since the early part of the nineteenth century that we have attempted to administer this possession of the Crown, and as recently as the sixties it was seriously discussed whether we should not withdraw from these localities altogether. But there is undoubtedly " money in it." A glance at the statistics show, as a satisfactory *quid pro quo*, that the imports of the Gold Coast have been doubled during the last few years. This colony extends in reality only up to the river Prah, seventy miles inland from the coast, but we have lately taken over, when Germany, France, and Britain divided up this part of the map amongst themselves, a large and valuable tract of the hinterland, now called the "Northern Territories Gold Coast." The natural outlet for all the produce from this region was straight through Ashanti down to Cape Coast, but the Ashantis did not agree with us in regarding their country as a short cut for our merchandise, and interfered so much with the transit of commerce that much trade was diverted through the Protectorates of our European neighbours. Again, the Ashanti has a short memory, an easy conscience, and the usual low code of honour common to the savage. The war indemnity of twenty-seven years' standing still remained unpaid, human sacrifices and slave-raiding were continued, and the beautiful road they had promised to make to facilitate traffic through their country had not even been started. Consequently, when they actually went to the length of rebellion, nothing remained to us but to give them a sharp lesson, with the endeavour to make it of such a kind as to be remembered. It seems a fairly common, though none the less erroneous, belief that Ashanti was British territory. Such was not really the case : although we nominally annexed the country in 1896 we have only exercised a suzerainty over it. The fact must not be lost sight of that the Ashantis, until now, have never been a conquered race. They are probably the most warlike tribe in Africa, and certainly have been the terror of all the others for miles around them. This influence is very noticeable, and explains why others joined them in this war. In past days they overran all the countries around their own, right down to the sea coast, and even the white merchant had a wholesome dread of them. After the Ashanti invasion in 1821, the Governor of the Gold Coast, Sir Charles M'Carthy, organised a small expedition against them, but was entirely defeated. He himself was killed, and his skull is now supposed to be in use amongst the enemy as a drinking-bowl. In 1863 another force met with total failure. The strong forts on the sea-board bear silent witness to the difficulties and pertinacity of the early traders, who, although unable to do little exploration, made much money by barter with the natives. It was in 1873 that Sir Garnet Wolseley, for the first time, formed an adequately powerful column, and drove the Ashantis completely out of the colony, penetrating to their capital, which he burnt. Even at that time the country north of the river Prah was, unfortunately, never fully traversed by troops and the rebellion everywhere stamped out, as has now been done. Lord Wolseley's fortifications for the defence of Cape Coast can still be seen, but few of the Ashantis, with whom we have conversed, remember this lesson at all clearly. The tribe abandoned, indeed, their raids across the Prah, but continued the old practices, so seriously retarding development, civilisation, and business, that in 1895 Sir Francis Scott got together and took up a fourth expedition. For some reason or another, probably owing to the presence of the white troops, this warlike nation offered no resistance, and permitted their king Prempeh to be removed; they even accepted, without reluctance, a permanent British Resident in their capital, who was to supervise the native legislation; and it was chiefly on account of the installation and appointment of this new official that the present fort was built in Kumasi. But one Resident could never cope with the needs of such a large district; it must be borne in mind that such a person requires to be more than an ambassador at a civilised court. A race like this one must be moulded into shape by the effective military occupation of their country, be it but temporary. There must be armed force behind the orders before the barbarian can be expected to obey orders and respect the white man's position. There is now every reason to feel positive that after Sir Francis Scott's column was disbanded the Ashantis again longed for their independence, and the restoration of their king; but the fact that every available soldier we had was compelled to take part in the Transvaal War was the chief reason why this particular time was selected by them. Their enormous stores of arms and ammunition testify to the rising having been long premeditated, and it is an undeniable fact that the educated Ashantis kept their less enlightened fellow-countrymen informed of our political situation. These traitors were mostly traders at Cape Coast, Accra, and other places on the sea coast, and some of them have even been to London; they certainly never expected that we should be able to collect a sufficient force to suppress this outbreak. The Ashanti openly avowed his contempt for the black soldier, and his opinion of his own superiority to him as a fighting man. An opportunity was offered to them when the Governor, Sir Frederic Hodgson, K.C.M.G., went to Kumasi in April, 1900, on his first tour of inspection, with only a nominal escort; and a cause for revolt appeared when they were reminded that the white man still remembered they had never fulfilled their bargain of 1873, and insisted that its stipulations must be completed. Now, however, the Ashanti knows that the European, with only his black soldiers, can not only beat him at his own game and in his own country, but can mete out a commensurately severe punishment, and he will think a much longer time before again offering armed resistance. In fact, with the removal, root and branch, of the fetish-consecrated dynasty, the execution of some of the leading and most powerful chieftains, and the effective garrisoning of the country by troops, there ought to be little cause for apprehension in the future. One must conquer the savage before one can be kind to him, or introduce the gentler methods of civilisation and religion.

CHAPTER I

SCORED OFF

THE news of the disturbances in Ashanti reached the Frontier Force in Northern Nigeria before we or the public had realised that anything very serious was about to take place. That the unexpected always happens seems to be particularly the case in West Africa, owing largely to the difficulty of transmitting news. Certainly, our two bases were then connected by wire with the coast, but most of us were away from them, often at such distances that weeks were required before communications could reach their destinations.

At dawn on April 22nd a letter was brought to me by an express native runner, at the post where I then was, five days' march north of Jebba. The prolonged enervation induced by a pestilential climate of alternating misty damp and scorching sun, is bound to have its influence upon the temperament of a European. It was, therefore, without the slightest feeling of excitement that I opened the envelope, marked "very urgent" underscored deeply in red ink, and read that the Secretary of State for the Colonies had cabled for as large a force as possible from the W.A.F.F. to proceed with the utmost expedition from Northern

Nigeria to the Gold Coast, on account of trouble with the natives. A general move of almost all the troops was ordered in consequence by the Commandant, and it became necessary to evacuate temporarily some important posts.

Personally, I was on the eve of completing my tour of service in West Africa, twelve months' continuous residence in these fever-stricken parts having been found to be the longest limit advisable for a white man. Twelve months' service, often on lonely duty with one's company or detachment of native soldiers, many days' march from any other white comrade ; twelve months' service in a sickly climate, when you can count the days on which you feel fit on the fingers of one hand ; twelve months' service of dull routine, whilst your native land is waging the greatest war of the last half century—twelve months' service under such conditions gives one an insatiable longing for release, so as to be off to fresh fields of labour, even though but for a time. It was, therefore, no great surprise to me to learn also that I was to proceed from Boussa in East Borgu, where I was in command at the time, to the base, as soon as my relief arrived. Little realising what important service was before me, I rashly concluded that I should be paid off and sent home. I even calculated I could just catch the homeward-bound mail steamer which left our port, Forçados, at the mouth of the river, on May the 19th. Travelling is always tedious in these parts, particularly at this time of year when there is so little water in the river that no steam craft can be utilised, and the many hundreds of miles to the sea have to be traversed in open native canoes. These are dug out solid tree trunks, and are slow, incommodious, uncomfortable, leaky things at best. I could see no

immediate chance of any active service where I was; it
was stiflingly hot—at times nearly 120° Fahr. in my hut
(which was the official quarter); and a short time previously I had lost all my kit in a fire; so it was not
unnatural, under the circumstances, that my orders to
be once more on the move, and this time in the right
direction, brought a pleasurable feeling of relief. There
was yet time to get out to the South African War, and
I had already made all possible arrangements to give
up my six months' leave and go there as soon as
possible after my arrival home: and I was hopeful of
success. It never entered my head, at that time, that
the Ashanti news was so momentous, and I quite
thought that matters there would very shortly be put
straight. In fact, I was much more anxious to go
southwards than to prolong my stay in West Africa,
that temple of health, which had already changed my
life into an existence, and my muscle into pulp. The
immediate changes, now ordered, did rather surprise
me, I admit, but, as I was leaving, I concluded I would
meditate upon them in detail on the deck of the mail
steamer.

In anticipation of my early departure, I bade farewell
to the king, presented him with my ostriches and
similar property which I could not very well take home,
made arrangements with him for a canoe to take me
down to Jebba, and sent on my pony by land, with the
horse-boy, to await my arrival. On the 25th, Frontier
Force orders arrived, from which I learned that the
W.A.F.F., alone, was supplying four hundred and fifty
infantry with some guns, all with white officers, N.C.O.'s,
and medical officers. "E" Company (Nupé), 1st Bn.
W.A.F.F., with Captains Hall and Wilson, was starting
forthwith, picking up at Illorin "D" Company, under

Captain Beamish, and marching to Lagos, *en route* for
Cape Coast. Lieutenant O'Malley's company, from the
2nd Battalion, was going from Lokoja, and Lieutenant
Edwards, R.A., with the guns.

When emergency requires, one can work wonderfully
quickly. My relief arrived about ten a.m. I gave him
breakfast, and at once took him away to the important
duties of handing over all the station, district, troops,
magazine, treasure, and such like, and by nightfall all
was finished. My scanty packing was soon completed,
and by sunrise next morning I embarked in my canoe,
with a circular grass roof in the centre of it to keep off
the sun, and with a double relay of paddlers. In this
delightful drain-pipe I stewed until the evening of the
28th, when I reached headquarters. The journey
through the rapids had been quite exciting; they
were luckily navigated without any loss, and with only
a few partial swampings. Then I received the cheering
information that the High Commissioner had just gone
away to meet the Governor of Lagos, which, of course,
necessitated my remaining inertly where I was until
his return. Jebba, up till now the capital, is, I ought
to explain, an island, on the rocky summit of which is
a standing camp, where the headquarters of the 1st
Battalion are situated. Below lies a native village and
swamp; the right bank ascends some hundreds of feet,
on the top of which live the High Commissioner and
the civil staff; the left bank is flat, and contains the
artillery camp, bordering on another large swamp which
has had the most deadly effect upon the European
garrison. The river at this point passes through a deep
gully, which often induces terrible wind-storms; the
rocky nature of the ground also makes this spot
intensely hot. In fact, it has never been popular; its

only redeeming point is the beautiful view down-stream;
but beauty in Africa is usually associated with some
danger to health.

It was just dark when I disembarked. My small stock
of baggage was left with my orderly and "boys" for
removal to the first vacant officer's quarter they could
find, whilst I hurried up to the mess hut. Here I found
some limp friends, refreshing exhausted nature with
pre-prandial drinks; it gave me quite an anticipatory
feeling of home-coming. I still remember that bottle
of lager beer they offered me. It was delicious. I had
not seen such a luxury for months! A tropical thirst,
when you can quench it, is in a sense delightful, but all
that sultry day I had only had Niger water, with a little
whisky in it to disguise its nauseous taste. Dinner later
on, with really clean knives and forks, a white table-
cloth, and decently cooked food, was no common
experience at that time. It was also nice to be off
the water, and less tormented by sand-flies and mos-
quitos. There was not much Ashanti news to be
learned, but I heard for the first time that Major
Wilkinson, the second in command of our 2nd Battalion, had been offered and accepted the appointment
of Inspector-General—in other words, the command—
of the Gold Coast Forces.

Unalloyed good fortune is rare, and I was horrified
to hear the unofficial rumour that officers might be
required to stay on over their time, because their reliefs
did not appear to be forthcoming from home in a supply
that was in any way sufficient. Events in this colony,
as we know, demanded more, and not less, than the
normal complement. This information proved to be
only too correct a few days later, and the feelings of
those immediately concerned may be easier imagined

than described.   Things certainly were at a low ebb
in Jebba ; there were practically no guns left behind,
and hardly more infantry than what had once constituted the garrison of an important outpost.   It seemed
scarcely credible that there could be so few officers.
Colonel Willcocks was on the eve of his departure to
take command of the combined columns operating in
the Zaria district ; there was only one officer in the
Brigade Office ; Major O'Neal, C.R.A., was the only
artillery officer.   The P.M.O., Dr. McDowell, his year
being completed, was about to return to England.
Lieutenant Walbach, who was our Quartermaster, had
had to be transferred to the Transport Department, and
Captain Wright, the only other infantry officer besides
myself, was performing the duties of C.O., Adjutant, and
Quartermaster, in addition to looking after the mess.
Captain Molesworth was in charge of the Engineers,
and was to leave in a few days with the Commandant.
Mr. Harrison, the Treasurer, had only one white assistant
to help him.   These then composed the garrison, and
the favourite topic of conversation was overwork.

CHAPTER II

CONFINEMENT TO BARRACKS

THE next day I officially reported myself, and found out that nobody could proceed home without the High Commissioner's personal sanction; so there was nothing to be done but to join in the numerous routine duties of the station, resignedly "marking time" until one's fate should be decided. The command of F Company, 1st Bn. W.A.F.F., was then given to me; and it was with these Hausas that I subsequently went through the campaign. On May 2nd, the Commandant, together with Major (local Lieutenant-Colonel) Kemball, R.A., the second in command to Colonel Willcocks, left us for Zaria, and Major O'Neal assumed military command at headquarters. The worst of living on a small island is the difficulty of getting off it when neither bridge nor ferry exists. The interval between sundown and dark is so short that a journey to the mainland is scarcely worth one's while, all the more so as there is but little to shoot in the immediate vicinity. The exhaustion due to the heat of the day is also conducive to physical idleness, with the net result that the average individual seeks his daily recreation at the cost of the least possible exertion. Athletic diversions were limited; games of tennis or short rides were the most common ; any attempt at boating was more or less of a failure, owing to the extremely strong current in the river Niger ; the fishing really was not good enough, and anything one caught was uneatable.   Life, therefore, was dull.

It was nearly a year since I had seen a white woman, so once during this period of captivity I was glad to pay a call on the European Sister at the hospital.   Tea-fighting is not most soldiers' strong point, but it really was refreshing again to see a fully dressed woman with a white face—out here, unfortunately, too often bleached by the climate.   The female form divine may be, poetically, a beautiful thing, and the study of the nude useful to an artist, but I think one gets very much bored with it in savage Africa, and begins to develop a leaning towards even the conventionalities of civilisation.   A life of frequent isolation in a virgin country. such as this, curiously affects men at times, and its influence, other than physical, is perhaps not wholly injurious.   Lying sometimes at the close of the day in a canvas deck-chair, surrendered to *dolce far niente*, disinclined for more exertion than the smoking of one of those horrible American cigarettes, which were all one could get in West Africa, one's thoughts would occasionally wander back to the old country.   Men of the pioneer type must not be sentimentalists, but all have their softer feelings, and miss, ever and anon, the refining influences from which they live in banishment.   In moments such as these and under such conditions, the sweet, lingering memories of home revive, the scent of fresh-mown hay, the quiet domestic landscape pictured from some favourite garden nook, and the music of the birds one used to hear, insensibly recur.   The gay night in town, the whirling waltz, the crowded play, the rattling

hansom are forgotten. The humble chop and glass of
beer at the wayside inn are remembered even in preference to the Parisian *déjeuner* and champagne at the
crowded restaurant, when one tackles in this wilderness,
sans appétit, one's tinned meat, biscuit, and filtered water.

On the 3rd of May, Captain Melliss, I.S.C., under
whom I immediately served during the majority of my
time in West Africa, reinforced us. To my satisfaction,
H.E. the High Commissioner also returned, and the
following day he was officially visited by all fresh
arrivals, in due course. Shortly after this we were
instructed to stay on where we were, as no officer's
services could then be spared. One or two were offered
appointments, carrying a little more pay, to comfort
them. But I got no such sop. After this I spent many
disconsolate odd half-hours in my match-boarded,
galvanised-iron-roofed dog-kennel, otherwise called my
quarter. It was wretchedly small and horribly hot.
Why people send such structures to the tropics I could
not understand; they would have been miserable accommodation enough even in a colony with a temperate
climate, where one could have lived much out of doors.
I temporarily became a shocking heretic, whilst I
grumbled to myself over this state of things in the
solitude and seclusion of my official pigeon-hole. I
constantly asked myself what we could possibly want
with so many colonies; assuredly they could only be
useful as places to which to send our surplus population.
I experienced quite a feeling of consolation when I
remembered that this particular one was too unhealthy
to colonise in this way. Had not the Spaniards already
tried it, and failed, in Fernando Po? From what I had
personally seen, I was convinced that only the discovery
of alluvial gold in large nuggets could make the sterile,

rocky province of Borgu pay its way. Yes, patriotism was distorted—it was commercialism. Imperialism was the most hopeless nonsense that had ever emanated from the politician's intellect ; I, for one, certainly had no ambition to help to paint the map of the world pink. In short, I became a confirmed Little Englander during these days at Jebba and did not change my views until I left. It was useless to expect sympathy from others whose time out here was not yet completed ; they either laughed at one's grievance, or said it was quite fair no one should go unless replaced ; they, anyhow, did not wish for any more work.

Thus the days dragged on ; they were, none the less, busy ones, fully occupied with the same sort of comparative trivialities which can be met with under pleasanter conditions at Aldershot or at any military centre. Soldiers in any part of the Empire must be trained, fed, paid, and tried by court-martial. Their wives quarrel ; they never keep their lines and the Government property entrusted to their care quite as clean as one could wish ; but, excepting obvious racial and climatic differences, our camp and men here would compare favourably with any similar place at home. On the 6th, Dr. Tichborne, who had just been serving with the Anglo-French Boundary Commission, arrived. On the 7th, very serious information reached us about Ashanti, namely that Kumasi was besieged by the rebels in such force that a column from outside must be formed to relieve it. The only good point of the matter, as far as we were concerned, was that our Commandant, Colonel Willcocks, had been offered the supreme command of the expedition. My first stroke of luck came to me on this evening of the 7th of May, when Captain Melliss and I were told that we should

be required to proceed on active service to the Gold
Coast almost at once. F Company was to go too;
many more troops than at first estimated being required,
owing to the increased gravity of the situation. A
British N.C.O., with an escort of thirty rank and file,
left the next morning by forced marches (*i.e.*, of double
the usual distances) to overtake Colonel Willcocks and
hand him the urgent despatches, the contents of which
we had just heard. Preparations now began in real
earnest. The company had to be got ready for service
forthwith, and ammunition and stores drawn to take
with us. Thanks to careful forethought, the forces in
Northern Nigeria were well supplied with warlike
material, and it was due to the possession of an
adequate supply of cartridges that our troops were
able to commence hostilities as soon as they arrived,
for the magazine at Cape Coast Castle was subsequently
found to be unable to meet the heavy unexpected calls
made upon its resources. Then there were all our own
private arrangements to be made, and, having now to
provide myself with a new kit, I was particularly busy.
From the outfit of a recently deceased officer, whose
popularity made his loss very severely felt by all, I
rigged myself out with clothing, civil and military, and
bought a revolver; these I supplemented with certain
articles from the Niger Company's store. The three
items I could not purchase anywhere were a saddle and
bridle, sword, and water-bottle, all of the highest importance. However, thanks to the kindness of the
Acting Commandant, I was allowed to take the first
out of the Government stores; the two latter were lent
to me by our Sergeant-Major, and many times since
have I gratefully remembered his timely loan.

In a country like Northern Nigeria, troops are always

more quickly got ready for immediate service than is the case elsewhere, for they live in an atmosphere of antici- pation of hostilities ; at the same time there are special local conditions that are apt to cause delay, and so it was now. One can make up and arrange one's loads to their proper weights (50 lbs. on active service, 65 lbs. at other times), but it it not always possible to collect carriers for their transportation. Perhaps I ought to mention here that throughout West Africa, where the non- existence of roads prohibits wheeled traffic and the tsetse fly makes the employment of pack animals an impossibility, everything is, perforce, moved about by human labour. The natives carry their loads on their heads, and, owing to this practice having been in vogue for centuries, they do so with wonderful endurance and cleverness. The column which was being got together, though not strong in soldiers, was a long one, as every possible kind of stores which could be spared had to be taken, owing to urgent need of *matériel* at the seat of war. Orders were sent to all the chiefs for many miles around to collect and bring in varying contingents of men, the exact total each one was required to furnish being based upon a rough estimate of the number of natives over whom he exercised authority. Carrying loads for the white man is, and ever will be, a most uncongenial pastime to the black man : in this respect, even the pay fails to conciliate his distaste.

Another company, B, 2nd Battalion, under Captain Beddoes, was also to go to Ashanti. It was to concen- trate with the one from Jebba at Ogbomoso in Northern Lagos. A march to the coast was the only possible course open at the time, for the river was too low to admit of transport by water. Captain Beddoes' company was split up into detachments along our south-west frontier, on preventive service. As all these units would have to be collected, and it was clearly impossible for them to make this junction in the time it would take us to get to the rendezvous ; the date of our departure was postponed for a few days. In addition to everything else, F Company was put through a hurried course of musketry, the results of which proved that one cannot give the black soldier (or for that matter the white or brown) too much practice on the range. The two most important qualities of a good soldier, ability to march and shoot, both require constantly to be kept up. The West African are equal to any troops in the former respect, and there are no reasons why they should not, in time, become so in the latter.

The following day, I selected an orderly from my new company, by name Somilu. He was a genuine Hausa, fortunately spoke English remarkably well, and, I am glad to say, turned out to be an excellent man in all respects. I also informed my small Yoruba boy, who rejoiced in the pseudonym of Dan Leno, that I was going on service, and that, as he was only about twelve years old, I did not care to subject him to the dangers inseparable from campaigning ; I would, however, pay him up and let him either take a holiday or seek another master. To my surprise, Dan Leno's face fell so much at this news that I was compelled to ask him the cause. He then told me that, as he had served me to my satisfaction for about half a year or more, he thought it very hard lines to be cut out of the fun now ; he did not fear the Ashanti or anybody else (a fact which he subsequently proved under much severer tests than either of us then dreamt of), and, please, he wanted to go. The prospect of seeing, for the first time in his life, a railway train (called by the natives land-canoe, after the

river steamers they have seen), and ocean-going steam-
ships, appealed very strongly to his funny little black
mind. Finally, I was compelled to give in, and he went
off, wreathed in smiles, to tell the other boys of his
superior luck. My cook was such a scoundrel that I
abandoned all thought of taking him, and now that our
destination was the colony, *par excellence*, from which to
get trained servants, I resolved to wait for one until I
got to Cape Coast. At 5 p.m. on the 13th, Colonel
Willcocks returned, after a splendid bit of travelling
averaging over thirty miles a day. The 14th was a hard
day; nevertheless by sundown, the ponies had been
swum over, all the soldiers and the loads ferried across,
and an encampment made on the mainland. Lastly,
the band played us down to the water's edge, tents were
pitched for the four white men, Captain Melliss, myself,
Colour-Sergeant Foster, and Sergeant-Major Bosher, R.A.
(who was to come with us), the ponies picketed out, the
loads stacked, and all finished in the nick of time. The
Commandant, with Sergeant Farini as his clerk, and Dr.
Tichborne, were to leave the day after us and, travelling
light, were to overtake us.

That evening, Captain Melliss and I were the guests of
the mess. We were given a very good dinner, a most
hearty send-off, but perhaps a rather generous quantity
of "boy" for a reveille at 4 a.m. "Fizz" is poor stuff
to go on, particularly in a hot sun, but this prospect
did not detract from an enjoyable evening; and, as a
matter of fact, not a single ill-effect from the late hours
or the merrymaking was traceable next morning.

CHAPTER III

THE MARCH TO THE COAST

THE start on the first day is always the worst one, but our column, which extended for about a couple of miles, fell in and filed off in a wonderfully orderly manner shortly after daybreak on the 15th. At last we had fairly started! Curiously enough, this was the very day on which Captain Melliss and I had completed our year's tour of service, and ought, in the ordinary way, to have been leaving the mouth of the river for England. When should we really find ourselves walking down Piccadilly again, in frock-coats and top-hats, looking at the kaleidoscope of fours-in-hand and omnibuses, Highnesses and hawkers, plutocrats and paupers, and all the heterogeneous elements that make up the traffic of the streets? The prospect now seemed so far away and doubtful that wisdom prompted forgetfulness. One philosophically set one's face to gaze at stern reality, and tried to believe that ammunition boxes and bags of rice were the only things worthy of consideration.

Thanks to a terrific tornado and drenching fall of rain the night before, the journey was cooler than is usual at this time of year, and fifteen miles were traversed with as much comfort as is possible in this

country. The halt for the night was ordered at a
village called Babambodi.

The general procedure at the conclusion of any march
in West Africa is usually much the same. The loads
are stacked, the soldiers pile arms and sleep in their
immediate vicinity, the guard is mounted, and the
sentries posted. The men light their fires, around
which they sit in groups, jabbering incessantly in the
style common to all negroes. Cooking their "chop" (the
universal term for any kind of refreshment) is to them
always an agreeable occupation; and in cantonments the
women take much time and trouble in providing their
husbands' meals. The West African's staple diet consists
of the produce of that part of the country to which he
belongs, and he devotes as much time as possible to its
preparation. In Ashanti, fruit is the commonest form of
sustenance, whereas in most other colonies corn, rice,
and yams (a kind of potato) are the usual fare. The
grain is ground to powder between large stones or
pounded into pulp, and mixed with peppers, palm-oil,
or similar relishes. This dirty-looking mess is placed
in a calabash (a hollow gourd universally used in
Africa), the guests squat round it in a circle, and
devour the contents with the help of their fingers.
When it can be obtained, meat is a very popular
addition to any repast, but it is not eaten by natives
in the constant and liberal way in which it is by
Europeans. The white man, at the end of the day's
march, is invariably tired, and so, when his duties are
finished and his orders for dinner have been given to
his "boy," he prefers to take things easy, unless there
happen to be good shooting in the locality. In that
case the love of sport proves stronger, as a rule, than
the feeling of fatigue. An officer's menu is wearisomely

A NATIVE MARKET, CAPE COAST

similar.   Many of the local productions, when such can
be got in a friendly country, can be utilised, and the
ubiquitous fowl, a small sheep, or even a goat make a
welcome change from Maconochie's well-known Army
Rations.   The luxury of an evening bath is beyond
the power of words to express.   Hot, dusty, travel-
stained, repugnant to oneself, one understands the
stimulating virtue of soap and water as it could not
be felt under other conditions : the refreshed feeling it
induces surpasses even that of the subsequent drink at
sundown.   It is advisable to have a look round one's
pony to ascertain that it is not galled, and that it has
been fed and watered.   It does not do to place much
confidence in the horse-boy ; he belongs to the most
idle class of a very unenergetic race.   In times of peace
it is native etiquette for the local king and his head
men to visit any passing stranger of importance.   After
a little practice this interview need not detain one long,
for the ceremony is invariably mercantile in character.
Presents, usually food stuffs — called "dashes" — are
brought to one, whether wanted or not.   It is very
bad form to refuse them, but the equivalent monetary
value is expected in exchange, so that the hospitality
does not appear, in our way of looking at things, to
have quite the charm of unselfish generosity.   Even at
such times, it is impossible to escape from the petty
worries inseparable from this life ; they need the
customary settlement ; and not infrequently, a little
amateur doctoring has to be done.   This would be
difficult, even to a responsible medical man, as soldiers
and carriers can never give more enlightening descrip-
tions of their symptoms than that they are "sick" some
way or another : in practice a dose of something or
other generally satisfies them.   There is little to tempt

D

one to sit up late when on the move, but this evening, at about 9 p.m., when we were preparing to turn in, the head man of the gangs of carriers from Illorin suddenly came and reported that one hundred and twenty of his charges had deserted. This was gratifying intelligence to sleep on, because it either meant one would be completely hung up, or that much delay would be caused on the morrow in trying to replace them. Several parties of soldiers were despatched to endeavour to find the fugitives, but failed. Luckily, the next morning we learned that the report was as inaccurate as most native ones are, and that only twenty carriers did not answer to the roll call. This number was speedily commandeered from the locality, but the incident, none the less, made us lose some of the cool of the early morning, when one can get over the ground so much more rapidly and pleasantly than when the sun is beating down in all its fury.

The succeeding stage of our journey began to impress upon us that we were approaching an older colony than our own, and that the aboriginal Yoruba had improved by his slight acquaintance with civilisation. The houses were better built, the villages were cleaner, and the country improved the further we penetrated into it, both from the point of view of cultivation and population.

Our camp was pitched just outside the village of Longwar, where we were fortunate in getting some good eggs. We had not quite succeeded in settling down, when, to our astonishment, Colonel Willcocks with his guard of honour (half Hausa, half Yoruba) and carriers came in sight. They were pushing on as rapidly as possible, and, after a late lunch, they continued on their way. We were told that no fresh news had arrived from the Gold Coast since we left, except a message to the effect that haste was imperative. We, of course, had hitherto been unable to get any information, as we had been away from telegraphic stations. Despite the fact that the Illorin carriers were put under a guard, we had a bad night; a pony got loose, and went round savaging all the rest, and an awful storm, which blew half a tent up into a tree, fairly washed us out. Nevertheless, in the morning we were away in excellent time, though perhaps not as refreshed and happy as might have been desired. It was with very genuine pleasure we sighted Illorin just before sunset, but we found, with some chagrin, that it took one hour and twenty minutes' steady marching to traverse the town and reach the barracks on its further side.

Illorin is a very large city, the capital of the Yoruba country, and one of our posts. It is situated upon high ground, with delightful scenery on every side, and green undulating meadow-land, which reminded one of English downs. This was the first time for a great many months that I had beheld any landscape which extended as far as the horizon, and it brought quite a feeling of relief, somewhat similar to that which one experiences when coming out of a clammy fog into the warm sunshine. Some years ago Her Majesty, through Major Sir Claude Macdonald, K.C.B., K.C.M.G., at that time H.B.M. Consul-General of the Niger Coast Protectorate and now holding a similar appointment in Japan, sent to the Emir of Illorin a General's presentation sword. This potentate saw fit some three years ago to differ in opinion from Sir George Taubman-Goldie, K.C.M.G., who promptly sent a force of the Royal Niger Company's Constabulary, which discomfited him and took away the sabre.

The old garrison having already proceeded to the Gold Coast, the barracks were empty; there was nothing left behind except the soldiers' wives, who had been making themselves very obnoxious to the citizens of Illorin. In these cantonments we got excellent quarters, and were most grateful for them after twelve hours' steady going in the heat. Here we found the Commandant, none too pleased at having to remain the night on account of the Emir's tardiness in changing his carriers. We were now at a telegraphic station, and were enabled to see some encouraging Reuters concerning the Transvaal War.

The following morning we woke to find that Captain Melliss' " boys " had disappeared in the night, evidently having considered that so much fatigue was not worth their while. This was awkward, for we were compelled to cast Dan Leno for cook, the first time he had appeared in this *rôle*. Fortunately, nothing high-class was required of him, but much of what he did manage was uninviting to the eye and dyspeptic to the stomach. The country we marched through that day was the same rolling sward which had recently charmed us so much. We spent the night at Bodowi Egba, with more rain and another violent tornado. Colonel Willcocks had got away from Illorin before us, and we did not meet him again until we reached Cape Coast.

Our next halt was at Ogbomoso, where we were to join Captain Beddoes' Company and column of carriers. Captain Sabine had been sent here specially from his station at Ibadan to collect carriers, as the demand upon the local manhood had been heavy: this work he had accomplished on our arrival. There was another telegraph office here, and we heard that Sir Frederic Hodgson was expected to be relieved shortly by the

forces then on their way to Kumasi ; that one body of
the Gold Coast Hausas, under their Deputy Inspector-
General, Captain Middlemist, had got into the fort
unopposed ; that another one of Lagos Hausas, under
their Inspector-General, Captain Aplin, C.M.G., had met
with serious opposition when within one day's march of
the capital, but had succeeded in getting through the line
of investment, and it then appeared probable that the
relief had been effected. We knew, of course, that
Captain Hall's column of the W.A.F.F. could have done
little more than arrive at Cape Coast. Although glad
to know that the Governor had now such a strong
garrison with him, I must admit we felt a little disappointed at the thought that the main object in view,
namely, the relief of Kumasi, was probably accomplished, and that all we should get in for were punitive
operations.

Ogbomoso has a bad name from a health point of
view, and Captain Melliss had a smart attack of fever,
which left him very weak at a most awkward and busy
time. The fact that we had to wait here four days
furnishes a good illustration of the difficulty of making
accurate arrangements in this country.

The only person who enjoyed our stay here was Dan
Leno, whose home it was. Sure enough, he appeared
on the first opportunity with some sisters, whose big
fishy eyes were proof of the genuineness of the relation-
ship ; to them I had to be introduced, and to be
mendaciously complimentary. The missionary at this
place took a particular fancy to my pony, Charles Dilke,
and as I did not know how I could dispose of him when
I got to my immediate destination, I sold him, on the
understanding that I might ride him as far as the
rail-head. It was a sad day for poor Charlie Dilke

when he descended from the position of an officer's polo
pony and charger to that of a black missionary's hack ;
however, he got a good home, and, under the circumstances, his feelings could not very well be considered.

Colour-Sergeant Foster was the next to be laid up
during this stay ; and I, though not actually sick, was in
a state of great discomfort, as the heat of the sun during
this march had turned the backs of my hands into two
enormous blisters. The opportunity afforded by the
delay was utilised to wash our clothes and collect supplies. These, happily, were plentiful, for our rations
were diminishing, whilst our drugs had almost completely run out. These days were far from comfortable :
the prevalence of sickness made the want of a cook
and doctor acutely felt, and even nature turned against
us, rain falling incessantly. The soldiers, and horde of
carriers, required superintending, especially the latter,
who had to be counted twice daily on account of their
trick of deserting at the most critical junctures.

On the 22nd we were all delighted to hear of the
relief of Mafeking, though we were not in a position to
celebrate the event as it deserved. In reply to a telegram, we were informed that no news had been received
from Kumasi since the 8th inst., the Ashantis having
cut the wire. At 6.30 p.m. on the 23rd, the expected
column, wet to the skin, came in ; one officer and one
British non-commissioned officer, however, had had to
be left behind, too ill to travel. The junction having
now been effected, it was decided that we should go off
on the morrow, the other column following a day later :
firstly, because they were tired out ; secondly, because
more carriers were now required than had been originally ordered ; and finally, because a movement in two
short columns would be more convenient. So on the

morning of Her Majesty's birthday, but in very far from
Queen's weather, we moved on.   We had now struck
the Government road, constructed by impressed native
labour, and it was found to be in excellent condition all
the way.   We halted at Tinbar, and were off the following morning at 6 a.m.   The excellent pathway enabled
us to make good going.   We stopped at Oyo for lunch
beside the American Baptist Mission House, but, I am
sorry to say, the inmates were so churlish and inhospit-
able that they declined even to supply us with water.
The night was spent in an evil-smelling little village
named Fadeti.   I should imagine, from their number,
that it must be noted for its pigs or its insanitary condition.   Although the exposures inseparable from most
marches in this climate are nails in one's coffin, the
country compared favourably with Northern Nigeria,
which, as far as my experience has gone, is rocky and
arid to the verge of being a desert.   At last we successfully got to Ibadan, the most important up-country
station in Lagos.   This was Captain Sabine's post, and
he put us up in a very comfortable bungalow to await
Captain Beddoes' arrival.   There was also an Assistant
Resident, who had quite an imposing official quarter,
perched up on the hill-top overlooking the town.   After
a year of makeshift in our new colony, the civilisation of
this place impressed one.   It was fortunate that we had
settled to have a day's rest there, for Sergeant-Major
Bosher, R.A., the third out of the four of us, went down
with fever on arrival.   Next day Captain Beddoes' detachment came in, and thenceforward we all went on
together.

The united column had rather an unpleasant time of
it between Ibadan and the rail-head.   The good road
had given way to the course of the advancing railway.

At first it was only clearing, then levellings, cuttings, and embankments ; further on, the track was strewn with sleepers, thrown down preparatory to laying, and finally we came to the completed permanent way with the rails fixed. The sleepers were steel, like those used in Uganda, this being the most suitable material for countries with a moist climate. To square timber for making sleepers would be an immense labour, and they would require constant renovation. This railway is the longest and best in West Africa, although it is only a 3 ft. 6 in. gauge single line. Captains Melliss and Beddoes disposed of their horse-flesh to the white engineers, so that only the Government ponies, used by the non-commissioned officers, were left. These returned by easy stages to headquarters, after they had had a short rest. Our last day's riding was over cut-up ground, disastrous at times to our footsore beasts : twice my pony fell with me, his legs going clean through the rickety bridges at the side of the track. The heat seemed worse than ever, inasmuch as there was no shade to give one even a temporary respite. At the final camp a special train was to meet us at nine a.m. on the morrow, and we were glad to pay off our carriers and send them home. We actually steamed out at about ten o'clock. The first part of the journey had to be undertaken in open trucks, drawn by a small engine of the kind one sees in America, with a big chimney funnel. None of the soldiers had ever seen a train before, and their astonishment and delight were most amusing. The distance to the Lagos station (the town is built upon an island) is about a hundred miles, and we went at the very creditable pace of about twenty miles an hour. It was quite exhilarating, at one time dashing over dangerous-looking bridges, at another rocking over a regular switchback piece of line. The first stations passed were rather primitive, usually just a tin hut, but further on they were not unlike the ones seen in India. We had to stop at intervals for water, the various spots being dictated by the lie of the land. Shortly after mid-day we changed trains for one with a sort of Continental corridor carriage and a more powerful engine; this was preferable to sitting in the open trucks, though anything was better than the slow marching of the past few days. The terminus of the main line is called Ebuta Metta, which we reached at 6.30 p.m. We were only about an hour late, though we missed a kindly welcome from some of the officials, who had been good enough to come down to meet us, but had been unable to wait.

The troops spent the night in a large shed, and the white men were comfortably housed as the guests of the railway officials, who appeared, after what we had been accustomed to, to be living in palaces. Mr. Knight, the head official of the Lagos Government Railway, dined all the officers, who much appreciated his generous hospitality. The ozone of the strong sea-air, inhaled for the first time for over a year, and the fatigue of our railway journey, conduced to sound sleep. We found that we should have to wait for further news of the rebellion until we reached Cape Coast, but we were told that Colonel Willcocks had gone straight from the train to the boat and embarked for the Gold Coast. Beyond the fact that matters wore a gloomy aspect, we were unable to obtain further news, but we now knew for certain that Kumasi had not been relieved.

CHAPTER IV

ARRIVAL IN THE GOLD COAST

OUR return to such luxury as Lagos could afford was to be of brief duration. We had embarked upon no picnic. Though most of us had by now some experience of West African vicissitudes, I doubt if any quite realised what was in store for us ; but even if we had been able to do so, I am certain we could not have appreciated more thoroughly the comfort and civility which we met with in this place.

The specially chartered S.S. *Ekuro*, a cargo boat, ordinarily running between Forçados and Lagos, was waiting for us in the harbour, formed by Lagos Island. With the exception of the railway buildings and the houses of the *employés* connected with the line, almost the whole of Lagos town is built upon this island. As is customary in this part of the world, Government House and the various official quarters constitute the greater part of the dwellings. This pretty spot is as insalubrious as the other sea-board places, and has a large cemetery, in which lie many good men who have fallen victims to disease whilst serving their country.

The grey dawn of the coming day was heralded by

the blast of bugles, and peaceful sleep was exchanged for renewed activity. A hurried *chota hazari* discussed with our kind host, and we were once more engrossed with the multifarious duties now pressing upon us, the embarkation of the troops and stores. Sir George Denton, K.C.M.G., who was then acting for the Governor, and other officers, came down to see us off. They gave us an account of the severe way in which the Ashantis had handled Captain Aplin's column from this colony, telling us that all the white men in it were reported to have been wounded, and that it was now shut up in Kumasi with the others; that Captain Middlemist's death in the fort from fever was now confirmed; that Captain Slater was reported to have been killed in action in an ambush near Kwisa; in fact, that the position could not well be graver, and that the enemy was in great force, the estimated number of those now in the neighbourhood of Kumasi being something like thirty thousand.

Lieutenant McClintock, R.E., and three British N.C.O.'s, who had been stopped on their way home and landed here, joined us on the boat. All the men's kits and other paraphernalia were safely on board by 8 a.m., when we slowly steamed out of Lagos Roads, and successfully navigated the bar, which is always dangerous to shipping, so that only small craft now attempt to cross it. The soldiers were enormously impressed and pleased with their first introduction to an ocean-going steamer, but they soon lost their new-born enthusiasm, for we were no sooner clear of land than we ran straight into dirty weather and a rough sea, which continued unceasingly until we were disembarked. I think I am correct in saying that every black man was seasick, and almost every white man. Poor Dan Leno repented of his former ardour for fresh experiences, and was absolutely useless, spending the whole of his maiden voyage huddled up in a heap on the deck, with an unwonted partiality for starvation, taciturnity, and solitude; the most eloquent proof possible that something was wrong, seeing that the opposites of these three characteristics had invariably been, in former times, his chief attributes. My wretched orderly was speechless, and seemed only to long for an immediate end to his military career. The majority of the Europeans became more pallid than is their wont, even in the tropics, and appeared to care for nothing but an occasional inspection of the storm-swept ocean from the taffrail of the squalid upper deck. Nevertheless, duty had to be done; rifles and Maxim guns, after the long march and exposure to the sea-air, required careful cleaning, and, of course, they got it. At 3.45 p.m., on the third day, June 1st, we anchored off our destination, rolling abominably in the heavy swell. Alongside of us lay a gunboat, tossing about like a cork, and, simultaneously with our arrival, in came the S.S. *Jebba* from home, signalling to the shore that she had some thousands of Government packages, whilst we for our part hoisted the flags in the code for " Troops on board."

Cape Coast from the sea, the point of vantage for most West African views if you wish to have a pleasant remembrance of them, looked quite attractive to us then. There, prominent in the central foreground, was the old Dutch fort, standing as it had done for centuries, rock-girt and surf-beaten, its whitewashed walls glittering in the evening sunlight. On the hill behind, the lighthouse showed itself against the sky line, flying, in response to our signal, the disappointing answer to stand

THE INTERIOR OF CAPE COAST CASTLE

by for orders as the surf was too bad for landing. To
right and left, extending for some couple of miles, was
the town with its stores and traders' houses, hospital
and Government offices. But the chief object of
interest to us all was the Cape Coast-Kumasi road,
skirted by telegraph poles and wires, winding round the
back of the town until lost to sight over the crest of the
low ridge of hills which formed the background of this
picture. There was nothing for it but to reconcile ourselves to another night on board, and here we were,
"rocked in the cradle of the deep" with a vengeance,
our vessel being small and accordingly sensitive to the
slightest heave of the ocean swell. There could be no
deliverance from this tedious confinement. It was impossible to lower any boat with so rough a sea on ; so
our only amusement was to look through our glasses at
the naval officers on the gunboat and the military ones
on the liner, vainly trying to forget that our home
letters were on board the latter, shortly to be taken on
to the very place we had just left, the object of
desire, as in the case of Tantalus, being just out of
our reach.

Early next morning a boat succeeded in getting off
to us with orders from Colonel Willcocks, to the effect
that as the surf was too bad at present to land the
troops and discharge our cargo of stores, we were to
proceed to Elmina, disembark there, and then march
back to Cape Coast. The former place is some nine
miles further up the coast, and affords a better landing,
as a promontory of rocks breaks the force of the
in-coming sea. Steam was accordingly got up, the
anchor weighed, and before midday we were at our
haven, whistling for boats to come off and transport us
to the land.

Smartness is not the negro's characteristic, so I was enabled to get a light and early lunch before my duties as disembarking officer could commence, thanks to the non-appearance of the surf-boats. In one of the first of these I was ordered to go ashore, make all arrangements with the District Commissioner, and superintend the disposal of the boat loads as they came in.

A surf-boat is capable of taking some ten or twelve passengers at a time, and has a high sharp-pointed prow and stern, so as in launching to cleave the in-coming breaker and mount upon its summit without being capsized. It is usually manned by eight Krooboys (the only West African race accustomed to this work), who, with curious three-pronged paddles, sit on the bulwarks, whilst one stands in the stern, steering with a long oar. The getting-off and the landing are always the most ticklish times, and many fatal accidents occur through upsets and swampings; nevertheless the passage is somewhat exciting. The paddlers are most dexterous, and chant an inspiriting song the while to set the time and keep the crew together. The method of navigation is to reach the top of one of the enormous swells before it breaks into foam, and fly with it into the trough formed between this wave and the next. At this moment nothing can be seen save a wall of water before and behind. Then one is picked up and hurled on by another roller, and so on, until, on the crest of the last, with the boat's nose straight for the shore, one finds oneself high and sometimes dry on the beach, and not uncommonly unseated by the violence of the concussion.

The serious hindrance to shipping caused by this mode of landing, prevalent at most anchorages down the coast, is so great that breakwaters, anyhow a intervals, ought to be built, and joined by a light railway running along the fore-shore. The enterprising French have both a breakwater and a jetty at Konakri, their principal port on the Ivory Coast, and here the surf is not at all bad. Surely if our neighbours find this investment pays, so should we, and the reduction of risk to life, not to speak of inconvenience, would be enormous.

The District Commissioner, who lives in the picturesque old castle, similar in appearance and style to the other Dutch fifteenth-century, slave-built structures at Axim and Cape Coast, was most obliging and kind. Elmina is certainly the most fascinating spot I have ever seen in West Africa. To stand on the lofty balcony of the castle in the starlight and watch the foaming breakers on the palm-fringed shore below, and the pretty little town behind, was an indescribable treat to any one whose hunger for the beautiful in nature had been unappeased for one whole year. But behind all this loveliness lay in wait subtle death, for, just out of sight, lurks a large and swampy lagoon, whose fever germs are wafted by every wind from that quarter; and so terrible has the havoc been in the past, that no white man is now stationed here, although once it was the headquarters and barracks of the Gold Coast Forces.

It did not require a very practised eye, or long experience of Africa, to show one that it would be impossible to do more than finish the disembarkation before nightfall, and that the march into Cape Coast would have to be postponed until the next day. Consequently, this information was wired to the Commandant, and all arrangements made to quarter the men and house the loads for the night. The calculation was fairly accurate, for Captain Melliss, the officer commanding the troops, and therefore the last to leave the ship, only arrived in the glow of the sunset.

Every one was only too grateful to be once more ashore, and not a discordant murmur was to be heard. Colonel Willcocks had already sent our carriers down for us, and Dr. Tichborne rode over on a bicycle—another unusual sight—to see us. Lieutenant McClintock returned with him, having just received the good news that, as the Commandant had no Staff Officer, he had been appointed to this desirable post, and had been given the local rank of captain.

"Last post" was not sounded until rather late in the evening, owing to the progress in the courtyard of a noisy market from which the lately seasick troops could obtain any quantity of much needed and most welcome food, the delicious bread sold in it being unknown to most of them.

One cannot say much that is favourable about the Fantis, who inhabit this part of the Gold Coast, because they are not only as idle as other native races, but distinctly cowardly, and therefore useless for recruiting purposes. However, I must say a good word here for their women. Contact for generations with Europeans has wonderfully refined them. Their features are naturally cleaner cut than those of other natives, and their complexion is often toned down to a yellowish tint, by the previous mixture of white blood. The frizzled hair is longer and always carefully plaited, the favourite *coiffure* being in twists, standing out like horns or upright on the crown of the head. The *tout ensemble* is made very effective by a bright-coloured, daintily folded turban, which artistically hides all the weak points. The figure, again, is fully draped in loose flowing garments, an easy graceful effect being obtained

by some pretty piece of cloth, twisted, plaid-like, round
the waist, and thrown across the breast and over one
shoulder.   One little maiden, named Gertrude, some
fifteen years of age, originally of Dutch and Fanti
descent, was of such an unusually light colour, and so
pretty that she might have sat for the picture of an
Italian flower-girl; and her low sweet voice and taking
manners harmonised with such a notion.

Camp-beds, great improvements on the bunks of the
Ekuro, were put up for us in cool stone rooms at the
castle, and at rather a late hour we had an excellent
little dinner with the District Commissioner in his
comfortable and really well furnished quarters. We,
found, however, that we had to wait until our arrival at
the base next day for more detailed news of the state
of public affairs than that which we had received at
Lagos.

E

CHAPTER V

PREPARATIONS FOR THE FORWARD MOVE

THE nine miles' march into Cape Coast was rather trying, and the too liberal breakfast which our host insisted upon our eating, added to our recent experiences on board ship, did not help to make us any fitter for the exertion. The road skirting the sandy beach was certainly very good, but the hedges which shut it in on both sides almost uninterruptedly, in really English rural style, kept off the breeze, and the blazing sun made the heat almost unbearable. As a matter of fact, when we did get in, one of the white men was found to have been so severely " touched up," that for some time it was feared that he might have got a sunstroke.

About a mile out of Cape Coast we met Colonel Willcocks, in a little rickshaw cart, accompanied by his newly appointed private secretary, Mr. Russell, a local merchant, who had volunteered his services.

The Government schools were temporarily turned into barracks for the men, and the officers were either billeted about the town or quartered in the castle. Colonel Willcocks occupied, as both domicile and office, the house next to the police barracks, and this building

was subsequently taken on by the Base Commandant,
Lieut.-Col. Man-Stuart, C.M.G., when he arrived some
weeks later. Another house, which had been similarly
utilised by Lord Wolseley in 1873, was now occupied
by the medical officer appointed to the charge of the
base hospital. He was assisted by two of our Northern
Nigerian nursing sisters, who, in a truly self-sacrificing
spirit, had asked to be landed here on their way home,
and pluckily nursed the bad cases from the front until
the end of the campaign. We were all glad again to
meet our P.M.O. of the W.A.F.F., Dr. McDowell, who
had also been stopped on his return to England, and
had been appointed P.M.O. of the Ashanti Field Force.
No better man could have occupied this important
position, either as an organiser, doctor, or considerate
comrade, under circumstances peculiarly calling for
kind-heartedness.

We now found that a short halt at the base would be
unavoidable. There was, however, plenty for every one
to do. Unostentatious work done within the four walls
of an office is frequently of the greatest importance,
though often not appraised at its full value by the
public. If I may be permitted to say so, it was here,
and at this stage of affairs, that Colonel Willcocks laid
the foundation of his eminent success in this campaign,
and demonstrated his exceptional power of organisation. To any one with a competent appreciation of
the situation, such as was shown by our Commandant,
it was clear that until larger reinforcements had arrived
and especially until a much greater quantity of food and
ammunition had been accumulated, it was most un-
advisable for a forward movement to be made, even if
a force could have been thrown into the beleaguered fort,
seeing that this would have been but the addition of

mouths to consume stores which were already fast
running out. The difficulty, however, was greater even
than this. It was not only necessary to collect food
and ammunition, but to provide carriers to transport it
and a column of sufficient strength to fight its way
through with the convoy. Besides that, carriers and
soldiers would themselves require feeding, and, at
present, there were not sufficient soldiers and carriers,
ammunition or food in Cape Coast.

It was mainly for these reasons that the former
parties which had reached Kumasi had failed to raise
the siege, whilst the small bodies of troops at different
points along the road were too weak, numerically, to
make any effective advance, owing to the formidable
proportions the rebellion was rapidly assuming. Slow
and sure is a good motto, provided you do not overdo
it, and people who say, "Weren't you a long time
accomplishing the relief?" probably do not appreciate
the above circumstances.

Those employed in connection with the telegraph
during this war have not had an easy time of it. Our
Commandant had not long set foot ashore before he put
the wires in motion, and placed himself in direct communication with the Colonial Secretary in London.
Very definite results were soon apparent on every side.
Ammunition and food began to be despatched with all
possible speed from home; the fact having been
grasped by Colonel Willcocks that big reinforcements
would be required to carry through successfully the
enormous task before him, troops were under orders
from several other colonies; the absolute necessity for
an immediate supply of carriers, and that on a large
scale, had been realised, and also that men from other
colonies would be preferable for this purpose to the

aborigines of the Gold Coast. It is true that carriers might have been obtained by the institution of the Labour Ordinance, but this step would have decreased the supply of men available as native levies, which it was intended to raise later on. Consequently, several thousand carriers were immediately ordered from Sierra Leone. It was no small advantage in the case of these outside men that it was a very difficult thing for them to desert. However, it is not for me to say more upon these points, important as they were: the unbroken series of successes which marked the Commandant's forward course, when he did move, the masterly and economical way in which he successfully brought this campaign to a close in less than six months, speak for themselves, and can not only be understood, but appreciated, by every competent judge.

The number of white officers and N.C.O.'s was fortunately not too great to preclude our being made the guests of the Gold Coast officials during our short stay at the base. We found that considerable anxiety existed at Cape Coast amongst the civilians, both white and black, and at Accra, the other large coast town and seat of government of this colony. Somewhat later, matters bordered on panic, the volunteers being called out, and preparations made to meet an attack, in case one should be attempted.

Barely two days were allowed us for the many preparations requisite before leaving the only place at which anything could be obtained from local stores and shops. We arrived shortly before noon on June 3rd, and we had marched out by midday of the 5th. The troops had to be clothed in their new khaki uniforms, which had just been sent back from Forçados for them.

The men had to be rationed, every bag of rice had to be taken over and got ready for immediate transportation, together with all available boxes of ammunition. These latter were of three sizes, five hundreds, eight hundreds, and eleven hundreds. The last kind was heartily detested by us all later on, for the wretched men who had to carry this heavy weight invariably became prematurely exhausted ; and it was frequently very troublesome to find substitutes with so few men available. Carriers, who were at that time all Fantis, had to be collected ; this, always a difficult job, was especially so at that moment, because the preceding columns had already drained the local population for this purpose, taking very rightly too many rather than too few for their needs.

The women, who in this respect were wonderful examples to the men, carried loads throughout the campaign as far as Prahsu, up to which point the road was always safe, and an escort of troops never required for the protection of the transport. It was a funny spectacle to see these merry little ladies thus engaged. All African mothers carry their babies about in the same fashion. The youngster sits astride the small of its parent's back, with one leg on each side of her body, and is dexterously supported in this position by a cloth tied round it, and fastened in front of the woman's chest. It looks to us extremely insecure and uncomfortable ; but I have never seen or heard of a fall, and the infant is, more often than not, quite contented or sound asleep. This domestic addition is quite extra to the load on the woman's head, which is, as a rule, of the same weight as that taken by the male carrier. Thus doubly encumbered, they amble along in an easy manner, and at a very good pace, always jolly, and, unless they have their much-appreciated pipes in their mouths, keeping up a ceaseless flow of pleasantries with their neighbours.

We were glad to hear that one hammock would be allowed between every two white men as far as Prahsu. Beyond this point they were generally confined to the hospital train, and indeed the work became far too anxious for any of us to allow ourselves to use them, because it was impossible properly to supervise one's men or carriers under such conditions.

A hammock in the tropics is made up in this fashion. A light, strong ridge-pole of some ten feet supports the weight, and to it is attached a light cover, which more or less successfully keeps off the sun and rain. At either extremity of this pole are attached at right angles to it flat boards, of some three or four feet in length, the ends of which rest on the carriers' heads. Under the roof, and between these cross-trees, is suspended a canvas or string hammock, in which one lies. This method of travelling is really most restful when one gets accustomed to it, and the rhythmic movement of the marching quite often rocks the inmate to sleep, weariness and heat lending their help. The general allowance to each hammock is eight "boys" in relays of four, and they do their work excellently. It is rarely one finds oneself brought into contact with a tree-stump at any of the numberless sharp turns in the pathway, or experiences a fall, be the track ever so slippery after a deluge of rain. For all this, I preferred to walk, unless too done up to permit of this exertion.

At this early stage of affairs there was no free issue of Government rations, and we were, consequently, compelled to get our supplies in the interim (that is for about two months) at the stores in Cape Coast. Not only was this expensive, but it was rather a bother, when so many other important and pressing duties had to be performed.   But this European " chop," in water-proof canvas-topped boxes of 50 lbs. weight, was destined to play its part later on in the relief of Kumasi.   We now knew that seven officers, some turned back at the islands on their way home on leave, had come in on the *Jebba;* they were, however, not going on with us, but were to bring up more supplies when these arrived, a little later on.   As we had rather expected it, we were not surprised to hear that we were to get a somewhat short allowance of carriers for our personal kits, and that our tents, which we had brought from Northern Nigeria, each of which represented two loads, would have to be left behind.   The whole of the 4th, and the forenoon of the 5th of June, an apparently hopeless chaos of soldiers, carriers, servants, and others, not to speak of ammunition and stores, was transforming itself into the orderly and business-like looking column, which marched out at noon on the latter date ; and orders were being issued, and final preparations made, late into the night before we left.   The District Commissioner, who was to act as Civil Officer at the base, unfortunately selected this time for a go of fever, and as he was my host, this made matters rather awkward for me.   Nevertheless, I succeeded in getting a cook at an extravagant wage, and was deceived into the opinion that I had made a fortunate find, owing to his having recently been servant to a friend of mine at Jebba.   This personage, a few days later, gave me a terrible shock, and, curiously enough, so did my faithful Dan Leno on the same day.   It is the custom, and a very wise one, in these parts, to give " boys " in addition to their main-tenance only a little of their pay at a time, as pocket-money, the bulk of their wages being kept in reserve as a wholesome check upon their behaviour, and to lessen the chance of suddenly finding oneself deprived of their services. I was not, therefore, surprised when, later in the day, Dan Leno, his fancy inflamed by the many beautiful things he had seen, bashfully approached me begging for a sovereign out of his " book-money." As I knew that he could not very well clear out, and that I was his debtor to a considerable amount, I concurred. Rounding a corner of the street a little later, I was convulsed with laughter at the apparition which suddenly presented itself to view. There was my twelve-year-old hopeful, idly lounging along, in company with a promiscuous acquaintance, smoking a large new pipe, twirling, in the most approved military fashion, a swagger cane, a large C.I.V. sort of hat jauntily cocked on one side of his head, and frightfully overdressed. I had never hitherto seen such a striking turn-out for 20s., and I never want to again. But this wardrobe was to figure in the future, and no warnings from me about its making a rather conspicuous target for the enemy could ever induce him to change his opinion as to its desirability and good taste.

Before concluding this chapter, I must briefly describe the enemy's particular weapon, the one we were so soon to face, and which I had never before closely examined. The Dane gun, as it is called, is about six feet long, with an enormous barrel, down which the charge is poured, and the wad and shot rammed. It is fitted with a flint lock and powder chamber at the butt-end, and resembles the firearms of the Middle Ages. Its range is about two hundred yards, and it is deadly at about half this distance. The missiles employed are of various kinds, telegraph wire cut up into little pieces having been used a good deal in this war, but lead and iron slugs are the commonest. These are sold as bars, which are chopped by the natives with a large knife into small irregular cubes. The favourite charge is a couple of dozen or so of these, mixed with one or two big iron ones. Both guns and bars are obtained from the traders; the former are manufactured in Birmingham, and sold out here at the small cost of about 16s.

The Ashanti's warlike nature makes him prefer the possession of a gun to anything else. The powder is sold in small barrels of two sizes, and is also imported from Europe. The savage carries the quantity he immediately wants in a small dried gourd, plugged with a piece of cloth, or corked with a twig; this is suspended round his neck or waist, and his slugs are similarly carried in a bag made of hide. These trade guns, or as they are nicknamed, "gaspipes," carry like a shot-gun, and the charge spreads, thus making them more dangerous at close quarters than a rifle with its single bullet. Once hit in a vital part by a ragged-edged slug, one has a poor chance of recovery, whereas a modern bullet often makes a clean wound, from which wonderful recoveries are made. We subsequently found out, however, that the enemy had many rifles, but chiefly of obsolete pattern, such as Sniders, Martinis, and others, also muskets, but whence they got the ammunition for them is, up to the present, a mystery. They also had other firearms, captured from us during the war, such as a few ·220 rook rifles, obtained at the enemy's seizure of the outlying buildings round Kumasi fort, and some ·303 carbines, taken from our soldiers who fell into their hands on a few deplorable occasions. The Ashanti also wears in his girdle a long knife in a skin scabbard, for hand-to-hand work, but he prefers to fight with firearms without coming to close quarters. These Dane guns are always kept loaded when the enemy are on the war-path, and the first three or four volleys are the most formidable. Loaded at leisure, the barrels are filled up with a carefully rammed and extra large charge both of slugs and powder, whereas when an action has once commenced the loading has perforce to be more rapid. This work is generally done by their slaves, who sit in a trench in the rear, screened from fire. The organisation of the Ashanti army was quite wonderful, and seemed to one almost incredible for any savage race. It was sub-divided into units of different sizes, the smallest being a company. The various chieftains held commands pro-portionate to their rank. Royalties had large bodyguards of picked men, and the commander-in-chief had a staff and intelligence department of linguists and fetish men. Dispersed forces, such as that on the Cape Coast Road, were, none the less, under the command of a single individual, the particular officer in charge of the one referred to having held the post of chief executioner to King Prempeh. Each war-camp also had its general. The usual method of fighting was in three lines, each formed of a company under its own captain; these would double up and fire successively, running to the rear when they had done so to get freshly loaded guns : this accounted for the unceasing fire they were enabled to keep up. The noise of the discharge was terrific, being at times absolutely deafening, and, in consequence, our difficulties in giving orders, and keeping our men in hand, were greatly increased. The hunters, the enemy's crack shots, always had rifles, and were usually placed in trees or in rifle-pits, with special orders to pick off the white men. Some of the neatest and most cleverly made things I have seen were the ramrods which the enemy made out of telegraph wire, miles of which they removed for this purpose. It was closely twisted, and had a looped handle at one end, with an empty cartridge case fixed on at the other to facilitate the ramming down of the charge. Such were the weapons and methods of the enemy we had to encounter.

CHAPTER VI

POSITION OF AFFAIRS WHEN WE LANDED

DURING our few spare moments at the base, there was no lack of subjects for conversation, for the air was full of rumours. Now that we had actually reached the fringe of the zone of operations, we were able at last to get a little authentic information, but even here the wildest stories were in circulation. First and foremost, there was little doubt that the wire had been cut by the enemy; this alone discredited three-quarters of the reports. We steadfastly refused to credit such fairy tales—sprung from goodness knows where—as that the Governor had got out of Kumasi and was making his way down through the bush, or that Lady Hodgson had succumbed in the fort to fever and anxiety. Speculation ran riot at this time. Some of the more daring local newsmongers made the bold statement that the enemy were aided by white men from somewhere or other, whilst others were convinced that retired Senegalese under-officers from the admirable French native regiments were responsible for the Ashanti plan of campaign, which was deemed to be superior to that of mere savages. Even the truculent Samory, who had fought the French so stubbornly was (though a captive), credited with having joined the rebels.

The removal of the Ashanti ex-king Prempeh (Kwaku Dua III., to quote his native title) from Elmina jail, where he was first lodged after his capture in 1896, to Sierra Leone was not a sufficiently far-reaching measure, and he was wisely transported to the Seychelles Islands a short time ago. There was little doubt that this despicable potentate had been continuously in touch with his old subjects, who were known to wish to have him reinstated. These considerations gave colour to the statement that some of the uncaptured rebels from the Sierra Leone rising of 1897, who were the first to fight behind stockades, had joined the Ashantis and taught them how to make these fortifications. Certain it was that the Adansi tribe, whose territory is situated between the river Prah and the southern confines of Ashanti, had definitely thrown in their lot with the insurgents. This people in 1895 had produced Major-General Baden-Powell's best scouts, and in return for their services had been given arms and ammunition. They had, moreover, built field works of timber under the tuition of British officers, and it was probable that the knowledge thus gained would be used with these very guns in opposing us. There was good evidence that no enemy had crossed the Prah and come southwards; we had consequently a clear seventy miles of open road, which meant about half the actual distance to Kumasi. The most important fact of all that we learned at this time was that the fort had *not* been relieved. That, then, would be our objective, but we were not there yet, by a very long way!

After the Governor's arrival in the Ashanti capital, when his eyes were finally opened to the fact that determined fighting was really intended, he sent a telegram for reinforcements. The first which joined him were a party of Gold Coast troops from the south, under their Deputy Inspector-General, Captain Middlemist. This was the only contingent permitted by the rebels to enter Kumasi unopposed.

The next column to reach the besieged garrison was one from Lagos, composed of two hundred and fifty men of that colony's Hausa force, with four British officers and a doctor, under the command of Captain Aplin. The Adansis had not then revolted, and this contingent reached Esiago in the Ashanti country without opposition. Here they were ambushed and attacked, the enemy using their favourite tactics of gradual envelopment, sniping from the trees, besides keeping up a heavy fire from the bush. After a couple of hours or so, during which time the village was shelled, the advance guard saw their opportunity and rushed it with the bayonet. After passing the night there, they burned the houses, and in due time crossed the Ordah River, shortly before noon, when more determined resistance was met with from the enemy, who were then entrenched behind a stockade. The fight lasted until 5 p.m., when the situation of the troops became critical. The Maxim had jammed, an enormous quantity of small-arm ammunition had been expended, and that of the 7-pounder exhausted, the gunners being reduced to firing stones. At this juncture, Captain Cochrane and thirty men were sent into the bush to turn the position, which they successfully accomplished. The stockade was then charged, and the double kept up until Kumasi was reached just before dark. The danger had been extreme, as is shown by the facts that, firstly, all the white men had been wounded, and one hundred and thirty casualties had occurred among the two hundred and fifty native soldiers; secondly, the 7-pounder gun had had to be deserted ; indeed it was not seen again until surrendered to Colonel Sir James Willcocks six months later. That this force had used nearly all its rounds was a great misfortune, because ammunition was found to be the most urgent need of the garrison. It was on April the 29th that this reinforcement reached the fort—the very day that the Ashantis made their attack upon it.

The third effort to relieve Kumasi—the only one from that direction—was made by the Gold Coast troops quartered in the northern territories under Captain (local Major) Morris, D.S.O., Acting Commissioner and Commandant of the district. This force, consisting of seven British officers, two hundred and thirty soldiers, and eighty-two native levies, reached its destination on May 15th. This was the last reinforcement His Excellency got, and brought the strength of the garrison up to seven hundred rank and file with about a dozen British officers. Besides these, there were in Kumasi Sir Frederic and Lady Hodgson, two or three white traders, seven Basel missionaries (three of them ladies), about three hundred friendly native levies, and nearly four thousand Fanti and Hausa refugees. The whole of this large number of human beings were hemmed into a few acres by an almost continuous cordon of stockades erected by the Ashantis.

Although the major part of the opposition was met with from the south, the following short account of the trials of the northern column will show how widespread the rebellion had become, even at this early date. On the 18th of April the first news of what was in progress reached Gambaga, three hundred and forty miles from Kumasi. Three days later, four British officers and one hundred and seventy men, with a 7-pounder gun and a Maxim, started away under the command of Major Morris. Six days after this they received the Governor's urgent appeal for help. After thirteen days' marching they arrived at Kintampo, and left it on May 9th, having increased their numbers at this station to the strength above enumerated. Till then the country traversed had been quite friendly, but at the river near N'Quanta the enemy were met with for the first time, and a couple of hours later successfully engaged at Sekedumasi, only three casualties being sustained by the column. On the 14th, however, they walked into an ambush and incurred twelve casualties. The succeeding day and that following it were occupied by more or less continuous fighting, and in charging a stockade across the road, after the 7-pr. had failed to dislodge the enemy, Major Morris was severely wounded. Captain Maguire headed this charge in the same plucky manner as he subsequently did when he was killed at Bantama, in a sortie that failed to demolish the stockade which had been built to the north of that village. Major Morris's wound was so painful that he had to be carried in a hammock, but he was able to retain command until the fort was reached at 3 p.m. No further resistance was met with, though two more stockades were passed, one of which was the large investing one a quarter of a mile from the fort. This apparent want of enterprise on the part of the enemy was due to a short armistice having been arranged with the beleaguered garrison, and the arrival of Major Morris's column on the particular day that this was in force was an extraordinary piece of good luck ; in fact, it was even more a matter for congratulation than Captain Aplin's timely advent. The Ashantis, to give them their due, had strictly and honourably adhered to their agreement, and they did not credit the fact that

F

this column had come in by mere chance on this identical day, but were under the impression that the game had not been fairly and squarely played on our side.

Before this anxious month of May was far advanced, the first contingent from Northern Nigeria arrived at Cape Coast under the command of Captain Hall. It consisted of two companies, 1st Bn. W.A.F.F., under Captains Wilson and Beamish, and one 75 m/m gun in charge of Sergeant Griggs, R.A. They immediately proceeded up-country, and were, in fact, the last body of troops to traverse the Adansi country unopposed. Kwisa, situated on the Monsi Hills, the furthermost point reached by the late Prince Henry of Battenburg in 1895, was made on the 21st by ordinary marches, without mishap or incident. Here two miners, Messrs. Jones and Cookson, who had purposely come from Bekwai, met the troops with information about the recent Ashanti movements and the hostile preparations of the Kokofus, whose country lies immediately east of the main road between the northern boundary of the Adansis and the southern one of the Ashantis. Captain Hall drew up a treaty and got the Adansi king to sign it ; wherein the old ruffian promised the utmost loyalty to the Queen, an allegiance which he substantiated with votive offerings, till such time as it suited him to violate it. The two miners were left with an escort of twenty men, and asked to remain in charge of Kwisa till the arrival of Captain Slater, an officer of the Gold Coast Hausas, then quartered a little south of this place. Captain Hall's party then moved on to Bekwai, and finally took up its quarters at Esumeja. This village is the usual halting-place on the main road, one day's march south of Kumasi and a similar distance north of Kwisa. Close to Esumeja lie Bekwai and Kokofu, the former about a mile to the west, the latter about half that distance to the east.   The Kokofus are really an Ashanti tribe, fierce and warlike ; for this reason, they were a great source of disquietude and danger.   The occupation of Esumeja was an exceedingly wise move, for the presence of a garrison on the direct line of communication kept the rebels in check and inspired the loyal Bekwais with confidence.   Here Captain Hall's column concentrated with the second contingent from Lagos, one hundred rank and file under Captain Anderson, and the first one from Sierra Leone, fifty men of the S.L.F.P. under Lieutenant Edwards.   Captain Haslewood and Dr. Barker, both belonging to the Gold Coast Colony, were also there.   Although this force never succeeded in getting any further, it was of the utmost service ; in fact, had it not been where it was, it is almost certain matters would have gone very differently. The Bekwais are a tribe of bastard Ashantis, and were dependents of and paid tribute to their pure-blooded progenitors, until put upon a privileged footing for their loyalty to us in 1895.   Ever since the burning of their capital, and the heavy loss inflicted on them by Lord Wolseley in 1873 at the battle of Amoaful, the kings of Bekwai have been staunch supporters of the white man.   This political attitude is, I do not deny, the outcome of fear combined with a sufficiency of common sense to enable them to appreciate the superior strength of the European, and to see that, do what the black man will, it is only a matter of time before he has to undergo the unpleasant process of being subdued, or crushed. The king of Bekwai was at this time invited to join the rebels, and then threatened by them with invasion if he did not ; had he done so, or had he even decamped into the Denkera territory, as he was once on the point of doing, nobody can imagine how much more difficult our task would have been. Under such circumstances Kumasi fort might never have been relieved, and the consequences, had it fallen, would have been too awful to estimate. I do not mean to suggest that the Bekwais helped us much in any other way, or that they were superior to the neighbouring tribes, for I do not think they were at all more civilised. Their predilection for human sacrifice certainly was the same, but they never indulged in these cruel fetish orgies when the white man was near enough to hear of them. I remember well when the headquarters of the Ashanti Field Force were at Bekwai and one of the rebels was hanged, the interest their barbaric chieftain took in this unpleasant spectacle, and his comment : " Yes, it is good, but the death is too quick."

The next incident was the rising of the Adansis, three days after having made their agreement of peace. On the 24th, Messrs. Jones and Cookson set out in the course of business for Bekwai from Kwisa, a day's journey, but near the town of Dompoasi they were fired upon ; their terror-stricken carriers fled, their loads were lost, and they themselves just succeeded in escaping to Kwisa. Captain Slater, who had then arrived there, was much surprised to hear of such an unexpected act of hostility, and forthwith started off with twenty-six men to investigate the cause. Much about the same place they were also attacked, one soldier being killed and ten wounded, whilst two were missing. This necessitated another retirement to Kwisa, where it was deemed desirable to remain until the arrival of fresh troops. The two missing soldiers from this party, who fled in the most cowardly manner, never stopped until they encountered Major Wilkinson. By way of excuse for their conduct they concocted a report of Captain Slater's death.

After this experience, a large number of European gold miners and prospectors made tracks for the coast and home, but it is painful to have to record that two were caught by the rebels. One was sacrificed, tortured to death, the inevitable end of any white man who falls into their clutches. For this reason even suicide was considered preferable to being taken a prisoner-of-war. The other one was more fortunate ; he was a powerful man, and made such a good fight for his life that the hope of capturing him alive for a lingering death was abandoned, and he was decapitated from behind in the struggle. There were some sixty Englishmen at the Obuasi gold mines, which are on the western frontier of the Adansi and immediately south of the Bekwai country. In response to their appeal, Police Commissioner Donovan with fifty men left Cape Coast on May 24th with arms for them, and carried out his mission without any mishap. A few days before Colonel Willcocks' arrival, Major (local Lieutenant-Colonel) Wilkinson, the newly appointed Inspector-General of the Gold Coast Forces, arrived in the Colony with troops from Northern Nigeria, including Lieutenant O'Malley's company, and a 7-pr. under Lieutenant Edwards, R.A. The passage down the river Niger had greatly delayed them, the journey having been a series of groundings-upon and gettings-off sandbanks nearly all the way. This party had only started a few days, when Lieutenant-Colonel Carter, C.M.G., Commandant of the forces of Southern Nigeria, landed with some two hundred men, two British officers, and a doctor, and started for the front forthwith. However, Colonel Willcocks was in time to catch him, and at once ordered a concentration with the former party, sending telegraphic instructions to that effect to Lieutenant-Colonel

Wilkinson. The latter, therefore, remained at Fumsu to effect this combination, which took place on May 31st. There was then not the slightest reason to doubt that this force was amply strong enough to effect a junction with Captain Hall's at Esumeja.

To sum up, then, the Ashanti Field Force, of which Colonel Willcocks found himself in command, consisted of four hundred and fifty men under Captain Hall at Esumeja and Bekwai ; Captain Slater, with a handful of men, was at Kwisa ; Lieutenant-Colonel Wilkinson was at Fumsu with a company ; and Lieutenant-Colonel Carter was on the line of march with two hundred soldiers to join the troops at Fumsu, whence the combined units were going to push on together. Beside these there were our three hundred from Northern Nigeria, who were to accompany the Commandant in person, and some nine hundred reinforcements on their way to the Gold Coast, who could not be expected for a while. It was indeed an unsatisfactory command, inasmuch as the units composing it were cut off from one another, the size of the force being no criterion of its strength from the fact of its dispersion. It was scattered along one hundred and forty miles of lines of communication, and numerically only equal to the garrison it was essaying to relieve. It had only three field guns, no reliable means of transport, and, up till this time, there had been no organised scheme of operations. The dearth of white men for supervision was keenly felt ; even the Commandant had not a single political officer with knowledge of the colony to help him. There was a hopelessly insufficient supply of carriers for the transport, and a glance at the telegraphic despatches, which were sent home, will show the false and conflicting information which was the only guide upon which to base our strategic plans.

CHAPTER VII

THE ADVANCE FOR THE FRONT

THE morning of the 5th of June opened with drizzling rain, instilling gloom into all around; the suddenness of our departure, following as it did a conference held at ten the previous night, suggested the receipt of bad news, and a feeling of vague anxiety was experienced by those of us who knew no details. However, before the bugles had brayed out the advance and the column moved away, the sun broke through the misty clouds as if smiling approval on our mission. But much as we had wished for warm sunshine in the chill damp of the dawn, before the march was completed that day, parched and faint from its reflected heat, we longed intensely for the red glow and lengthening shadows which would herald its discontinuance.

Away through the quiet streets we went, Colonel Willcocks and his staff in front, the whole populace turning out to see us off. It was a strangely silent crowd which lined the roads; scarce a cheer or God-speed was vouchsafed to the men who were going to fight for the Empire. But a native is always undemonstrative, and on this occasion there was no reason to think him unappreciative; it only meant that our way was not his. There was no martial music to play the column off, no flag-bedecked arches under which to march, no sentimental mottoes, no handkerchiefs fluttering from fair hands, no tear-stained faces at the windows; but the very silence, broken only by a sharp word of command or a brief farewell, made the departure perhaps more impressive.   On through the slums of the native quarter tramped this band of men in single file: soldiers with glinting rifles, carriers with loads of every size and shape, here and there a white officer in an inconspicuous khaki uniform.   Over the low, scrub-covered sand-hills behind the town wound the long, snake-like column, until lost to the eyes of those left behind, and little by little the topmost roofs of Cape Coast faded from the sight of those going forward. How long would it be before we should see again the sunlight dancing on the ocean, the town with its grim old castle, oftentimes to be so vividly recalled to mind during the next few months?

The Cape Coast-Kumasi road is broad at first, and, with the exception of bad bits at intervals, fairly good as far as Prahsu.   Beyond that, it deteriorates with each mile marched; the pathway is not well drained and is washed away at intervals during each successive rainy season.   I remember so well on my way back, when chaffing one of the officials of the Public Works Department who had been specially employed on repair work, how amused I was at his reply to a remark of mine anent the celerity of his progress: "It was in excellent condition for the return of the troops and the Commandant, was it not?" said he, "what more was wanted?   It was no good doing too much to some parts of it during that ceaseless going to and fro of transport carriers; they only undid all one had accomplished."

The first day's march — owing to our late start a
short one—was through the only country approaching
what one might call open that we passed through during
the campaign.   The next day we struck into the forest
belt, three hundred miles wide, which runs along the
coast in unbroken similarity.   One's first impressions
were deceptive ; the shade afforded by the foliage was
a very welcome protection from the merciless rays of
the tropical sun.   But how deadly sick one got of it !
The gloom and tedium became almost intolerable, and
the prospect, which charmed at first, was soon looked at
with a feeling akin to disgust.   The hushed silence of
the forest was maddening, and one felt at times in-
clined to cry out from a feeling of utter loneliness.
Nothing broke the silence of nature but the occasional
hoarse scream of some gay-plumed, restless bird by day,
and by night the plaintive call of the sloth, like the
cry of a woman in pain.   The bush, so dense on
either side that one could neither penetrate nor even see
into it more than a yard or two, engendered a sensation
of oppression that became appalling.   The damp,
malarious mist, the monotonous drip of water from the
leaves overhead, the fœtid mire under foot, the dank
clammy feeling of the atmosphere, the pungent, sickly
smell of decaying vegetation, all combined to create
loathing and weariness.   The giant cotton and mahogany
trees, vast columns lining the forest tracks, were magnificent in themselves, but their endless number blunted
all perception of their grandeur.   In close proximity
have they stood for centuries, amid pools of stagnant,
muddy water, united by twining creepers above, and
never - changing undergrowth below.   Close - woven
between their trunks, a maze of brambles, graceful
banana plants, nodding stalks of corn, and stunted

timber kept ever sodden a carpet of rotting leaves.   An occasional orchid peeped out between the branches of some silver-tinted stem, scattered clusters of garish scarlet flowers looming through the purple haze of death, but for the rest—an embodiment of sorrowful silence, a never-changing sequence of dissatisfaction, a wilderness of superabundance.   Does the lover of nature blame one for a dulled appreciation of the beautiful?   If so, let him come and experience for himself what month after month of this eternal lack of variation in scenery means. It is the earth brooding moodily, bereft of heaven's bright sun, weeping in darkness for the light.

To look at this country from a practical point of view does not improve one's opinion of it.   The narrow, tortuous track compels a force to move in single file, which makes its length enormous and renders it exceedingly vulnerable.   The path in places is next to impassable, since, in the absence of sunshine, there is nothing to dry up the slimy, slippery mud and surface water.   At frequent intervals, great fallen trees lie across the road, and nobody would believe how such an apparently slight obstacle delays a march, nor what gaps are made in a long column by such checks.   It is the most impossible country in which to fight and manœuvre. The only way to extend one's front is for each man to cut his own way through the jungle, which is such a perfect natural ambush that one's nerves are strained to the extremest tension by the knowledge that a murderous fire, at a few yards' range, may be poured into your men at any moment.   Is it wonderful, then, that with experience one gets to hate the African "bush," as it is rather inappropriately called?

Our first night was spent at Akroful, which was reached just before dark, making it pretty late before

A BUSH PATH

all the soldiers and carriers had been disposed of and the loads stacked. Again we had rather an amusing difference with a local missionary, who had, much against his will, to submit and make the best of it. Rice, the usual food carried for the consumption of the natives in West Africa, is made up in 50-lb. canvas bags and generally becomes mouldy if allowed to get wet. The ordinary symptoms informed us, in most unmistakable terms, that a storm was brewing, and we knew we should have to use caution in this matter. The bags were not waterproof, nor had they even been tied up in banana leaves, which are of assistance in keeping out of water—a device which came into common practice later on in the campaign. What was to be done with the precious bags? Where could they be put? The very thing! There stood the iron-roofed mission hall, aggressively suggesting its services. There was nothing for it; it was the only eligible building and must be requisitioned in the emergency. After all, why not? Was not the rice to feed our starving compatriots in Kumasi? Did not Cromwell, in time of war, even turn cathedrals into stables? So it was done.

Sleeping five in a small room, with nowhere to cook one's food and none of one's kit unpacked, was not comfort; but at such times comfort is not expected, and it is wonderful how quickly one learns to shake down and become accustomed to these trifles. The rain came down and the room was stuffy, but we slept through it all and arose betimes next morning. We were off soon after dawn, despite the desertion of some carriers—that everlasting trouble—and some recently acquired white men's servants. The march of some twenty miles through the primeval forest was uneventful, except for its inherent annoyances. Some carriers dropped their

loads and bolted, whilst more went sick, and others had
to be impressed at the first village to replace them.
The next rest-house was at Dunkwa, but we went right
through to the one at Mansu, which was reached at
5 p.m.   Here an excellent two-storied *dâk* bungalow
afforded every one good quarters.   At this place we
heard by telegraph from the coast of the fall of Pretoria,
and by native rumour the report of another unsuccessful
sortie at Kumasi.   Next morning brought the same
amusements again, more carriers gone, despite the guard
that had been put over them, and more boys ; amongst
the latter my beautiful new cook, to whom I had weakly
advanced money for his lonely wife before starting and
who had seemed over-night too footsore to make off in
this abrupt fashion.   These *contretemps* placed such a
serious complexion on affairs, that the Commandant
wired to the Base Commandant to have all these camp
followers arrested and tried for desertion ; but they were
never caught, and we had to get on without them as
best we could.   How we longed for the substitution
of Mendis from Sierra Leone (two thousand and fifty-
three of whom had left there the previous day), for these
Fanti carriers.   I was sent out with a party of soldiers
to raid the neighbouring village for men, to make up
their deficiency, and was not only fortunate enough to
succeed at once, but was personally rewarded by getting
another cook, a " boy " who had just been given notice
by a white official.   This was great luck, because, once
off the coast, servants were unobtainable, particularly
when it was known that their would-be master was
going on active service.   I must admit I could not
blame them.   We reached our destination, Fesu, by
tea time ; there was another rest-house there, but so
much smaller than the one at Mansu that most of the

white men had to go into the village like the troops and
carriers. The road had been chiefly noticeable for two
points: firstly, for its deterioration underfoot ; secondly,
for the magnificent clumps of bamboos which grew to a
great height, arching over the pathway and rendering
the tunnel, thus formed, comparatively dark.

The midday halt, when on the march, had been, as
usual, made in a village, of which there are very many in
this colony. This rest generally lasted about an hour,
and was occupied in breakfasting. Nature does not, in
this climate, assert her requirements by giving one a
healthy appetite as at home, but by a passive feeling of
exhaustion which is far more eloquent, though less pleasant. One of our two companies, Captain Beddoes', was
left behind to bring on the first gang of five or six hundred Mendi carriers, as soon as they arrived. In the late
afternoon of the next day, the 8th, Prahsu was reached,
these twenty miles being the last march known to be
safe. This place now became headquarters, and its very
fair, double-storied rest-house came to be looked upon
quite as a home by many of us. It was, however, far
too small for what was required, the ground-floor alone
being entirely taken up by offices and storerooms.
Had it not been for two or three tents, the subsequent
erection of bamboo huts, and a small native village to
take in the surplus, it would have been impossible to
put every one under shelter, however makeshift and leaky.

The river Prah at this time was about a hundred and
thirty yards broad, flowing rapidly, and quite unfordable. It circled from a north-westerly direction round
the north, west, and south-west sides of the town. There
was no bridge, so two wooden pontoons, relics of the
last expedition, and a couple of large native canoes had
to do the subsequent transportation—a very awkward

procedure. On the opposite bank the enemy's country began, and it was the general belief that they had worked down thus far. As a matter of fact, they were never seen south of Fumsu, eighteen miles further north on the road to Kumasi.

CHAPTER VIII

RETARDED BY REVERSES

IT was during the halt here that all the bad news of the campaign came surging in, until the chance of ever relieving Kumasi fort looked well-nigh hopeless. The reports of the succession of misfortunes and reverses which were received at this period would have daunted any man not possessed of the indomitable pluck of our Commandant. With him it was otherwise: he only laboured on the harder, often late into the night and sometimes without food.

If I may be permitted to anticipate for a moment, the following summary of events, which occurred in quick succession, will assist the reader to understand the feelings of those who took part in the early stage of the relief operations. The first misfortune was the rising of the Adansis, which doubled the difficulties at once by isolating the units of the field force, and trebling the extent of hostile country we had to pass through south of Kumasi. Captain Hall and his force were thus neither able to go on nor to come back; he had attacked Kokofu, but was repulsed. A southward-bound party of carriers, with their escort of soldiers from Esumeja, were massacred. Captain Beamish's company was severely attacked when returning for supplies, and had to fight its way to its destination, but was unable to get back. Lieutenant-Colonel Carter's column joined Lieutenant-Colonel Wilkinson's on its way northwards, had a tremendous fight, and was practically repulsed, inasmuch as its heavy losses prevented its advance. Captain Wilson started with his company to reinforce them : he was attacked, the company decimated and himself killed. The Obuasi miners were crying for military assistance, which the sadly lessened little relief force could not furnish. All the troops were clamouring for food and ammunition, which it was next to impossible to send up as every convoy was fiercely attacked. Lieutenant-Colonel Burroughs afterwards assaulted Kokofu again, but was repulsed with a heavy list of casualties. There was no certainty that the Bekwais would remain loyal. Several despatches were received from the Governor, to the effect that he would have to break out if not relieved by various dates, which were past when the letters were received. There was no mention made in them at first of any intention to leave a garrison behind in the fort, should this plan be adopted : a detail of such importance that it would have altered the course of the campaign completely. Then news came that the Governor had fought his way out and had left a garrison behind him, but with rations for a very limited number of days. Finally, there was no possibility of immediate reinforcements. Colonel Willcocks received all this information without turning a hair : he perceived that a fresh scheme of strategy and new tactics must be devised : he devised them and put them into action.

To return now to the situation as it was when we arrived at Prahsu. The earliest wires were urgent orders. Every available officer and carrier in Cape Coast was to come up forthwith; all the road to the south was to be repaired at once to facilitate transport; moreover, martial law was declared in the colony.

The morning after our arrival, a despatch dated May 24th arrived from Captain Hall at Esumeja. It narrated the details of his attack on Kokofu, which he considered so threatened his right flank that no advance to Kumasi could be made in safety till it was destroyed. Within half an hour of his departure for this purpose he had met with severe opposition at a small village between his headquarters and the enemy's war-camp. The position was taken after a short struggle and the village burnt. Before his force was quit of the place some thousands of Kokofus, reinforced by Ashantis, engaged it again, this time with such determination that after an hour's fight a withdrawal had to be made. Two Europeans had been hit and six soldiers wounded; worst of all, the prestige of the white man was lowered, the rebels encouraged, and their influence increased with those tribes whose loyalty was wavering.

On the heels of this runner came another, from Lieutenant-Colonel Carter at Kwisa, with a message dated the 8th. It appeared he had been ambushed several times between Fumsu and Kwisa, which he relieved on the 4th, having lost four men killed and seven wounded in one attack alone from the bush. Four of these casualties were significant of the enemy's intention to pick off the white officers. Lieutenant-Colonels Carter and Wilkinson and Dr. Fletcher were walking together, followed by their three orderlies and the Regimental Sergeant-Major. The four natives were dropped by a sudden volley, the three white men fortunately escaping untouched. On the morning of the 6th, Lieutenant-Colonel Carter, with

G

one 7-pr., three Maxims, and three hundred and eighty
men, started from Kwisa to join Captain Hall at
Esumeja. The column moved out in the usual formation. The foremost officer was Captain Roupell, who,
depending more upon his own sagacity than that of the
natives, went with the " point "—the few men who move
along the path in front of the advance guard. At any
likely place for an attack volleys by some half-dozen
men of the " point " were fired into the undergrowth,
Lieutenant-Colonel Carter having found by experience
in Southern Nigeria that, if fired upon, the native
invariably disclosed his presence by replying. This
procedure took the place of scouting in the bush, the
necessity of which was as little known then as was the
enemy's mode of warfare.

The village of Dompoasi was a large one, and behind
it was an extensive Adansi war-camp, in which was a
garrison of several thousands, including Ashanti and
Kokofu reinforcements. The natives of this town, we
learned subsequently, had sworn a solemn oath to stop
any further columns going up to relieve Kumasi, and
their method of so doing and the way in which they
fortified themselves were both cunningly conceived and
cleverly carried out. On the south side of the village
and a short distance from it, they erected a six-feet
high and six-feet thick stockade of two rows of tree
trunks, the interval between which was filled with
timber, stones, and rammed earth, so that it was not
only absolutely proof against rifle fire but also against
7-pr. shells. This formidable entrenchment was built
in zig-zag shape (so that a flanking and cross-fire
could be kept up from it), about four hundred yards
in length, and with both ends doubled backwards to
prevent its being turned, and to bring an enfilading fire

up and down the road. In the rear was a trench in which their guns could be loaded with immunity from our fire, and a path, so cut as to give them a line of retreat and connect them with their village. At points of vantage neighbouring trees were prepared and rifle-pits dug to accommodate marksmen, the undergrowth in their immediate front being left untouched, so that there might be nothing to excite suspicion. The stockade itself was roughly parallel to the road, on our right when coming up, at a distance varying from twenty to thirty yards from it. Thus anybody coming along the path would see nothing abnormal, although himself in full view of the defenders, who could easily concentrate their fire on him. On the northern side of the village a similar stockade, about three hundred yards in length, had been constructed, so that, from whichever side the white man might come, they were ready for him. Captain Roupell with the "point" became aware as he approached Dompoasi that the enemy must be in force in the neighbourhood, to judge from the numerous footprints and little tracks running off at right angles into the bush, but he never expected such a gigantic trap as the one into which he walked. The rebels, however, lay quiet and allowed him to proceed to the far end of their position, so that the majority of the column was in front of it when they opened fire with a terrific volley, which dropped Captain Roupell and many others. Then the battle began in earnest with a continuous, deafening roar all along the line. The troops were momentarily paralysed by the hail of lead suddenly hurled into them ; then, facing the unseen, unknown enemy, they replied with their rifles, whilst the Maxims and 7-pr. were got to work. Captain Roupell, who had staggered to his feet, and Lieutenant O'Malley worked two of the former, Lieutenant Edwards, R.A., the latter.   Captain Roupell was again dangerously wounded, and remained unconscious for two whole days and nights ; he was pluckily carried to the rear by Mr. Cookson, one of the mining engineers whom Captain Hall had originally left behind at Kwisa.   Lieutenant O'Malley was shortly afterwards so severely wounded in the arm that he was forced to discontinue firing.   Lieutenant Edwards, though hit early in the action, stuck gallantly to his gun, finally ramming home the shells himself with a stick, as all his gun team were lying around either killed or wounded. He was shortly afterwards shot again, this time in the left arm ; and being thus incapacitated for serving the 7-pr., he went and worked a Maxim with his right arm until a shot in the face compelled him to go to the rear and have his wounds dressed.   Lieutenant-Colonel Carter had, a short time before this, been shot in the head by a man in a tree, and had handed over command to Lieutenant-Colonel Wilkinson, who himself was slightly wounded in the back of the skull.   This was the first time that a man, whom we afterwards nicknamed "Ping-ping" from the sound made by his ·220 rook rifle, was met.   He was never caught (so far as we could ascertain), although he persistently turned up at every encounter, and was known to have been personally responsible for several of our casualties at various times.   This battle was one of the very nastiest fights in the whole campaign.   The men and carriers fell fast, the 7-pr. and a Maxim were completely isolated some distance up the path, whilst the fact of there being a stockade was only discovered by the intense fire having cut away the bush sufficiently to disclose its presence.

It was at this moment that Colour-Sergeant Mackenzie came up, and asked leave to charge the enemy, which was given, although it now seemed probable that a retreat would be absolutely necessary. The officer commanding D Company, 1st Bn. W.A.F.F., which had been in the rear guard all this time and consequently had not suffered heavily, was *hors de combat* in a hammock with fever, which accounted for the fact that Colour-Sergeant Mackenzie was in command. Without waiting for more than half his men to arrive, he, though himself slightly wounded, promptly charged the stockade at their head, other soldiers and some officers in the vicinity joining them. The enemy could not stand against this determined onslaught, and evacuated their position in headlong flight. Colour-Sergeant Mackenzie's self-reliance and initiative were beyond all praise. At the critical moment when he came forward a retirement might have been attended with heavy loss, if not worse, the gun and Maxim might have had to have been abandoned, and the prestige of the white man and his troops again been lowered. All these dangers were averted by Colour-Sergeant Mackenzie's judgment and courage. For this he has received the Victoria Cross, a well-earned honour.[1]

After this severe experience the force retired in a leisurely and orderly manner on Kwisa. Seven European officers had been wounded and over ninety other casualties sustained ; indeed, if the enemy had not fired high (as, mercifully, they invariably did), the column might have been exterminated. One of the Maxims had its water-jacket penetrated by a bullet,

[1] It is with pleasure I also record that this gallant soldier, with whom I have been closely associated on service, has since been given a commission in the Black Watch,

which rendered the gun temporarily useless.   As for
the enemy's casualties, they cannot have been more
than about half ours, for they were fighting behind
excellent cover.   Altogether the action lasted a few
minutes under two hours, and, unsatisfactory as it was,
the experience it afforded of the enemy's tactics proved
of great benefit to the other units of the field force in
subsequent engagements.

The same unfortunate day upon which Captain Hall's
and Lieutenant-Colonel Carter's bad news was received,
a letter arrived from the Governor, dated June 5th.   It
mentioned that Major Morris had got into the fort;
that the garrison was then seven hundred strong; that
the Europeans and troops were on half-rations; that
paucity of ammunition did not admit of much in the
way of offensive measures; that the health in Kumasi
was good, but that the native community was in a state
of destitution.   Some details of the opposition and
stockades that we might encounter were given, and
immediate assistance implored.

Orders were sent to Lieutenant-Colonel Carter, telling
him to remain where he was and await reinforcements
of men, ammunition, and food.   Instructions were also
forwarded to Captain Hall to send a company to
increase the garrison at Kwisa.

Captain Melliss and I, with F Company 1st Bn.
W.A.F.F., got orders to proceed instantly to the
relief of Kwisa, and within an hour we were off
escorting a convoy.   We were to force our way through
the enemy, ration the garrison, replenish their ammunition, and then return.   Dr. Buée, of the Gold Coast
Medical Department, accompanied us.   We fell in at
2 p.m., but it was four o'clock before we got across
the Prah; a delay which prevented us doing more than

THE RIVER PRAH

From the enemy's bank

ten miles on the slippery road.   It was a wretched
march ; the rain poured down, we were soon wet
through, and it was a quarter past eight—long after
dark—before we got in.   As we expected casualties,
enough hammocks were taken for each white man with
one to spare, but they were of little service for travelling,
thanks to the weather and the enemy.   An early start
the following day enabled us to reach Fumsu at
8 a.m., which place was then the advanced base on the
lines of communication.   White officers were so scarce
that this important post was being commanded by
Quartermaster-Sergeant Thomas, 2nd Bn. W.A.F.F.,
who was living in a roughly constructed sort of redoubt,
built of earth and timber round the rest-house.   He had
a cheering tale to relate : every party of troops and all
convoys had been attacked from this point onwards ; the
bush was swarming with the enemy ; all the troops
ahead were perilously situated, short of food and
ammunition, and crippled with casualties.   In fact, to
quote his own words : " You are simply walking into a
death-trap, sir ; it isn't fighting, it's murder.   I am sure
you will never get there with only a hundred men and
all those carriers."   However, we were going on, and
that as quickly as possible.   It was a grave emergency,
and we had our orders.   Nevertheless we realised, more
than ever before, what to expect, and the feeling of
responsibility became deeper and more anxious.

CHAPTER IX

GAINING EXPERIENCE

U NDER twenty miles from our destination, and not a moment to be lost! We had not yet appreciated what this meant, under such unfavourable conditions of nature, not to speak of hostile opposition. From the news which had just been received, and as we now knew that forty thousand rounds had been expended in the Dompoasi fight, it was decided that loads of ammunition were, on the whole, more urgently needed than even bags of rice. Our carriers were so limited in number that only a few days' food could be taken to the Kwisa garrison, if all our available cartridges were to go on also.

We now learned for the first time of the extraordinary way in which the enemy transmitted news. The moment we set out, a Dane gun was fired somewhere away in the forest. This signal was repeated by another, and so on as far as the enemy's next war-camp. A rough estimate of the strength and composition of our force was also given by the number of guns these scouts let off. Our departure from Prahsu had been known to the Adansis, it now appeared, and only darkness and pouring rain, which delayed their movements, had saved us from the ambush which had been planned to intercept us. Colonel Willcocks' personality was not only known to the enemy, but, like the Governor, he was "wanted," and a description of his hammock was in their possession.

There is nothing like food to instil comfort and confidence, when one cannot get it elsewhere; so, while the stores were being got together for our onward march, we breakfasted. To open one of the "Armour Canning" Company's tins of meat, get hold of a few "dog-biscuits," and boil a little water for tea, did not take long; in a hurry such as there now was, it required even less time to despatch our meal than it would have done had one been at home, and late for a train. When one gets a chance of eating while on service, it ought never to be neglected on the score of want of appetite or the irregularity of time. Both of these drawbacks were of daily occurrence out here: on this occasion, for example, we did not get another mouthful until over twelve hours afterwards.

Experientia docet; but two things were now done the inexpediency of which became evident very shortly. Firstly, one hundred extra rounds were served out to each man, in addition to the hundred he already had, for the apparently good reasons that in a fight there must be no risk of running short, and that the number of reserve ammunition carriers for the soldiers would be thereby reduced, thus enabling more loads to be taken for the force we were going to relieve. Secondly, when forming up the column for the march-off, a percentage of soldiers was distributed singly amongst the carriers, with the object of preventing straggling as far as possible —a very good idea, when one does not expect opposition. This plan did not, however, prove satisfactory.

The black soldier dearly loves to do his share of firing in an action, and, if left to himself, acts on the principle of quantity rather than quality. It does not answer to let him have too many rounds at once. If he wants more, it is better to open boxes and serve out cartridges even under fire. For the same reason, one must not let one's men move independently; they must never march except as a fire-unit, however small, when they would have at least a native N.C.O. with them, to control and direct their fire, keeping an eye on the expenditure of ammunition.

It is now time to say a word about the formation of columns on the march in this peculiar country, where the men have to move in single file, and the human transport makes supervision so hard. In time of peace, it is enough for a few soldiers accompanied by an officer to head the caravan as an escort for the white man, and to impress the natives as villages are approached. Then follow all the carriers, interspersed with single soldiers to keep them together, and behind is a small rear guard, to whip in stragglers, see that no loads are overlooked or lost, catch deserters and any carriers who bolt, and generally perform such unpleasant, though important duties. On active service this *modus operandi* is changed. The soldiers are then wanted for fighting, and to protect the carriers instead of merely driving them on. In front of all on the road comes a "point" of some half-dozen soldiers, whilst on either side, in the adjacent bush, a number of scouts move in extended order, looking for the enemy's ambuscades. Each one of these parties, which form the eyes and ears of the column in their rear, is under the personal control of an officer. Some twenty-five to fifty yards in rear of the "point" comes the advance guard, first a section of the leading company—a variable quantity, usually about thirty men ; then its Maxim gun and team, followed by the remaining three sections. Each section ought to have a British officer or N.C.O. to look after it effectively in action. In a large force there would immediately follow another entire company, after which would come the big guns with their escort of infantry, divided according to circumstances amongst them, and next the stretcher-party with the Medical Officer ; then, but with practically no interval, the head of the main body, composed of more troops, the Staff, and the like. Behind these, again, is a long string of carriers, with here and there a squad of soldiers to guard them. After the transport comes the hospital, with its own porters, hammocks with the " boys " for them, and the doctors. Last of all marches a strong rear guard, in a somewhat similar fighting formation to the guard in front, and between its infantry with their Maxims would probably be a field gun or two, if they could be spared. Also, as a rule, a few carriers march behind each company with its immediate supply of reserve ammunition.

A word about the scouts and carriers at this stage will perhaps be helpful to an understanding of future events, because they are more or less concerned in all movements. The constant ambuscades and the presence of small stockades, fallen trees, trenches, rifle-pits, and what not (as was especially the case at Dompoasi), plainly showed the necessity of scouting, by which alone such dangers could be reduced, if not obviated ; and, in the same way, another important change in tactics had now been clearly seen by us, namely, that a prolonged duel of fire with an entrenched foe was most undesirable, and would always prove costly ; but that he must be turned out either by flank movements, charged at the point of the bayonet, or, best of all, treated to a combination of both. By this means, the far from inconsiderable advantages accrued of giving the soldiers confidence in their own superiority, and a saving of ammunition, with a consequent reduction in the number of carriers requisite to transport it.

The principal drawback to scouting in the dense bush is the painfully slow progress made, and the greatly increased fatigue entailed thereby. Three-quarters of a mile an hour is the average rate, and a march of eight miles in one day is good going. Every scout should be provided with a long knife, as he frequently has to cut a way for himself through the undergrowth and tangled creepers. The work is done as silently as possible, nothing being heard save the rustle of the men's bodies, pushing and squeezing their way along, and the occasional chop of their *machêtês;* then the voice of the officer calling in an undertone, either to keep his men in line, or to ascertain from the "point" on the road whether he is abreast of them and maintaining the right direction. This is no easy matter when following an invisible path which never runs straight, and when constant *détours* are necessary to explore some small track running off at an angle into the jungle. This kind of work requires an expert; and the natives accustomed, like the Hausas, to fairly open country, are almost useless when so employed. They blunder bravely on, cracking branches, oftentimes falling, and generally making so much noise that a lurking enemy would get ample notice of their advance. But, though the Hausa may be a little deficient in such cunning and stealth, he certainly surpasses the forest-bred native when a charge in the open is required, and he can see the object he wants to get at. This constant search necessitated a killingly slow pace for the column on the road. The advance guard crawls along, and all loads become intolerable. Often complete halts are entailed, but despite this, there is continual straggling, and always gaps, which, sooner or later, have to be made up by stepping out, some inexperienced people even indulging in an occasional double.

The West African carrier is little better than a beast of burden, and his method of earning his living is, of all that I have ever known, the one I should select last. In all weathers, often for very prolonged periods, he is expected to do his monotonous weary grind of carrying his load along a winding track, with the same scrub on either side, and similar beings to himself before and behind him. He is not a high-caste native, but he is a wonderfully cheerful one. It was an astonishing sight to watch him going through swamp and water, and staggering over slippery mud with his load on his head, not infrequently falling, but rarely damaging anything. He has to go under fire like the soldier ; he is sniped at from the bush ; he runs the same risks of disease, without any reward beyond his pay, not even a medal as a record of his services. When the solid, dead-weight, compact little ammunition boxes were not so well known as they are now, it was an amusing sight to see these men rush and struggle to get them, when the order to pick up loads had been given, but it was much more funny to watch their faces when they tried to lift them. The 75 m/m gun carriers had the worst time of all, because the parts into which this weapon divides are mostly too heavy for single loads, and have to be carried by four men, slung between two bamboo poles. The trail, which is the heaviest, weighs about 340 lbs., making a load of over 80 lbs. for each of four men. It is an awkward shape, and a troublesome thing to carry, inasmuch as at acute bends in the road, or other nasty spots, four men cannot march, as they usually do, two in front and two behind when supporting it. At such times the whole burden has for the moment to be sustained by two of them. I have seen them, under such circumstances, straining with outstanding muscles and teeth clenched with their exertions to successfully surmount the obstacle, struggling manfully not to fall on the greasy ground at the imminent risk of being crushed under the gun. For the sake of convenience, all these hard-working labourers are divided into gangs of about twenty, each under its own head man, who is no help at all to the wretched officer on transport duty. His work is most arduous, both physically and mentally. It has not the same glamour about it as the combatant duties, and certainly is much less interesting. I have often sympathised with their difficulties.

CHAPTER X

THWARTED

IT was noon on June 10th before our column had fallen in, in the fighting formation which has been described; only a hundred odd rank and file, with one Maxim and some three hundred carriers. Captain Melliss in front, Colour-Sergeant Foster with the gun, Corporal Philpotts in charge of the immediate escort with the carriers, Dr. Buée next with his hospital train, and I, with Corporal Buchanan, in command of the rear guard.

The river Fum, which flows round Fumsu exactly like the Prah at Prahsu, was rising, but still fordable; so we waded it, and went off with a better idea of what to expect than on our arrival three and a half hours previously; but we knew we could not now afford the time to scout carefully all the way. Clearing volleys must be depended upon, and only particularly nasty localities looked into before the column passed.

It is always a wise course to conserve one's strength; and as there was no immediate probability of an attack, I thought I could safely take a short turn in my hammock. So I got in, but found that lying wet to the waist and with a revolver jammed into one's ribs on one

side, and an ammunition pouch on the other, was not
the height of comfort.   The swish of the rushing river
was scarce out of hearing when crash, bang, went a
volley.   I leapt out.   What ! were we attacked already ?
The alarmist rumours we had just heard must, then,
really have represented the true state of affairs.   No; a
false alarm : it was, after all, only a clearing volley into
a thicket with an ugly aspect.   Should I be carried a
little further ?   No, on the whole, I thought I would not.
Things looked business-like, and the enemy was no
respecter of any particular part of a column.   My
rear guard might, for all we knew, be their first fancy ;
nor were they averse to a pot-shot at a hammock, in
which only white and disabled black men travelled,
and the former were their favourite bag.   And now
what is that coming into view ahead ?   Yes, it is a
village, and what is more, there go a few Adansis
running for dear life.   The Maxim was mounted on
its tripod in a minute, and commenced belching bullets
at them at the rate of six hundred to the minute.
"Cease fire !"   We were too late : they were gone, and
the precious pellets must be kept for better sport than
running game.   One or two sparsely populated villages
flying white flags had been passed through just after
leaving Prahsu, but those we now met were deserted,
and mutely told the sorrowful tale of war.

Scarce two hours of this nerve-straining tramp, and
we halted.   What had happened now ?   The question
was scarce asked, when down doubled an orderly to tell
me I was required in front.   I went, and found a cheerful sight awaiting me.   There was the river, the same
old Fum, which had met us again at another bend, but
its volume and its width were more than doubled.   The
banks were now marshy, overhung with prickly thickets,

A DESERTED VILLAGE

rank grass, and obstructive bushes. On the far side of this whirling, rushing mill-stream stood another village, Akrofum. How many Dane guns lay hidden in the undergrowth between it and these unfordable eighty yards of foaming, eddying flood? What could possibly be done? Another West African problem which no manual had made rules to solve. There were no trees which we could cut down with our *machêtês* long enough to throw across; neither had we axes with which to fell the larger ones, nor rope with which to drag them to the river's bank. To right and left, a rapid reconnaissance only showed that no better place existed. Worst of all, the water was steadily rising with alarming rapidity; there was, therefore, the impending risk that the river behind would become impassable before we could get back, and that we should find ourselves cut off between the two!

Luck at last! Swept some distance further down, and caught in the branches of a fallen tree on our side, was a native canoe, but what a craft it was, with a heavy circular bottom which made it roll to such an extent that it was unsafe even when empty! Could it be a trick on the enemy's part? was the question which instinctively suggested itself to us. However, there was nothing else for it: an experiment must be made. A Maxim was got into position, so as to sweep the opposite bush should our attempt to cross be opposed. What a target we made, congregated together at the water's edge, discussing and arranging the preliminaries of the crossing!

Two naked hammock "boys," with long bamboo poles, volunteered to take this unseaworthy vessel over. If only a landing-party could be got over by driblets in the canoe, surely some better means of crossing

H

could be subsequently arranged. In got a couple of soldiers, having first been wisely ordered to take off their belts, and off they started. The little cockleshell rocked ominously in the quiet water near our bank; one heavier lurch, and it shipped a little water, yet it glided slowly on. Then an eddy caught it and swept it into the mid-stream sluice. Here the seething, boiling current admitted of no warning, and in an instant the canoe capsized, and shot, bottom upwards, down the swirling tide. Every eye was strained, an involuntary gasp escaped the lips of many of the onlookers. Without a moment's hesitation in plunged Captain Melliss, but he could not live unaided in such a torrent, strong swimmer though he was. On his way out from home he had won the Royal Humane Society's medal for saving life at sea, but he was much weaker now than then, for this climate soon saps strength, and so he was forced at once to call for help. Another European went to his aid, and at last the rescue was effected. The men were saved, but unfortunately their rifles were lost. Even then, however, many yards of boggy bank had to be waded over, while hosts of driver ants and the lacerating undergrowth left many painful reminiscences of the adventure. The intense chill produced by this sudden immersion in ice-cold water after the copious sweating of the hot march, the maddening bites of the ants as they swarmed over and stung their victims mercilessly, the knowledge of the imminent jeopardy of black-water fever or sunstroke, all urgently necessitated a rapid change of clothing. This done, a swig of neat spirits, a stiff dose of quinine, and all was happily over; but the river was still uncrossed, the obstacles remained still unsurmounted. The only good fortune was that no attack had been made during this time of unpreparedness to meet it.

It was getting late now, and we were fairly baffled, so the order "About turn" was given, and with our tails between our legs we disconsolately retraced our steps with all due speed. Our arrival was only in the nick of time. The river at Fumsu had risen in the incredible way so common out here in the rains, and was now unfordable. It was hours after darkness had fallen when the last man dragged himself over by a rope strained across, and the loads were floated safely to the other side. The wire was, fortunately, up as far as here, so Colonel Willcocks that night received a far from comforting telegram recounting our difficulties, together with the news that we should have to remain a day where we were for fresh orders, and to see what we could contrive to make further progress possible.

After a night of heavy rain we arose fatigued, but determined to try and do something to remedy yesterday's reverse. A survey of the river, which was now higher than ever, soon showed us that a bridge was out of the question, nor indeed had we any materials with which to construct one. There were no two opinions about it, we must build a raft, which might, if suitably made, have the advantage of portability. Moreover, we knew several other crossings would have to be effected, and judging by the experience of the previous day, they seemed likely to be worse instead of better. A friendly rivalry then began amongst the white men as to who would be the first to devise something suitable. I remember being chaffed with my slowness, and being told that the problem had been solved while I was still thinking it over. However, my thinking turned out in the end to be of some use. The raft designed was, nevertheless, not quite a success. It consisted of a platform of planks topping some barrels, a few of which had been found in the store-hut ; these latter were the piers, and gave the required buoyancy. They were lashed together with the only rope in the station. The structure certainly looked all right ashore, but when launched, weak points became noticeable. A couple of nude natives, with long sticks, clambered on top of it and pushed off. Their utmost efforts were quite unavailing against the current, and they were carried down stream. Then something seemed to be going wrong with the raft itself. First, their ankles became submerged, next their knees disappeared from view, then they were waist deep, and at last—yes, swimming! The raft—where was it? Horrors! it had sunk! Not only were the leaking casks gone, but the priceless rope which united them. We had learnt this much, anyhow : the science of the text-book could very easily be confounded by the freaks of Nature ; and she was very unkind here. True, the forest was full of timber, but nearly all of it was so heavy as to have too low a buoyancy for our purposes. The only procurable stuff of the required flotage was sodden with rain, and consequently useless. To get something sufficiently light and dry was what completely nonplussed us. The situation seemed hopelessly akin to thirst in mid-ocean. But help was near at hand, indeed staring us in the face, yet for a long time we could not see it.

The native huts throughout this country are built on one principle—four sheds facing inwards on a small quadrangle. These have three closed outer sides, and the inner one towards the enclosure open. The walls are often made of mud, plastered over bamboos, which not only support the gabled roof of leaves and dry grass, but furnish stability to the whole edifice. It was, then, these dry bamboo poles which provided the required

material and put an end to our difficulties. But a few
moments were required to pull down some of the least
desirable shanties, and a sufficient quantity of stuff was
obtained for our purpose. This was good so far, but
how was it to be fastened together without the lost
rope? Once again we were like some citizen of New-
castle, shivering with cold because he would not get
the coal required to make a fire. One remembered,
however, that the bush was interlaced with twining
creepers, actually called "tie-tie" by its inhabitants;
which, when their fibres are crushed, serve admirably as
lashings, if one does not expect much durability. Our
portable raft was made thus: four bundles of bamboos
were tied up, each a carrier's load, and joined together
by cross-pieces of the same material, so that the mass
could be carried by four men like a hammock. This
was half of the raft, which needed to be of some length
to prevent its head being forced under water by the
strong current. The other half was identical. The
two portions could be united, when it was required for
use, by two long bamboo poles, and got ready for
service in a few minutes. The telegraph wire was then
torn down by us from the tree on the bank where we
were, and lowered on the opposite one by shooting at
and breaking the insulator which held it up to a tree on
the far side. Thus the wire was brought down to the
water level in the form of a gently curving arc, due to
the fact that the next insulators were fixed to trees at
a considerable distance. One end of the raft was
attached to this wire by a noose which worked along it,
and this contrivance not only enabled the swiftest streams
to be triumphantly crossed and the loads of rice to be
kept dry, but did away with the need of punters, who
would either have been useless, or have steered everything to wreckage.

A great load was now taken off our minds, and a delightful sensation of independence possessed us. Yesterday we had been kicking against the pricks and hurt our feet, but to-day the way was clear. So it was with a feeling of relief that the telegraph office was visited, for the purpose of wiring the good news that we could proceed next day.

An escort of fifty soldiers, and some more ammunition, came in to reinforce this post, and the same day we learned that the Governor had given June 11th (that very day) as the latest to which he could hold out, but without any news of his intention to leave a garrison behind. This letter was sent to the Commandant. I remember a wild phantom appearing before one's imagination as to the possibility of slipping round by the Obuasi road, which was then open, joining Captain Hall's force, getting food at Bekwai, and then making a desperate dash for Kumasi, on the off-chance of its still being held. This idea would have been as mad and futile as its conception was rash and sudden. Obviously, if seven hundred Hausas could not get out, half that number would be unable to get in, and so this dream of fancy faded before the light of mature deliberation.

An effort was made to get a runner through to Kwisa. He was promised £10 if he accomplished the journey, but he had not gone much over a mile before he met some hostile scouts, and returned in abject fear, but another was induced to undertake the mission later.

The reinforcements we had asked for, we were informed, could not be spared, as a rumour had arrived that the enemy would endeavour to cut off the Sierra Leone carriers who were on their way up from the coast. There was now nothing to wait for; things seemed to be getting steadily worse; orders were no sooner sent than some fresh development made it necessary to cancel them ; conflicting and disquieting *canards* came in from all sides, until one knew not what to think, and much less what to believe. That the enemy had collected in front to meet us, and had isolated us in rear, was one of the many. So at midnight, with a 4 a.m. reveille to look forward to, I turned in, and composed myself for rest, to the lullaby of a dripping roof and pattering rain. I can even at this moment recall my sleepy thoughts as to the similarity of the stirring times and almost insuperable difficulties of the Indian Mutiny, to those in which we now were, and it was with a feeling of pity rather than of envy for our Commandant, who had this tangled knot to unravel, that I finally closed my eyes.

CHAPTER XI

AMBUSHED

OFF again next morning at an early hour, with the same formation, the same mode of procedure, and a determination, this time, not to be baulked. All went well until the fourth river was being crossed—in fact, we began to think that we should not be molested, having completed five miles out of the eighteen, with never a soul to be seen. We did not then know the favourite sort of place the enemy selected for ambushes—usually on the top or at the bottom of a hill, invariably just after some obstacle which would necessitate the column falling into some disorder, crowded here and there into groups constituting good stationary objectives. The exact spot selected in this case was where the ground sloped down on one side from the roadway. Thus their uphill fire is kept lower than its wont, the object is more clearly seen, and our fire in reply to theirs tends to go harmlessly over their heads, as it is impossible on the path to see what sort of ground lies behind the thick curtain of leaves and branches.

This first experience was a typical one. There were some fifty yards of swamp to traverse, a chest-deep river to wade, some more boggy land on the further bank, and

then a steep climb to reach the better and more level track
beyond. On the crest of this incline the ambush was
secreted—behind a large fallen tree, quite invisible, and
at a range of not more than a dozen yards; and patiently
did they wait their time until they considered they had
as good a target as they could get, so that the shock of
surprise might have the most damaging effect possible
upon the column. The advance guard, after crossing the
river, had been ordered to proceed some four hundred
yards further on, to make room for the ever-arriving and
straggling string of carriers, and had actually walked
leisurely past this carefully planned death-trap. The
carriers and escort were then closing up, preparatory to
the bugle to advance from the rear guard commander—
the signal that all was ready to move on.

Suddenly, like a salvo of field guns, or a clap of
thunder, rang out a startling b—o—o—m, followed by a
few reports of muskets and rifles. Astonishment staggered one's senses for a moment. Yes—that was the
enemy ; it was not the sharp crack of cordite cartridges
in a clearing volley. But from which side is the fire
coming? Would that this zigzag path made it possible
to be certain on the point even a few yards off! What
unequal terms upon which to play the game of war!
" Volleys left!" one shouts at the top of one's voice, but
the din drowns the order, and men not forty paces from
one deliberately turn to the right, enter the bush a few
yards, and kneel down as they have been trained.
" Ready: aim low!"   Thank God, the men always
march on service with fixed bayonets, which keeps the
fire down, and they are always ready for a charge.
" Present : f—i—r—e !"   Crash goes a shower of bullets
at the unseen foe. The growl of Dane guns continues,
and a hail of slugs and buck-shot whizzes overhead,

interspersed with the occasional whistle of a bullet.
Again a volley, and yet another. The shower of leaves
from above plainly shows the enemy's fire is high : is
ours going right, or are we merely wasting ammunition?
The officer cannot control his extended command,
neither his voice nor whistle, to check the firing, will
carry in this noise. "Section Commanders give the
orders!" one shouts, "and look for the signal to stop."
Bah! those scattered soldiers amongst the carriers are
out of hand and firing recklessly, without word of command or careful aim. "You senseless ass, stop, will you!"
One hits down the barrel of his rifle, and races on up
the line, at the imminent risk of being shot by either
side. Merciful Heavens! the firing has ceased, and one
instinctively realises that never again must the men be
so broken up that they cannot be efficiently supervised.
But this is the first experience of an ambush that they
have had, and, to their credit be it said, they never lost
their heads again ; henceforth they were cool and careful,
with one eye along their sights and the other ex-
pectantly fixed on the white man for any order he
might give. There was no further need to hurry to and
fro, or worry the Recording Angel with one's language.
I returned relieved, though breathless, to find Dan
Leno squatting on the root of a tree, balancing my
sword on his knees and grinning from ear to ear—his
first time under fire, but perfectly happy and highly
pleased with the diversion caused by all he saw. "Get
up, you little fool! hide behind that tree, or you'll be
shot!" I shouted. Not a bit of it: he was quite comfortable where he was, and there he intended to remain.
Round the next bend of the path and nearer to the
ambuscade matters had not fared so well. From that
point was heard at this moment the "Cease fire!"

and then the "Charge!" Hurrying, stumbling over the prostrate figures of the carriers, lying along the track and seeking such cover as their loads afforded them, we soon reached the locality of the ambuscade. Into the bush we dashed with a yell, and then, some falling, all struggling, forcing a way onwards, made into the enemy's lair. A little blood, a gun here, a knife there, to show our fire had done good work. But where was the foe? Ahead there was a fresh-cut track. Down it we bounded—but to no purpose, save the imminent risk of losing one's way, or being cut off. Sound the "Retire," bugler—now the "Assembly."

The sight on the road was rather a sad one for a twenty minutes' fight. There lay the little advance guard bugler on his face, riddled with slugs, stone dead, poor little chap! A few yards further down was Corporal Philpotts, the blood streaming down his face, shot in the forehead, luckily only a flesh wound ; while scattered about were some dozen soldiers and carriers, hit in sundry places with varying degrees of severity, and Dr. Buée busily engaged amongst them with bottles, lint, and bandages. Such is a West African ambush.

All this caused considerable delay, and filled the hammocks and some of the stretchers. We subsequently learnt at Kwisa, from Lieutenant - Colonel Carter, who had the heir-apparent to the Adansi stool a prisoner, that they had heard through this man that we were to be attacked in this place, but, of course, he could not send us warning, and never expected us to force our way through. It appeared that a company of the enemy, under its captain, had been sent down the previous day for this purpose, and that our heavy fire had done great damage, which accounted for our getting through so successfully. That evening was spent by them in burying their dead, whom they always take away unless absolutely routed, chanting dismal fetish dirges to their departed spirits.

Then our onward plod recommenced, and so did the rain. Our force was a little weaker now with the wounded, but there was no time for extra precautions. Innumerable causes of delay beset us in our efforts to recover lost time, yet scarcely a hundred yards but some great fallen tree, barricade, stream, or quagmire was encountered ; and every now and again, a bit of road was reached, metalled with empty cartridge cases, showing where some previous party had met with opposition. Several villages were passed through ; and one wondered when we were going to halt. At last we arrived at Sherabroso, the worst water-obstacles, so far as we knew, being left behind. Here we stayed for breakfast, after nine hours' hard work on only a cup of cocoa and a biscuit. The bugler was buried by his fellows in a patch of plantain trees, just outside this hamlet. It is patent that we must have been followed and watched, because, on our way back, we found the poor boy's body dug up and beheaded, despite the care which we had taken to keep his grave a secret.

The rear guard is always the most fatiguing part of any column : incessant checks makes its progress wearisome to a degree. It is a continuation of stops, and then spurts to make good the never-ending gaps. This must be done, or else the chance of becoming isolated would be very great.

Just outside Sherabroso was another river, and a swamp over half a mile in length. This locality, and the Monsi Hill, at the foot of which, on the far side, stands Kwisa, were the two bugbears of the transport,

being the worst places on the lines of communication.
Sheramasi was our halting-place for that night, as the
approaching darkness forbade further progress. There
was no time to do much in the way of defensive preparations : a small clearing was made round the place
by cutting down the banana plantation (which invariably surrounds all domiciles in this country), a strong
in-lying picket was posted, and double sentries were
thrown out all round. Captain Melliss and I occupied
a hut at the far end of this village, in close proximity
to which was a characteristic look-out station of the
enemy's. It was a tall, straight tree, with a rude ladder
made up its smooth trunk by lashing cross-sticks to it,
until a fork was reached, high up and out of sight,
where a sentinel was placed. Interred here were the
victims of one of the ambushes set for Lieutenant-
Colonel Carter's column, this side of the long swamp we
had just passed. They also had been exhumed and
decapitated.

To account for our non-arrival that day, and protect
our inadequately escorted convoy against the enemy,
who, we were told, were collected in force in the Adansi
Hills, about three miles ahead of this place, to stop
us, it was imperative to get a letter through to Kwisa,
asking for some troops to be sent out at dawn to come
and meet us. After much trouble, and in response to a
big bribe, a volunteer was at last obtained, a head man
of carriers, who set off after nightfall, when the enemy
were not so likely to catch him, and safely reached
his destination. Nevertheless, he met several Adansi
scouts on the road, whom he successfully bluffed by
rushing at them with a drawn sword, his only weapon.

The white men had a poor time of it all round. Dr.
Buée, in his extempore hospital, was busy until all

hours, endeavouring to extricate bullets, whilst the combatants in turn went round the sentries at short intervals, to see that all was well, and were on outpost duty hour and hour about. We were ignorant, at that time, that the enemy had such a fetish dread of the demons of the dark, that they never make concentrated night attacks; but, in any case, precautions could not have been omitted.

Marvellously quietly can movements be carried out in this land of bare feet. At 3 a.m., without bugle, whistle, or shouting of orders, the crowd of sleeping forms arose in ghostly silence, and fell in. A misty moon afforded just sufficient light to enable the column to pick its way through the sombre shades of the forest. This unexpectedly early start of the two converging parties, our convoy, and the troops from Lieutenant-Colonel Carter, had the desired effect upon the enemy, and they left us alone. Kwisa, in its dire need, was saved. These were some of the most anxious times of the campaign, for the enemy, thinking they were carrying all before them, were filled with the courage of intoxication, and glutted with blood and victory. But there was a heavy reckoning in store for them, and the mill that now appeared to grind so slowly was soon to crush them to powder. The duel between savage cunning and civilised organisation admitted of but one solution in the finish.

At dawn the foot of the Adansi Hills was reached, and beautiful they looked in the rosy light of the approaching day! The precipitous pine-clad slopes towered upwards, bathed in the morning mist, and beyond these, rocky crags stood silhouetted against the sky, until they too were lost in fleecy clouds. The earth blushed as the sun arose and kissed her; Nature seemed to sigh with sensuous languor, and silence to kneel in wonder at the shrine of solitude. How fraudulent is Africa! Its fascinations dwindle and disappear like the mirage of the desert.

What a disillusion was to come when sweating humanity toiled up that slippery mountain side! Where was our hoped-for reinforcement? What an impregnable position for our foe! One such experience was more than enough. I little knew then that seven times more would I have to prove the difference between practical experience and the mockery of appearances. Winding, climbing, panting, cursing, at last the top was reached, and then down a lane of our comrades, standing with shouldered arms, we started the descent. Captain Beamish, and D Company 1st Bn. W.A.F.F., had wisely waited here to welcome us. In a few minutes Kwisa was sighted, and then in we marched, to our own satisfaction and the joy of those whom we had come to help, including Captain Slater, whose death had been supposed to be so satisfactorily substantiated that he had been reported home as killed in action.

CHAPTER XII

BACK AGAIN

ONE'S first impressions were that one had walked into a field hospital by mistake. Every third man one saw had some part of him tied up, but was none the less cheerful for all that. By far the saddest sight of all was poor Captain Roupell, lying on his bed in the rest-house, which was used as a ward for the wounded white men. He was still dangerously ill; his haggard face and emaciated body showing unmistakably what he had been through, without taking into account his bandaged arms and head. With over half a dozen slugs in him, it was miraculous that he had lived through it, and the great fear then was that an attack of fever might supervene and prove fatal. Half of Lieutenant-Colonel Carter's face was hidden by a covering over his wounded eye, and it was amusing to notice his devoted little fox terrier wistfully watching him as though conscious that something were wrong. During the fighting at Dompoasi this little animal had been in a state of high excitement, madly rushing up and down and barking loudly as if divining by instinct the dangers threatening his master. The one-armed officers had considerable difficulty at breakfast in com-

plying with the requirements of table manners, and
were compelled at intervals to use their fingers as well
as their knives and forks. One, whose personal appearance was much disfigured at the time by a slug which
had gone through his upper lip, and made it swell to an
enormous extent, was unceasingly twitted by another
with his inability on arrival home to demonstrate his
affection for his—well, let it be—relatives ! He retaliated
by pointing out to his gay tormentor, whose left arm
was in a sling, that he could not put it round his
partner's waist—the reference being, we presumed, to
dancing ! And thus the merry meal progressed, the
fare as good as the company. Some boxes of stores
left behind by H.E. the Governor, on his way up to
Kumasi, had been found by these hungry, foodless
officers, and, naturally, looted ; the comical consequence
of which was, that the officers of the replenishing convoy
became the guests, and not the hosts, at this convivial
party. But to cast one's eyes for a moment beyond
one's laughing *vis-à-vis*, sitting in perfect contentment
upon an upturned box, showed one the sterner aspect of
affairs at once.   Hasty fortifications met the eye on
every side ; that small stockade round the loop-holed
rest-house ; those Maxims enfilading all approaches,
the ever-watchful sentries, all spoke plainly of another
side of affairs.   One had only to leave this extempore
mess-room, and go into the make-shift office, to learn
the truth of the situation, the terrible tale of reverse and
suffering these men had undergone, and of the horde of
investing savages, and we realised our own good fortune
in having arrived here with as few losses as we had
experienced.   The officers were on half rations, the men
practically dependent upon what they could find in the
surrounding bush at the risk of their lives, and there

I

was not enough ammunition left to allow even of a
retirement without grave risk being incurred.   One felt
a cold shiver run down one's back on hearing that, but
for our last message, Kwisa would have been evacuated
last night.   The rice for the rank and file, medical
dressings for the wounded, and comforts for the sick,
were the most appreciated of all we had brought.   The
Europeans now got full rations, and there was ammunition enough and to spare.

Lieutenant-Colonel Carter heard the news we brought
about the Governor with much gravity, and at once held
a council of war with two or three of his senior officers.
The result of this was that he decided that, all the
circumstances carefully considered, it was his duty to
evacuate Kwisa, and retire on Fumsu, from whence not
only could the Commandant's sanction be obtained by
wire, but, by the Obuasi route, a junction could be
effected with Captain Hall's force, so far as was known
with comparative safety ; the loss of prestige to the white
man by thus giving up a post on the lines of communication being, in his opinion, worth the stake.   But
subsequent events proved this not to have been the case,
particularly as the Commandant and almost all the
units were out of touch with one another.   Only a
man in simultaneous control could direct the now
complicated operations, and he would be hopelessly
confounded in his efforts and plans unless his instructions were implicitly carried out.   The emergency of
Kumasi's need was probably better understood by him
than by any one else.   We then knew, from what we
had heard before starting, that the Governor might
already be out, and the fort in the enemy's hands,
although we could not bring ourselves to believe that
this had really happened.

There was much to be done that day by officers and doctors alike. The Europeans all had some hovel or other to hide in, but the troops were reduced to shelters of leaves for protection. Off duty, the light-hearted superstitious Yorubas amused themselves by making war "ju-ju" out of sundry little relics they had taken from the enemy's dead, while the more stolid and stoical Hausa, with his superior belief in Allah, was quite happy looking on. Even in Africa, religious feelings are strong, and the Mohammedan has as much contempt for the simple pagan as some of us have for the two combined. I recollect that my recreation took the form of a brief but delicious sleep, to make up for the night before and prepare for the one to come, which would end in another 3 a.m. reveillé, without bugle call. A start in the dark was again necessary, so as to get away before the enemy found it out. With such a dismally long string of wounded, all possibility of attack must be avoided, and it was necessary to get over the dangerous hill under cover of night. This put the enemy's calculations out, and accounted for our unopposed march back. Going away from Kumasi, one was usually unmolested, and the Adansis, having seen our convoy come into Kwisa, at once jumped to the conclusion that this was a reinforcement for the purpose of again attacking Dompoasi. Accordingly, we filed slowly out in the darkness, on the following morning, a few hundred yards at a time. Nothing broke the silence, save an occasional stumble on an unseen stone, a splash into some unknown pool, a groan from some wounded victim on a stretcher, or a whisper, passing up the order to halt, to go slower, and then finally, "All's well —advance." When the advance guard reached Monsi village at the foot of the far slope, the greatest danger was over. Here a short halt was called to get well together. It was a spectral caravan that came slowly down in the dim light, not a thing being left behind us. This hamlet was formerly a telegraphic post, but the native clerk and instrument had been carried off by the enemy, together with twelve boxes of mails, for their own intelligence staff, the unfortunate man being finally done to death by them. Forward once more, slowly and watchfully as ever. With vivid recollections the various little battle-fields were passed. So and so fell here; this is where the man next me was hit; such were some of the remarks at these points of the journey. What trying work it was, getting those numerous burdens of wounded through those slimy, sticky bogs; how bravely they clenched their teeth, and dug their nails into the palms of their hands to stifle a cry of pain when some slip, some false step, caused some torturing jar to broken limb or unhealed wound. Only one short halt for food in the livelong day. Fumsu, the first place of safety from pursuit, must be reached ere night; and so it was, in the lengthening shadows of evening, and after fifteen weary hours on the road. The accommodation was strained to its utmost limit, but necessity, as ever, found the solution of all difficulties. Being always wet, as one was at this time, rendered every march a trial; sodden boots covered with stinking slime, made one very footsore; and the struggle next day to get them on was exhausting and annoying, in the short time available for dressing, with a flickering candle for one's only light. Yes, we had been to Kwisa now, half way between Kumasi and the river Prah, and only two ordinary marching stages from the former; but we had had to go back again. Should we ever reach our goal? so near, yet how far off it seemed to be at the moment! How welcome would have been the short, comfortable marches, without reverses or delays, in the dry season, too, of the last expedition, with prepared rest-camps at each halt, and plenty in the place of want.

The garrison had been increased since we left. Captain Beddoes and the rest of his company had come in with Dr. Tichborne, and most generously did they dispense to us every available refreshment from their scanty stores.

The following day, the 15th of June—a month to the day when we fought our way into Kumasi—we remained here because of the inability of the wounded to go on without a short rest; but there was plenty to do, and much to hear. Captain Beamish, with fifty men, was ordered to the Obuasi Gold Mines to protect the white men and property at that place. Lieutenant-Colonel Wilkinson, with every available officer and man, some three hundred strong, with all stores and ammunition which could be spared, went at the same time and by the same route to join Captain Hall at Bekwai, where he safely arrived two days later. The object of this move was, though it denuded all other posts, to help the beleaguered garrison in the event of their having broken out, in which case Bekwai was expected to be their objective. Thus there would be a really useful force with which we could hope to combine for further operations, for the Governor's retirement direct to the coast, with all his troops, was never anticipated. Taking into account how ill these three hundred men could then be spared, and also the danger of isolating this body of troops, it was, none the less, a most wise move. They were urgently needed at the place to which they went, and their presence there had a most salutary effect. An urgent runner had been despatched to Captain Hall to cancel the order previously sent him to send a company to reinforce Kwisa ; which, of course, was then known to have been vacated by the forces south of that place, but not by those to the north of it. Unfortunately, this messenger arrived too late, and the delay led to serious consequences ; for Captain Hall, in response to his previous instructions, had already sent off E Company 1st Bn. W.A.F.F. to Kwisa. Captain Wilson, though he had learned through the Bekwais that the Adansis had risen, that a small convoy and escort from Esumeja had been massacred, and that Captain Beamish's and other parties of troops had been attacked, did not know that Dompoasi was stockaded in the manner in which it was, nor was he aware that it was so strongly held by the rebels. It was this which entailed the sad results to which allusion has already been made, and which must be now related.

On the 16th, Captain Wilson, with his company, one hundred and twelve strong, started off, and was first attacked at the stockade on the north side of Dompoasi. This was passed after a sharp running fight in which considerable losses were sustained. In the village a halt was made, for the purpose of refreshment and attending to the wounded. These objects having been attained, part of the place was burnt down as a lesson to the enemy, who were, however, contrary to all expectation, waiting for our exit in the southern stockade, where Lieutenant-Colonel Carter's column had suffered so severely. It is a merciful thing that any of the company escaped, and greatly to their credit that they got through. The foe, enraged at the loss of their houses, attacked this party more fiercely than ever as soon as it got abreast of their entrenchment, killing Captain Wilson and six soldiers, and wounding Sergeant Payne, R.A.M.C., twenty-five soldiers and sixteen carriers. Colour-Sergeant Humphries then took command, and saved the survivors from extermination by a steady advance, with no attempt at a stationary fight. The men behaved extremely well, and clustered round poor Captain Wilson's body when he fell, with fixed bayonets, until it was put into a hammock, in which it was carried to Fumsu, a forced march of thirty-three miles. What the feelings of those unfortunate men must have been when they discovered that Kwisa had been burnt to the ground by the enemy and found not a soldier there is not hard to imagine. The first idea which presented itself to their minds was that all was over, that they were cut off, and would probably be annihilated. When Fumsu was reached the wounded were sent on next day to the advanced hospital at Prahsu, and Captain Wilson's body interred on the left bank of the river, between it and the rest-house. Volleys could not be fired over it lest the enemy's notice should be drawn to the exact position of the grave, but the " Last Post " was sounded and all other military honours rendered to our brave comrade, whose name was now added to Africa's list of heroes. But the rebels, by every such action, were only increasing the long account which had yet to be paid off to the uttermost farthing, for, in times like these, one neither forgives nor forgets. This was a much-felt loss at a most critical time, and in the person of Captain Wilson many of us lost an old and valued friend.

The same morning that the party for Bekwai set out we started for Prahsu with the wounded, leaving only a small garrison of sixty men, under Corporal Philpotts, at Fumsu. This place was then in a most insanitary

condition, and the smell revolting. It was only surpassed by what we met with when we reached Kumasi.
In this respect alone did the rain serve any good purpose by washing away innumerable germs, and by the
manner in which it enabled the sickening stench to be
kept under. Both occasions were indescribably repulsive. The injured all safely reached their destination
the same day, completely exhausted, poor chaps, and
soaked with rain ; whereas the loads and most of the
soldiers did not get in until the one following. This
was due, partly to the constant breaks-down and repairs
to the stretchers, whose joints gave way owing to the
damp causing the wood to swell, and partly to the
rising of another small river, which did not exist on our
way up, and had now to be crossed by one small raft.

Nobody who has not been in such a country as West
Africa can understand what this last-named obstacle
involves. It took hours before the passage was completed, and we were thus employed, toiling long after
dark had fallen, and in constant fear of some mishap.
I remember an officer, who met us with some ammunition just before we reached this spot, who had been
sent from Prahsu for the purpose, remarked : " There is
a swollen stream just ahead of you, but it will be all
right as there is a small raft, which is good enough for
its purpose, and will soon run you all across." The
crossing took, however, something like six hours. Next
morning the last of us got into Prahsu, very glad to
think we might get an eagerly-looked-for, though brief
rest, and heard, for the first time, of the war in China
and the advance on Peking of the Allied Forces.

CHAPTER XIII

WAITING AND WONDERING

WHAT would the Commandant do now? Had Kumasi fallen? Were the lines of communication to be *viâ* Obuasi or Kwisa? When should we be able to move forward? Would reinforcements soon arrive? Such were the questions which we constantly asked. We might speculate, but we could not know. Colonel Willcocks was always careful to keep his plans to himself. Information reached the enemy in the most extraordinary way. Absolute secrecy was the only safety. Rest was rather a misnomer for our condition during these days, but we were dry and stationary, and that was something. Make the best of it while you can, and let to-morrow take care of itself, is a good motto for the inquisitive mind. Surprise is clothed in red tape; she lurks in that make-shift office, and leers at you from behind a pile of mysterious orders and despatches. When you neither want nor expect her she will pounce upon you, drag you out, and send you where you least anticipate.

Herrings in a barrel must be in quite comfortable proximity compared to what we were in that rest-house, which was the European hospital and headquarters, as well as everything else. There was only one room for the able-bodied officers in which they could feed, sleep, work, and carry on their official and private intercourse. It was littered with beds and boxes—a confused collection prohibitive of anything like order. If one raised one's voice above a whisper it disturbed some invalid or staff officer, and one soon received a message to that effect. We crept across the creaking boards in ammunition boots as noiselessly as any stocking-footed burglar. One scarce dared to squeeze one's sponge when bathing lest it should create discord. One pointed out his errors to one's "boy" at a distance from this house varying according to the turpitude of his misdeeds, and pitched one's voice proportionately. At night one respected the reckless mosquito buzzing at the top of his voice for his independence, as he visited every one in turn, from Commandant to native clerk. Nervous buglers retired out of our hearing to blow their calls ; soldiers and carriers wore worried looks when in this immediate vicinity. But though it might have been better, it might have been worse ; and, with the exception of Kumasi, we never had such comfortable quarters again, so they must be remembered gratefully.

Prahsu, as subsequently occurred in the case of all other posts, was in a state of rapid transformation. Bamboo, grass-roofed sheds, for stores and barracks, were in course of construction, but they were not ready yet.

As there was no Röntgen rays apparatus in the colony it was found impossible to extract some of the slugs ; consequently, Lieutenant-Colonel Carter, Captain Roupell, and Lieutenants Edwards, R.A., and O'Malley, were invalided and left for home, together with a convoy of over a hundred wounded for the base at the Coast.

Captain Neal had got together some fifty selected carriers, henceforth known as the "pioneers"; they were utilised for rough engineering, such as improving bad bits of road, and were at this time engaged in making a raft which was to take stores and troops across the Prah.

At last troops were coming: over four hundred of the W.A.R., with nearly twenty officers, under the command of Lieutenant-Colonel Burroughs, had just arrived at Cape Coast. Captain Wilkinson, with a company from Jebba, was also on his way. Mr. Haddon Smith, Assistant Colonial Secretary of the Gold Coast Colony, had arrived, and assumed the billet of Political Officer to the Force.

Major Cramer was to leave in a few days to raise some native levies, and Captain Hall, Commissioner of Civil Police, was shortly to quit Cape Coast on a similar duty in the western Denkera country, whilst Captain Wilcox, Adjutant of the Accra Volunteers, with Captain Benson, was going to do the same in the Akim district, on our right flank. Dane guns, slugs, and powder were also to be purchased for their armament by Captain Wright, who was Acting Base Commandant until the arrival of Lieutenant-Colonel Man-Stuart, in addition to his duties connected with the despatch of supplies of all kinds as they arrived. Numberless rumours about more troops from all parts of the world were discussed, but at present nothing could be hoped for, except from West Africa, until August at least. The Commandant spent many of his spare moments in practising the troops in "bush drill," firing a few volleys, and then charging into the bordering forest with the bayonet; he also spoke very seriously to them about the need of economising ammunition, and never firing unless directly ordered to do so.

During our absence, a letter of earlier date to the one we had seen had come in from the Governor, with news of Major Morris' arrival from the north reinforcing the garrison of the fort. It gave some other minor details, including the sad intelligence of poor Captain Maguire's death in action on May 29th. But where was the garrison now?

As a specimen of information carefully extracted by questioning, and a native's style of narration, the following verbatim account of an occurrence may be interesting. The bearers had just brought in the Governor's despatch :—

"Supplied. Prahsu, June 19, 1900, by Charlie and Teacup, two Krooboys, the former a Government *employé*, and the latter a servant of Messrs. Russell & Co., at Kumasi.

1. "We left Kumasi about fourteen days ago, and went to Bekwai *viâ* Esumeja. It took us four days to reach the latter place. We did not go on the road, but travelled through the bush. At Esumeja we met some white men and soldiers. We gave the white men a letter we brought from the Governor at Kumasi. We were promised by the Governor that if we delivered the letter we were to receive : Charlie £5, and Teacup £12. At Esumeja we stopped a day, and then went on to Bekwai, where we also rested a day. We then proceeded to Obuasi, which we reached in one day, travelling through the bush. We stopped two days at this place, coming on here through the Denkera country.

2. "When we left Kumasi there were large numbers of natives in the town, viz., Fantis, Accras, Krooboys,

Hausas, loyal Ashantis, Bouris, Bekwais, and Mendis. The number exceeded two thousand, and included many children. The Fantis and Accras predominated. The Ashantis have erected barricades across all outlets from Kumasi, and refused to allow any natives to leave the town, many of whom, through starvation, attempted to get through the Ashanti lines, but I believe most, if not all, were beheaded, a few being kept as slaves. They are killing the Fantis as well as the other natives. Three of our brothers (Krooboys) were amongst those decapitated, having been caught on the Kintampo road endeavouring to get through.

3. "There were many white men in Kumasi, also four white women, but no children. One of these women is the wife of the Governor; the others are lady missionaries from the Basel Society, and include Mrs. Ramseyer.

4. "When we left there was no 'chop' in Kumasi for the native population. Many were dying of sickness and starvation; the numbers were so great that they were being put two or three into one grave. The soldiers and carriers have some food, which is supplied by the Government. They were receiving when we left: soldiers—biscuits, three for two men, and one pound tinned beef for three men. Carriers—biscuits, one for two men, and one pound beef for four men. These allowances were a day's ration. The Bekwai people were fed on the same scale as the carriers. The native population was living on leaves and roots. Only two white men have died up to the time of our departure; one was killed in a skirmish, and the other died of fever. Some of the officers were wounded, but we believe they and the white ladies were all in good health. After leaving Kumasi we saw plenty of

Ashantis, although we ourselves were not seen. We were afraid to return to Kumasi, as we knew this would be much more dangerous than to go on. Near Kumasi we saw the headless bodies of many natives, which we presumed were the remains of refugees from the town. We also saw heads, some of which we recognised. Furthermore, we came across many bodies in the bush.

5. "There was a fight in Kumasi some two months ago ; many Ashantis were killed. The Ashantis tried to take the fort, but never got near it. They attacked from all the roads converging into Kumasi. The cantonments and some other houses were burnt about a week before the attack. They did not burn the Basel Mission, though they sacked it. They burnt the Wesleyan Mission on the Kintampo road, but were unable to touch Russell's house as soldiers were living there. Then the Ashantis again endeavoured to take the fort, and succeeded in occupying a house belonging to the Government engineer. A large number secured an entry ; they were, however, surrounded, and all killed to a man. We think in this engagement there were more than two hundred Ashantis killed, as the Government labourers were occupied for four days afterwards burying them.

6. "It is most difficult for any one to escape from Kumasi, as the Ashantis not only block all the roads, but have built huts or shelters which completely surround the town, and in all of these huts they have soldiers.

7. "The Governor told us himself that he, the white women, and most of his soldiers would shortly be leaving Kumasi, though he intended to leave a garrison there ; that he expected a lot of soldiers from the south,

and that if we met any we were to tell them to go on quickly.

8. "When we left Kumasi we were very thin ; we have eaten well since then."

This statement of these "boys" was the first we had heard of a garrison being left in the fort, although we presumed such would be the case in the end. This evidence as a whole was, I think, some of the best obtained during the campaign.

Over two thousand Mendi carriers were on their way up already, out of the five thousand Sierra Leone men eventually sent in batches of various numbers, who had been organised and despatched with great promptitude. The news of the offer and acceptance of the Jamaica Militia for service in Ashanti also reached us at this time ; but, in the end, they did not come, and as things turned out were not required. Special service officers were also coming out from home, and the second party had already sailed from Liverpool, together with large quantities of ammunition and supplies. Some few of these substitutes and helpers had arrived prior to this date. Considerable treachery appeared to be going on in the way of supplying the enemy with arms and ammunition, but nothing was directly traceable. Needless uneasiness was increasing amongst the Cape Coast traders, and numbers of fugitives were flocking thither daily. Captain Holford was the next to arrive, and at first held the appointment of A.D.C. to the Commandant, but was afterwards made an Executive Staff Officer. That the Colonial Office was sending three hundred men, with seventy-three Sikhs from South-east Africa, seemed to be authentic, and further reinforcements were being prepared and sent off from Northern Nigeria ; Captain Eden's Company, 2nd Bn. W.A.F.F., of one hundred and fifty men, which had been lent to Southern Nigeria for garrison duty pending the Cross River Expedition, actually arrived at Prahsu on the 25th. The half battalion of the W.A.R. was immediately inspected on its arrival at head-quarters, and sent on to Fumsu, as there was no accommodation for it at Prahsu ; its subsequent destination was to be Bekwai. From what we could gather from the newspapers, and those who had just come out from England, it appeared that people at home thought so seriously of the state of affairs out here that it had been stated that a brigade of British infantry would be needed to quell the rebellion, and successfully end the war. Whether this be true or not is now of little consequence, but should it have really been the case it only reflects more credit upon the way in which the Commandant has managed the business with native troops only.

As no post then had sufficient accommodation for a large number of troops and the W.A.R. was expected shortly, Captain Melliss and I, with F Company, were sent to Tobiasi, roughly speaking half way to Fumsu, to put the place in a state of defence, and prepare it for a subsidiary depôt. We had an impression then that both the Obuasi and the main roads into Bekwai were to be simultaneously used as lines of communication, and, to a modified extent, this surmise was correct. Before we left, we had heard with much satisfaction that we were to be given free rations. This saved an infinity of anxiety, trouble, and expense, when they did arrive. Already the stores which we had bought and brought up with us were very much reduced ; and, although more were ordered, it was a chance whether they would reach one in time. There was also to be an issue of fresh meat, when such was possible, and the ever-thoughtful P.M.O. had taken steps to try and procure beasts and fowls for this purpose. Medical comforts, too, were to be liberally issued when necessary, and what an inexpressible benefit they were! If they did not actually save life at times, they certainly enabled an amount of work and fatigue to be endured which would not otherwise have been possible. Sometimes when we arrived late at the end of a march, sick and jaded, when the very thought of tinned food was nauseous in the extreme, a pint of stout put new life into one, and sent one to sleep refreshed and fitted to cope with the duties of the morrow.

Our two days' stay at Tobiasi was memorable for nothing but its absolute dulness, and the ceaseless fall of rain throughout the time. We knew and heard nothing, and even our orders to advance were only made known to us by the arrival, at 9 a.m. on the 24th, of Lieutenant-Colonel Burroughs' advance guard. It was, on the whole, not an unwelcome experience to be shifted from the unsettled little world in which we then lived. There was no one with red tabs on his coat collar to vex one with sudden orders, or call for complicated returns in an impossibly short space of time; and to be off the wire is a pleasant relief for short periods. Ashanti, Chinese, and South African news were all critically interesting at the moment, but field telegraphs are put up on service, not for personal, but for official convenience. The exceedingly small supply of tools made our defensive preparations rather slow, and they would distinctly have been classed as "hasty fortifications." A clear field of fire, some abattis, and the like, composed the simple scheme, and would probably have been enough, even if we had been attacked in force. If one can only see one's enemy, and check any attempt on his part to make a

K

rush, a good deal has been achieved ; one can then take time about the lesson one wants to teach him, and a Maxim is undeniably a demoralising thing.

I have often been filled with a feeling of respect for the black sentry in this close country, where there was, as a rule, no opportunity for cutting back the bush, and much less of posting him out of range. In fact, the force itself rarely had the latter advantage, owing to the way in which the villages are situated in the very heart of the jungle. There he would stand, hour after hour, in wind and rain so boisterous that hearing was out of the question, peering into tangled undergrowth which might safely hide a murderous sharpshooter five yards from him. Yet he kept his watch, silent and motionless as a statue, a model of patient endurance and pluck. He had no protection against the fury of the elements, except his cape, and that was often soaked through before his guard was mounted. When one went round the sentries, one often had to call softly to him, so inconspicuous was he in his dangerous surroundings, nor was there usually in the forest depths even moon-light to disclose his whereabouts by a glint from his bayonet. Sometimes the only clue was the hacking cough which exposure had given to nearly all of us alike. And yet this very man, perhaps only a few months before was filled with the pagan's dread of darkness. Communion with his thoughts, and the phantoms of another world, who only come abroad under the sable wing of night, is more uncongenial to the negro than to us. Yet he does his duty manfully, guarding the lives, not only of his own black brothers, but of the white men whose seemingly cruel caution has put him to this task. Such is his implicit belief in his officer, and so capable is he of being moulded by discipline that he

A SENTRY OF THE WEST AFRICAN FRONTIER FORCE

will uncomplainingly submit to this ordeal.   Is it then fair to speak slightingly of "nigger" regiments? Greater devotion to duty could not be found in any other race.   Some may have almost animal stupidity,— intelligence is ever rare,—but if so, it is redeemed by the same brute faithfulness.   The birth of confidence in one's men removes an untold load of previous gnaw- ing dread: in Africa they are often almost strangers to one, because of the constant changing of the white men going home on sick leave and the like.   An old soldier is an almost unknown article as yet out here. Constantly it is difficult to be sure that one's orders are understood, on account of the numerous languages in vogue, which the white man cannot speak with fluency ; and dictionaries and grammars of these dialects have yet to be written in almost every case.

CHAPTER XIV

" HALLO! where do you come from?" So one greeted fresh arrivals of troops, in one's surprise and desire to know what was to be the next move. The advent of Lieutenant-Colonel Burroughs' force was the signal for our departure; a company of the W.A.R. being left to garrison Tobiasi, until it was found safe to abandon it, which in other words meant the suppression of the southern part of the Adansi rising.

Fumsu looked more uninviting than ever. Lying very low, it was from sunset until sunrise enveloped in damp mist, and the river had risen so much that the temporary footbridge, which had been recently thrown across it, was washed away, communication with the other bank having thus been again cut off. The going was as unpleasant as usual, no roads having yet been "corduroyed." This process simply means that at particularly swampy places large tree trunks are laid parallel to the path, and across them smaller round branches are laid, lashed together by "tie-tie." This measure is only a temporary one; and when crossing these spots, it is advisable to look out for gaps, often quite big enough to put one's foot into, and perhaps break one's leg, not to mention the disagreeable walking involved.

The rest-house was occupied by the newly appointed officer in command of this post, Major Ryde, W.I.R., and Dr. Tichborne, who was down with fever. Here we were given a cup of tea, a biscuit, and a little jam, which all tasted very good at the time. China and glass were now unknown luxuries to most of us, for they did not bear transport well, and were treated with even less consideration by black " boys " than by female servants at home. It would have been ungenerous in the extreme to have blamed one's invaluable factotum for not doing his work in good style ; it was enough to get anything finished, however late it might be. I know I often found it hard enough to conclude my own duties when I got in from a march ; and I can hardly imagine how little twelve-year-old Dan Leno and his *confrères* could set to work as soon as they got in, unrolling beds, filling waterproof canvas baths, and the like, and then starting to cook their master's evening meal, without refreshment or rest themselves. This tea-party was characteristic of many others : gaiters and boots removed, and if possible replaced by a pair of dry shoes, one's coat unbuttoned, helmet thrown on one side ; very hot and unwashed, one sat down upon anything that suggested itself as capable of affording a rest. The biscuit was broken with ease, in its pulpy tropical condition, by one's grimy fingers, into irregular lumps which represented mouthfuls. With a common spoon stuck into a tin, some jam (and most sustaining stuff it is) was put on each fragment, and down it went, without the familiar crunch heard elsewhere. The tea was rather spoiled, for an epicure, by condensed milk ; nevertheless, it slaked thirst, and revived one as

much in this form as in any other.   But hot fluids want
china cups much more than food does porcelain plates,
which after all can be replaced by tin ones.   The lucky
man of our party had a treasured earthenware jug, which,
though chipped, and liable to cut one's mouth, the
owner would not have parted with for any consideration.
I had an aluminium cup.   It was certainly light and
unbreakable, if not unable to be bent; but aluminium
does not suit hot drinks.   They must be allowed to cool
for some time, during which period one's thirst seems
to become almost unbearable.   Then, having carefully
wound one's handkerchief round the hot metal, in order
to protect one's hands, one gingerly tried to take small
sips, at the imminent risk of blistering one's mouth.
The conversation turned usually on the news from and
about Kumasi.   One learnt with interest that the
Ashantis strongly objected to missionaries, and did not
like schools any more than we did in our boyhood.
Amongst other persons, Mr. Ramseyer, the patriarchal
Swiss missionary, was mentioned.   He had had an
eventful career during some forty years among the
Ashantis, whose language he spoke fluently, and his is
a record spell of life for the West Coast.   The enemy
were anxious to get hold of him now, because they
thought it was he who had disclosed the whereabouts
of the Golden Stool to the Governor.   At one time this
enthusiast was a prisoner in Kumasi for over four years,
and he would have been put to death had not Lord
Wolseley arrived with his expeditionary force.   But his
and his wife's lives were spared in order that they might
be sent to intercede for the saving of the Ashanti
capital.

   The very first morning in a new post, and with
nothing special likely to occur, seemed to offer a good

opportunity for an undisturbed sleep; one would do
nothing until a gentlemanly hour. So one confided
this to the " boy," and ordered a cup of cocoa for 7 a.m.
However, darkness and light were still wrestling with
each other when up one started, and rubbed one's eyes.
Yes, there it went again, the " Alarm." One pulled on
something, anything, whatever came first to hand, and
raced off to one's post, where the company was falling
in. " Colour-Sergeant, what's the matter?" " I don't
know, sir." One ran one's eye over the men, to see
that all had got their arms, belts, and other necessaries,
though it was no time for the fault-finding minutiæ of
a parade-ground inspection, and then patiently awaited
orders. There was no firing, no sign of any enemy, and
one began to scent the game from afar. What a
wicked shame to perpetrate such a trick, when we had
got in, tired out, only the previous afternoon! Yes; it
had just been done to practise the little garrison, and
for the officer in command to satisfy himself that all the
units knew their places in case of necessity. Then the
" Dismiss" was sounded by the bugler at the quarter
guard, and back one went to bed, which had now lost
half its charms, grumbling and wondering whether to
get into it again, or to have some breakfast and stay up.

A refugee miner from Obuasi, on his way to the
coast, arrived that day, and reported the road still open,
and the Jim river, the only serious obstacle, fordable.
In return, he was safely rafted across the swollen Fum.
The men cleaned their arms *en règle*, and received pay
and rations. These last were at present only 1 lb. of
rice a day—less than their allowance in time of peace—
but it was subsequently increased, and at Bekwai
augmented by some tinned meat and biscuit. No meat
of any kind was to be had here, and indeed money was

rather useless, as no market existed. They were, therefore, only too glad to spend their time on fatigue duty,
building shelters for their own comfort and protection,
and the comical mass of booths which soon appeared
on all sides reminded one of a fair. The same afternoon, the three remaining companies of the W.A.R.
marched in, their Colonel travelling in state in a hammock. The advance guard with its important duties,
was entrusted to Captains Stallard and Tighe, D.S.O.,
both experienced old "bush-whackers" from the late
Royal Niger Company's Constabulary. The orders this
force had received were to proceed by and open up
the main road, finding out the ambushes and stockades,
and to join Lieutenant-Colonel Wilkinson at Bekwai.
This was the first column which had scouts, and could,
therefore, undertake such a task; and right well they
did it. On our way up shortly afterwards, we saw the
results of their work, and, in every single place where
cartridge cases on the road marked some former fight,
was found in the bush some ambuscade of timber, earth,
stones, fallen trees, rifle pits, or stockades, selected for
the cover they afforded from our fire.

These officers did not like the look-out any better
than we had done, but they made good use of all they
had heard about the enemy's tactics. They also
brought in with them the three soldiers who had
deserted from Captain Slater, who was also here and able
to give his evidence against them. They were to be
tried by a Field General Court-martial, and were
charged with having " shown cowardice in the presence
of the enemy." Lieutenant-Colonel Burroughs was
much upset when he saw what an obstacle the river
presented, and at once put his men on to raft building.
After our own experience, I could not help laughing at

the methods they adopted. They lashed tree trunks together, and of course, when launched, they went straight to the bottom, with never a chance of floating. The result was that they had to spend a whole day at Fumsu, during which, tools and materials being more plentiful now than they had previously been, a rude bridge was finally put across; but it, too, had no sooner rendered them its service than it gave up the ghost and disappeared during the next night.

Another sorry, though interesting, person came in that day. He was one of the Nupé soldiers from Captain Wilson's company, who had been left for dead, after being wounded no less than nineteen times. How he ever got in seemed a miracle; and what was even more marvellous was that he recovered. For days he had lain in the forest, crawling short distances at night, as far as his strength permitted, hiding by day, and living on the plantains he chanced to find on his way. To have covered twenty miles in six days under these conditions, was quite a feat, and furnished a proof of the extraordinary tenacity of life of the African.

Late in the afternoon of the 25th of June, four letters, as unexpected as they were important, reached Fumsu, and the contents were wired down to the Commandant at Prahsu. The documents were sent on by a runner, who, however, did not reach there until the next morning. The first letter was from Captain Hall at Esumeja, to Lieutenant-Colonel Wilkinson at Bekwai, where it had arrived at midnight of the 21st. It reported the firing of 7-pr. guns that evening from the direction of Kumasi: first five shots, then five more, and finally continuance of firing. Captain Hall had replied with two signal shots from his 75-m/m. Lieutenant-Colonel Wilkinson, on its receipt, immediately left

Bekwai with reinforcements, and arrived at Esumeja at dawn. Howbeit, it soon became evident that if the garrison were breaking out, they were not coming by the Cape Coast road, and so Lieutenant-Colonel Wilkinson returned. The second and third letters were from Lieutenant-Colonel Wilkinson, enclosing the fourth letter. These contained much valuable local news. They stated that a bamboo stockade had been erected round part of Bekwai in case of attack, and contained a request for more supplies, especially tinned stuffs, in case of a siege, and also for more troops. This fourth letter on a scrap of paper a couple of inches square, written in French for security, in case it fell into the enemy's hands, was from the Governor in Kumasi, and dated the 17th. It stated that the garrison would hold out until the 20th, after which His Excellency stated that he would have to "*faire mon jeu.*" Relieving troops, and especially supplies, were earnestly asked for, and a warning given that there were two big stockades within an hour of the fort. The garrison, however, remained in Kumasi three days after the date assigned. I shall never forget the anxious discussion which a few of us held over the words "*faire mon jeu.*" What did it all mean? The Governor's previous letter of the 4th instant had given the 11th, on reduced rations, as the last day. It had arrived after that date was past : the presumption had then been formed that the garrison had fought their way out, and Lieutenant-Colonel Wilkinson with his force had been dispatched top-speed to Bekwai, to render them assistance. Then came this other letter, extending the limit more than a week. Was this, then, final or not? In any case, every nerve was being strained to reach the fort. One theory why the Governor had

decided to hold out at any cost until the 20th, was that
he might have received information from Colonel Willcocks of Lieutenant-Colonel Wilkinson's force having
been sent to Bekwai, where it had arrived on the
19th; and that His Excellency had presumed that
it could effect the relief. There was still no mention of
any garrison being left behind, save the unreliable
verbal evidence of a Krooboy, to whom it seemed unlikely that such an important confidence would have
been committed. Would the Commandant make a
dash for the capital on this chance, or wait to complete
the organisation of an efficient force to retake it, and
begin the punitive part of the campaign? Thus we
argued ; but none of us knew anything for certain. To
anticipate : it was not, as a matter of fact, until July 4th
that we became acquainted with the all-important fact
that two British officers, and a hundred rank and file,
had remained behind ; that they could hold out until
the 15th, at latest, after which they " must surrender,"
which was but another name for torture and death.
There were, therefore, only eleven days left before the
curtain must fall on this tragedy, or the prestige of
England in Ashanti be saved. The instant the Commandant received this despatch, which put him in
possession of the very facts he desired to know, urgent
special messengers were sent asking the Governor to
leave every possible man behind him to render assistance in the relief of Kumasi. But they missed their
destination, and so no help came from that source. Sir
Frederic Hodgson had then been out of Kumasi four
days, and was on his way down to the coast, through
friendly country, with an escort of six hundred soldiers,
less the casualties, together with all his officers. It was
then, on July 4th, that Colonel Willcocks wired home the

words : " I will personally relieve Kumasi by that date
(*i.e.*, July 15th), under any circumstances " ; which
promise he carried out to the letter, though at such
short notice.

On the morning of the 27th, Lieutenant-Colonel
Burroughs' force, having been reinforced by some of the
W.A.F.F., and numbering about five hundred, started
off on its dangerous journey north. The baggage had
been got over the river the previous evening, and a wire
had been received from the Commandant, wishing them
God-speed and success. The goodbyes were jokingly
said, but with an underlying tone of seriousness. I
must follow this column in its experiences before
returning to speak of those temporarily left behind.

The careful scouting practised made the progress
slow, and the first night was passed at Sheramasi, after
a prosperous day. Breakfast next morning was taken
at Brufu Edru, on the south side of the Adansi Hills,
and rather more than half-way to Kwisa. Here a
detachment had been ordered to be left to form another
subsidiary base. When this had been completed, the
advance guard again started, and slowly ascended the
Monsi Hill, when, just as the head of the troops arrived
at the top, and before the rear guard had got well under
way, it was ambushed from behind a fallen tree in a
similar position to the former ones. A sharp little fight
took place for nearly an hour before the enemy were
driven out by a flank movement, and a charge through
the bush by a company in rear, which had " front
formed " into line, and penetrated into the undergrowth.
Short as the encounter was, one man was killed, three
others severely wounded, and a long delay caused by
the occurrence. The spot was cleverly chosen by the
enemy, inasmuch as it was about the only one where the

scouts could not well perform their duties. Kwisa was reached after dark, and here another party was dropped to re-occupy the post. The place was not held, but had been levelled with the ground by the enemy, and every possible form of shelter, including the rest-house, burnt. So this little garrison had not only, like the one at Brufu Edru, to rapidly entrench themselves, but had also to build some cover against the weather.

Next morning the start was made, in the full expectation of a terrific fight at Dompoasi, that almost insuperable obstruction on the lines of communication. To prove what extreme caution and care were taken, this town was not reached by nightfall, though not four miles distant from Kwisa. When darkness had set in, with torrential rain showing clearly what the night was going to be like, and being unwilling to bivouac in such impenetrable jungle, with not so much protection as a single tent, and in such dangerously close proximity to a position known to be occupied by a large body of the rebels, Captains Stallard and Tighe held a hasty council of war, and decided to call in the scouts, who were useless in the dusk, make a dash for the village, and try to rush it before preparations for resistance could be made. It was a risk, but their defenceless situation warranted it. It ended in complete success, and was the first real defeat the Adansis had suffered. It opened up communication to Bekwai, and materially aided in reducing the southernmost part of the rebellion. The very inclemency of nature was the salvation of the venture. The enemy's scouts, who had reported the advance from Kwisa, had given up all idea of an attack that night, and they and the whole war camp were preparing their evening meal. The noise of falling water drowned the sound of trampling feet. The leading company was into the village before the foe knew what was about to happen. A scene of wild confusion followed. The enemy sprang up from their cooking fires, and rushed to a hut where their loaded guns were kept, whilst our men poured volleys into the *bizarre* figures flying madly here and there in the firelight. But savages have not enough discipline to rally when thus taken by surprise. Many fled pell-mell into the forest, whilst a number ran down their prepared path, manned the big stockade, from which they had so successfully given battle to the white man a few days before, and opened fire on the remainder of our column. But it was too late, and they were soon compelled to quit that, too, for the second and last time. Captain Tighe forthwith sent out half a company into the bush to snipe and follow up the disorganised warriors. All night it remained out, and the sound of desultory firing was heard, showing they were doing good execution. Picquets and sentries were thrown out in a complete circle round the place. At midnight our troops got a scratch meal, but they slept under protection from the rain, and with the comfortable feeling that an excellent bit of work had been accomplished, which was more satisfactory than anything else. The month of June had ended well: it was our first real time of success. Many guns, with their curious flue-shaped tin or hide coverings to protect the flint and powder from the rain, were taken; some Sniders, many kegs of powder, and much food, which had been thoughtfully cooked for our troops by the enemy; some of our own men's rifles, and three thousand rounds of ·303 ammunition were also found. Thirty dead bodies of the enemy lay about as visible testimony to their losses, and the rest of them were scattered, the whole having been achieved with no "butcher's bill" for ourselves.

Next day was spent at Dompoasi, destroying the two great stockades, removing the bush in front of them, cutting down the fetish trees, burying the enemy's dead, and resting the over-tired troops. During the performance of these duties, many headless skeletons and corpses of our soldiers and carriers were found in the village and in the surrounding jungle; to avenge which, the Mendi soldiers blew up many of the bodies of the Adansis with their own gunpowder. The evening of the following day Bekwai was gained, and their orders thus carried out with even more good fortune than could have been hoped for.

Lieutenant-Colonel Burroughs was so encouraged by the way in which this great danger had been removed, that he determined to get rid of the next by making another attack on the entrenched war camp at Kokofu, which so seriously harassed our right flank. The Commandant, however, had had other plans, which would have precluded this movement had they been known. At all events Lieutenant-Colonel Burroughs organised a force from his own, Lieutenant-Colonel Wilkinson's, and Captain Hall's, of five hundred men, with four Maxims and one 75 m/m gun; and having left one hundred and fifty men in reserve, he started out to accomplish his plan. But the task was more difficult this time. The enemy were quite ready for our troops, came out in great force, and engaged them fiercely for several hours, at one time having actually worked so far round as almost to envelop the hospital and rear guard. The fire was terrific, and our men were falling in large numbers. The attempted turning movement into the bush on our part had failed, and Lieutenant-Colonel Burroughs would not risk a frontal charge under the circumstances. The enemy never attempted to run away, but retired in the most orderly manner possible, one rank through another, not unlike the way in which our own skirmishers are taught to do, holding their enormous guns perpendicularly in front of them. Some few were said to have been dressed in uniforms taken from our own dead ; one of them is reported to have called out in English, "Don't fire!" immediately taking this opportunity to empty a charge of slugs, at a few yards' range, at the nearest white man. Lieutenant-Colonel Burroughs decided, therefore, to retire, and that evening reached Bekwai for the second time.

The enemy followed the column all the way to Esumeja, harassing the rear guard, upon which they inflicted twelve casualties, sometimes at such close quarters that our men killed some of them with their *machêtês*, and brazenly called upon the garrison and the loyal natives to come and join them as they had beaten the white man, and would soon drive him out of the country altogether.

The result of this disaster was the loss of many priceless white and black members of the relief force. Lieutenant Brounlie, W.I.R., a most promising young officer, who at his own request had been attached to the W.A.R. for the campaign, was killed. It is a strange fact that his particular friend and brother officer, Lieutenant Greer, who subsequently fell in action, should have been the only other volunteer attached to the W.A.R. Lieutenant Brounlie happened to be looking at his watch when he was shot, and it stopped at that moment. His body was rescued with difficulty, because owing to some superstitious fetish, his men were afraid to pick it up until his revolver was removed.   Six other officers were hit slightly, one British N.C.O. and three soldiers killed, and seventy-two N.C.O.'s and men wounded.   After this no fighting took place until the Commandant advanced in person, to accomplish the main object of the campaign.

CHAPTER XV

FACTS AND SPECULATIONS

" SITTING down," as the natives call it, in a place, is a dreary pastime, and was at this time invariably productive of sickness amongst the white men. When sustained by excitement and constant movement the fatigue inseparable from marching and fighting seemed less noticeable, but a halt of any duration always brought a reaction, and slowly filled the hut known as the European Hospital.

The trial of the three deserters in action was a rather painful duty. Their guilt was irrefutable, and they pleaded guilty. Then, for the first time in my life I was a member of a court-martial which passed sentence of death, and had to give my vote accordingly. The Commandant, however, in confirming the decision, commuted the sentence to penal servitude, on the ground that this was the first occasion upon which soldiers of the Ashanti Field Force had behaved otherwise than with great gallantry, and in recognition of the services of the remainder of the rank and file. This was read out on parade in the presence of the garrison ; the prisoners were stripped of the uniforms they had disgraced, and sent back under escort to Elmina jail, to undergo their sentence. The difference between the Mohammedan Hausa and the pagan Yoruba, in their methods of taking an oath, is worth recording. The former swears upon the Koran, or, if none is at hand, he verbally calls upon Allah to punish him if he does not give his evidence truthfully ; the latter takes a knife or bayonet between his teeth as a symbol of the death he expects if he lies. However, for all these formalities, the truth is often hard to obtain.

Shortly after the above disquieting occurrence, the only one of its kind in all those trying months, came a dangerous development amongst the Sierra Leone carriers, who, for the first and last time, attempted an outburst of independence. For gross insubordination to an officer, in combination with other misdeeds, one of them was punished. The result was that his mutinous comrades started a stampede, which was instantly suppressed in the sternest manner possible. The untutored savage does not appreciate the meaning of active service, nor why such a condition of affairs should change misdemeanours into crimes ; but he grasped it then, and the clockwork of the transport worked quite smoothly ever after.

Escorts with stores kept pouring in incessantly, and Captain Neal arrived at this time with his sappers, to bridge the Fum, which he duly did. His bridge was put some 12 feet above the water, and in thirty-six hours, had it not been for wire stays strained from it to giant trees on the bank, the whole thing would have been swept away. So rapidly had the river risen that it was washing clean over the central portion, which, like all natural timbers and prepared tree-trunks, had a downward bend instead of an upward camber. These pioneers were very amusing, and by virtue of their

present employment held other carriers in high contempt. It was interesting in the extreme to watch
them when, at last, some effort had been crowned with
success. The whole lot would then burst forth into a
sonorous song of triumph, which sounded exactly like
a distant organ. It was quite unlike our one, two, three,
heave! followed by a hoarse hurrah. To hear a roll
call of this gang was so diverting that one could have
laughed until one cried, partly because the individuals
saw nothing ridiculous in it, and solemnly replied as
they were addressed. The names in the older colony
of Sierra Leone, from whence they came, were originated
by the early traders, and many, I must say, were too
shocking to put on paper. The following are a few
specimens I remember:—Fine Boy, Salt Water, Sea
Breeze, Bottle o' Beer, Man-o'-War, Sambo, Blue Devil,
Snow Ball, Keg o' Rum, Cream Cheese, God's Gift,
Mother's Darling, Pride of Africa, Turkish Delight,
Glass Eye, Soft Soap, False Tooth, Plug o' Baccy, and
so on, interspersed with a few more conventional ones
like John Thomas or John Bull.

Any novel or newspaper was read to shreds during
this time, and one could not help remarking the
apparently small interest which was taken in the
campaign at home, some papers even indulging in
occasional flippancies about subjects of vital moment.
Conversation often reached the verge of boredom.
That we should have to cut our way through
thousands upon thousands of rebels if Kumasi were
ever to be relieved, seemed unquestionable; that our
entry might mean our being in the end besieged ourselves, looked at least like a possibility. But the
Commandant was surely coming soon, picking up from
here and there the scattered units which were to consti-

tute the relief force, and then we should, neck or nothing, do or die, make a determined effort to gain the fort, though well-armed rebels barred the way.

There was one most interesting, plucky, and nice old native, whose services were requisitioned as a messenger, guide and interpreter ; many pleasant chats have I had with him, in which I learnt some curious facts about the Ashantis. He was called " Peter the Great," and had got a medal and clasp in 1873, during which period, he assured me, he had been steward to Sir Garnet Wolseley. One's leisure moments were necessarily often sedentary because the bush was too dangerous to make exercise worth the risk it entailed. Where a body of troops might have gone with impunity a single white man would inevitably have met his death. Hitherto I had not seen many genuine Ashantis, but I had already noticed, and later on often remarked, that it was a general characteristic of the race that they had abnormally receding foreheads and high crowns. This, Peter told me, was considered a great point of beauty amongst them ; and to obtain it, the mothers were accustomed to press their infants' skulls into this peculiar shape. The enemy's tactics we had by painful experience begun to find out for ourselves, but I was interested to hear other important details, such as their trick of winding metal or cloth round our cartridges to make them fit the chambers of their large-bore Snider rifles. The stockades are built by slave labour ; and in order to complete them in time, wire or leather-thonged whips were so freely used, that the ground in their vicinity was usually covered with blood before ever a fight had taken place. A favourite plan of ambush, which had already been played off on Lieutenant-Colonel Carter's column, was to partially cut through one of the rough bridges which were sometimes met with; then, when it had collapsed under some heavy load, causing a check and some confusion, to blaze into the little crowd around it. It was no uncommon thing for the Ashantis to poison water-courses; indeed, they had freely done so in the past, when they were at war with the Accras. This was far from comforting, because it was a constant occurrence on the march not to have time to filter; and water-bottles had to be filled where, and when, opportunity offered, at the risk, in any case, of dysentery. But of all the complicated customs of this race which had terrified its neighbours, the one which appealed to me most was their involved fetish-system. This is, in other words, their religion; and as the climate no doubt influences mankind in his doctrines regarding the Deity, it is not wonderful that cruelty predominates in the ritual of these gloomy denizens of the forest. Peter rather failed me here. He could only tell me what certain things meant, and describe some of the usual tortures, but little more; and by these the impossibility of separating savagery from superstition was well illustrated. War was their god's delight, as blood was his favourite sustenance. When human victims were not obtainable, birds seemed the customary omens of evil. Beware of the fowl smeared red, whether its feathers are removed or not; something unfriendly is likely to occur. If one came upon a bird, or a human body, pegged out spread-eagle fashion in the path, it meant early resistance if one proceeded. One of our own soldiers had already been thus found near a battle-field, but his head, feet, and hands had been cut off. Human sacrifices were usually carried out much in the same way, save that the preliminary torments were varied somewhat for novelty, and the headless corpse was finally thrown into the sacred grove, for the edification of its presiding demons. The heads were retained as trophies, piled under "ju-ju" trees, stuck on stakes, or placed on the altar in the fetid bone-filled temple of the village. Hands and feet securely tied, the first to prevent resistance, the second to preclude escape to some holy precincts where his life would be safe, a knife driven through his cheeks, so that his tongue cannot frame the oath which would involve release, the wretched victim is seated with another's head upon his lap so that he may gaze the while into its glassy, staring eyes and nourish the acuteness of his misery with this spectacle of horror. The onlookers, gloating over their lust of blood, demand yet more. His ears are then cut off, and when the agony he has endured renders fainting nature incapable of further suffering, he is beheaded by the executioner, either as he sits, or kneeling with his neck on the prepared rim of the fetish bowl. But there are many other variations of this stereotyped religious rite; crucifixion is far from uncommon. Another form taken by these devilish diversions is to place the poor wretch upon his back, and tie him, in the shape of a St. Andrew's cross, by the wrists and ankles, to posts at the four corners of an ant-heap. He is then perforated and slashed with knives to give these insects the means of entering his body, and left there to be eaten alive: the eyelids, too, are sometimes removed, that the sun may blind the sight. Women, particularly white ones, are invariably outraged, prior to further proceedings, by scores of savage warriors, and other monstrous practices are resorted to, so foul and revolting that modesty forbids description. Burying alive is also in vogue amongst this race, but partial interment is preferred, so that the head or feet can be seen above the surface

of the ground. The few who are exempted, such as
Fantis, whose language they can speak, are made
slaves, and toil daily in cruel irons, in the burning
heat, without respite or sufficient food, until an early
death ends their wretchedness. Is it then to be
wondered at that the Ashanti is dreaded with a terrible fear, and exists only because of his superior force
and bravery ?

But one can be tormented also by flies and ants in the
economy of nature, and this we certainly were. There
seemed to be something in the red-coloured stucco with
which the natives face their houses, which attracts
insects, and makes rest an impossibility except during
the hours of darkness.

Lieutenant (local Captain) Willans, A.S.C., reached
headquarters at this period, and took over his duties of
Chief Transport Officer. His arrival completed the list
of those with whom I had originally come out from
home. With the exception of one doctor, who died
shortly after his arrival, we had better luck in the way
of the compensations that West Africa can afford than
most such batches of officials. We had been seven in all :
poor Dr. Hunter (dead), Dr. McDowell, Captain Melliss,
Captain Wilson (killed), Lieutenant Willans, Lieutenant
Philips, and myself ; and we were all destined, either by
wounds, disease, or other causes, to go back separately.

A runner came in about this time, and reported that
heavy firing had been heard round Kumasi on the 19th,
when the garrison's fire suddenly ceased. This, we
imagined, must have been a sortie, which had been
repulsed on account of the ammunition having run short.
But was it so ? Is anything credible in this land of
lies ? Certainly, we had been most unfortunate in
attempts at getting messengers through to the fort and

back again; despite our enormous bribes, they never returned. Possibly the enemy allowed a few of the Governor's despatches to pass, hoping his urgent appeals would induce some more small parties to rush up, either to be massacred or to flood the starving garrison with hungry mouths without bringing any appreciable increase of food or ammunition. The violence of the recent attacks on us did not, however, look like any further admissions being allowed. Such small bodies would certainly have only increased the Ashanti's bag when Kumasi was taken, and similarly have weakened the relief column, had they been permitted to pursue such a mad course. This time, without doubt, the rebels must be taught a severe lesson, as to their non-fulfilment of the treaty made with Lord Wolseley, by cutting down their crops, totally disarming them, decimating or transporting many of their "braves" and chiefs; and (since so much had been heard of it) this so-called Golden Stool would best be burnt in the presence of as many of them as could be collected to testify to the extinction of their reigning dynasty. There were innumerable old scores to be paid off in this century alone. Governor McCarthy's death had never yet been definitely expiated, and now the murder of another of Her Majesty's representatives had been attempted. A pompous procession from Cape Coast to Kumasi and back, would be useless; more must be done than was even accomplished in 1873. Moreover, Prempeh's supply of pocket-money might be cut down with advantage to himself and the tax-payer. The fine fort at Kumasi seemed to us to be a cause of weakness rather than strength at the moment, seeing that it had been so easily isolated, and the railway to it showed no signs of an early completion. Certainly, the contractor for this fortification was "doing time" for his swindling, but nevertheless, nearly all the stone and material had had to be brought from Europe; and the cost is reported to have been over £30,000.

One longed for some success, with such losses to our opponents that they would be anyhow temporarily crippled by them, if only to prevent the rebellion from spreading further. It might save the reconquest of the Northern Territories, where the tribes were then rumoured to be wavering. It would facilitate the raising of native levies, poor as their services were, though such high praise had been given to them. The friendly Ashantis then shut up in Kumasi were the only ones worth such a reputation. Would that our men were accustomed to this forest warfare, which was as new to most of them as it was to us; or that we might have the help of a naval detachment from the gun-boats, to practice the running fights they were reported to have so successfully waged of recent years! This, like everything else, required special training. There must be no thought of retirement, which is more difficult in this country than anywhere else, if only from the fact that in action the carriers drop their loads, thus making it well-nigh impossible to reorganise the transport with anything approaching rapidity. Mercifully, but we did not then know it, no more of those horrible Adansi stockades, parallel to the road, were encountered. The Ashanti builds his across the path, where it is, at any rate, visible a short distance off, with huge crescent-shaped flanking portions which run into the bush, to prevent turning movements and bring a cross fire on the zone within range to its front.

Convoys continued to arrive with greater frequency than ever, and at last, to our delight, several boxes of stores for Captain Melliss and myself. How good it was to vary one's diet a little, and to alternate wheat-meal with an occasional water biscuit ! Dried vegetables tasted quite different with a slice of bacon to help them down, and curry powder made preserved meat and soldiers' ration rice positively delicious, not to mention such luxuries as mustard, Worcester sauce, an occasional tin of almost forgotten fish, whisky, and sparklets. If the last two items had only been sufficient for such a purpose, one might have been tempted, at the risk of a permanently disordered liver, to renew too frequently the delicious sensation of that bubbling, refreshing, thirst-quenching nectar, rather than return to boiled water and Government rum. There was nothing to take away this feeling of pleasure, except that when I came to pay the bill, I found that, owing to the great demand occasioned by this war, the merchants at the coast had put up their prices ; which was not very patriotic of them.

The first messenger from Lieutenant-Colonel Burroughs' recently departed column came in on the 29th, wounded in two places. He had only managed to get away by knifing one of the enemy who waylaid him, but another made off with his despatches during the tussle, so we were no wiser. He could only tell us that Sheramasi had been reached without fighting. On his heels came another, from the detachment at Brufu Edru, with the report that distant firing had just been heard on the Monsi Hill, and it mentioned the arrival of the three wounded soldiers who had been sent back from there. Then rumours floated in that large numbers of the enemy had come south, and already surrounded our little posts at Kwisa and Brufu Edru, and were going to cut off Colonel Willcocks. If there was a vestige of truth in them, we argued, it looked very much as if Kumasi had fallen, and that the big investing force was coming down to take us on, otherwise they could scarcely be spared, or would have started this game before, while we were scattered about in driblets without stores enough to admit of any attempt at holding out.

On the evening of June 30th, the night before the Staff left Prahsu, information was received from the Commandant that, although both circumstances and nature had retarded him, he was going to leave next day for Fumsu, at that time the end of the wire. This, we clearly saw, must be the furthermost point to which headquarters could advance until news was received from Lieutenant-Colonel Burroughs. It was then impossible for any one to hazard an opinion as to what would afterwards take place. Doubtless the vexed question, as to whether the main road or the one _viâ_ Obuasi would become the line of our immediate advance, would be answered when it was known what had recently happened at that formidable barrier, Dompoasi.

At the same time Colonel Willcocks sent to Lieutenant-Colonel Wilkinson the unselfish order that, if it were possible for the concentrated forces at Bekwai to assist Kumasi (it being then unknown that the garrison had broken out, and that a portion of it had been left behind) in its great emergency, it was to be done, and the fort advised of his early arrival there with supplies and soldiers. The majority of the troops being then at Bekwai, instructions were forwarded thither to enable them to co-operate with those approaching from the south by keeping certain portions of the road open, if possible. The Commandant's column was very weak, inasmuch as it had so few fighting men for the protection of a very large number of carriers bringing all the stores intended for Kumasi. Two runners, who refused to go unless armed, and together, were at once sent off, each with his orders hidden in a harmless-looking bamboo stick.

Fumsu had become more unhealthy than ever, and some labourers, in their efforts to improve matters, had cut drains between the huts, with the natural consequence that the stench became intolerable, and the risk of black-water fever and typhoid extremely great.

At this moment of perplexity, a message from the king of Bekwai brought the intensely exciting news that the Governor and garrison had cut their way out of Kumasi on the 23rd, with heavy loss. This information had been sent by the king of Ekwanta, who had been confined in the fort with the troops, to the king of Pekki, who in turn had forwarded it to the king of Bekwai. The bearer stated that he had personally seen Sir Frederic and Lady Hodgson, and some ten officers. He had not observed any more white men or women. Allowing, as we might, for those white people whom we understood to have died or been killed during the siege, we were quite unable to make these particulars fit together, nor could we think what had become of the Swiss missionaries and their wives. The Governor, so we were given to understand by this man, was proceeding at once to the coast through the Denkera country, and we presumed, if all this was really the case, that the troops, after a short rest, would go to Bekwai, where they could quietly do garrison duty for a while. The bearer of these tidings had also heard that numerous bodies of Ashantis, flushed with their partial success, were then coming down the main road to attack our advanced posts, and oppose our advance, and that the Kokofus intended to storm Esumeja on July 1st or 2nd, the former being the very day this report was first communicated to us. Even then, nothing definite could be ascertained as to whether any men had been left behind in occupation of the fort, nor had any news of Lieutenant-Colonel Burroughs' success at Dompoasi come through. Could it be true, we involuntarily asked each other, after having come through no less than three natives, when one was unreliable enough as a rule? What an outlook! The other tribes would certainly rise after this. As there was, apparently, no fort to invest, our opposition would probably be worse than ever, and commence in force forthwith. Interest in the war was almost gone. All the plan of campaign would no doubt have to be changed ; no easy job when matters had progressed thus far, and with the troops widely scattered. Yes, possibly all that could then be done would be to pull our advanced posts out of the fire, then retire, and hold the Prah, waiting until the rains were over before continuing operations. But no, punitive measures must proceed, and the fort be retaken at once, to save the prestige of the white man. There was no time to wait for reinforcements from any distant quarter of the globe. It seemed useless to think at all in such a country of lies. Doubtless this last story about the Governor was as untruthful as the others had proved themselves to be ; but if not, what a blow to our Commandant!

A GROUP OF ASHANTI CHIEFS, RINGLEADERS OF THE REBELLION

CHAPTER XVI

THE COMMANDANT ENTERS THE ENEMY'S COUNTRY

COLONEL WILLCOCKS and Staff, with a train of soldiers and carriers, left Prahsu, the limit of friendly territory, and for all practical purposes the boundary of the Gold Coast Colony, at 5 a.m. on July 1st, having taken seven hours to get across the swollen river and an almost impassable swamp on its further bank. That night he reached Tobiasi, and was, for the first time, off the wire. Between 3 and 4 p.m. the next day he reached Fumsu, the slowness of the march being due to careful scouting, which appeared necessary on account of a plausible but really false report, that an army of thousands of rebels had worked their way round Fumsu with the object of intercepting him. His troops consisted of half the Tobiasi garrison company, W.A.R., and D Company, 2nd Bn. W.A.F.F., A Company, 1st Bn. W.A.F.F., being still at Prahsu. This was, as we rather expected, the prelude to our own departure.

Lieutenant-Colonel Burroughs had only rationed the two small detachments at Brufu Edru and Kwisa for a week, and this limit had almost been reached. Consequently, Captain Melliss was again detailed to take a convoy to them with twenty days' rations, with orders to return immediately on the completion of this duty. The escort was to be much stronger than our former one, partly because between six and seven hundred carriers were to go with us, and partly on account of rumours from various sources that such large numbers of the enemy had come southwards. My Hausa company, the majority of the Yoruba company, a 7-pr. gun, and a rocket tube, were to compose this fighting force, accompanied by a special Transport Officer and a doctor. The Intelligence Department also informed us of a new stockade, which was stated to have been erected between Sherabroso and Sheramasi, in close proximity to the well-remembered swamp in that locality. This turned out to be fairly accurate; but the enemy were not there. It was rather an anxious outlook, after our last experience of this thankless convoy duty; and as time was pressing to the last degree, there was again no chance of any scouting being possible. So we put our trust in luck and the black man, and prepared ourselves for any contingency that might arise. However, it happened to be another case of the saying that " when one expects most one gets least"; but this time in a favourable sense. So next morning off we went again for the same old trip, with that detestable bit of mountaineering, which would have been pleasant in Switzerland, but was not so in Africa; and at the last moment, in anticipation of heavy casualties, a second doctor was attached to our column.

Captain Neal's bridge afforded a dry start, but the next time we encountered the Fum, it was chest deep, once more wetting our scanty wardrobe most unpleasantly. And so it would have to remain until the next halt of sufficient duration to enable our things to be dried; but when that would be was too much of an outside chance to risk money upon. The river where we had previously been ambushed was quite unfordable, and a long delay was caused in bridging it with tree trunks. It was rather like tight-rope walking when completed, but it served its temporary purpose. We sent back a note regarding this matter, which led to its being subsequently improved by the pioneers under an escort, and the Commandant's column was not retarded by it. It is these seemingly trivial details which often put everything hopelessly out. I do not think I, for one, will ever again give vent to glib criticisms; Africa's practical way of imparting knowledge rubs it into one so effectually that there is every probability of its remaining. Yet once one gets home, one begins to forget extraordinarily quickly, and the past appears like a bad dream. The mere fact of putting on a dress suit seems to make one fastidious about the best fare; and one cannot walk in London mud because a cab crawls invitingly along the road near at hand. Yet in Africa one ate anything, and waded through feet of mire, quite forgetful of self in amusement at the comical misfortunes of one's comrades. Yes; Lieutenant-Colonel Burroughs' column had done good work. What a nasty place that ambush looked now, one could not but remark, on returning to the road again after a hasty inspection of one of these traps in the wayside undergrowth. It was marvellous, indeed, that the skulking blackguards had not wiped out scores of us instead of units, at such close ranges. But one has only to fire a trade gun oneself to realise the difficulty of hitting the target, let alone the bull's-eye. We could not get to Brufu Edru that day, because of the swollen river, so we halted for the night at the first convenient village, determining to reach Kwisa on the following day. The guide, however,

M

stated that the Adansi Hills were teeming with the enemy. Well, it could not be helped; they must be taken on if they came in our way. At present we had no time either to look for or avoid them.

Brufu Edru was reached in the nick of time. In desperation, the officer in command there was about to send his subaltern to Fumsu, with every man that he could spare, to get provisions, at the risk of possible annihilation. He could not know that the number of days' rations he had been left had been thoughtfully remembered. What a quaint little cage he had put himself and his men into—a couple of native huts, enclosed by a light stockade! It looked for all the world like a large hen-house with a fowl-run. The houses in its immediate vicinity had been demolished; and one could not help laughing on hearing that, at the time this was done, the ousted occupants set up howls and groans from the adjacent hills, to show their disapproval and dislike of their first experience of a military bailiff. Then we learned of the ambush the last column had met with on the Monsi Hill in front of us, and there were some wounded men here in proof of the fact. Was there any truth in the story we had heard, that this place and Kwisa were invested in force? we asked of the officer commanding this post. Well, the enemy were certainly plentiful about there; he could not say more, was the answer. His men, having no food to eat, had gone out in small parties, looting the surrounding farms, and some had been sniped at and several wounded. That certainly looked suspicious, and at the next post we heard the same yarn.

While the share of stores for this place was being taken over we breakfasted, and then pushed on. We peered rather more frequently and carefully into the bush on either side, as we made our way onwards, and the precipitous path was somewhat more slippery than it had been before. But we went on all the same, and reached Kwisa safely, in time for a cup of tea. What a scene of destruction this place presented in consequence of the enemy's visit after its evacuation; and how different it looked to what it did when we were there a few days before! The officer in command, having cleared away the filth left behind by them, was busy building quarters for the benefit of the in-coming troops, and a Public Works official had been left behind to help him. The officers' quarters were, for the present, the ruins of the old rest-house kitchen. This house had at one end only the remnants of its former walls; and this part was being got ready for Colonel Willcocks. One was shown with pride the light palisade round this wretched *enceinte*, then fast approaching completion, and the tambours (unless told the name, one would never have guessed it!) which were extra strong. In these the little force intended to congregate, and flank the sides of their position with a galling fire, if meddled with. But the weakest point was the water supply, which was some quarter of a mile distant in the thick bush. If the enemy had had the sense to get possession of this, Kwisa would have had to be evacuated for the second time.

There were no more of the Governor's " chop " boxes found this time, so we received the warm welcome of hunger and relief combined. We learnt that there had been a fight at Dompoasi, which had probably been successfully passed, as no more firing had been heard, and Lieutenant-Colonel Burroughs had not come back. Details of the ambuscade on the hill-top were then forthcoming, and we heard that several piles of ·303 empty cartridge cases had been found behind a fallen tree where the enemy had placed themselves. This little force was also *in extremis*, and serious thoughts had been entertained of a night march to Brufu Edru, so that, uniting with that post, the retirement might have been made with some chance of a successful termination.

I ended up the day with a talk to our guide, who was quite a little General in his way, and had some most common-sense ideas to propound. He thought the white man could do nothing without feeling his way with scouts ; and even when, in this country, the enemy were found, it would be impossible to inflict really heavy losses on them, as when they had had enough, they had only to "go for bush," and nobody could follow them. In future the enemy would doubtless confine their attention chiefly to the white men and carriers. Casualties in the transport would soon be more numerous than amongst the soldiers, as the Ashantis must ere long run short of food, and especially ammunition, and would adopt this means of supplying their needs. The "big white man" ought also to send troops up the Accra-Kumasi road, because this move would be unexpected, and in the villages along this route all the property, live stock, women, and children had been removed for safety. Thus soliloquised this black philosopher, and even if he had been propounding sophistries, they were certainly specious. However, we were going to run right into Fumsu next day, and had, accordingly, an extra early reveille. So I bade my wise friend good-night, and went to sleep, but not for so long as I had expected.

Shortly after midnight, two runners arrived with despatches, and the look of the envelope immediately made one start up, rub one's sleepy eyes very wide open, pull the candle a little closer, and commence studying their contents in real earnest, and—one may be forgiven for wishing such precautions to the uttermost ends of the earth—they were in French. But the interest of them was so absorbing that all else was soon forgotten. Some were for Lieutenant-Colonel Burroughs, and these were sent on at once. It was only with much difficulty that we were able to do so, for Dompoasi still stank in the nostrils of all friendly black men. We found that at last a native had reported correctly, and the truth had become known. Our goal could yet be reached. Only a matter of hours before, the Commandant had received a letter from the Governor at Ekwanta, some twenty miles south-west of Kumasi, revealing the fact that a small garrison *had* been left behind in the fort. The remainder had forced their way out on the 23rd, and taken a stockade at Potasi, which had been wisely selected as one of the weakest links in the investment. Then my suspicions about the 7-pr. shots which Captain Hall had heard on the 19th were correct. The noise of the firing of this gun, in this enclosed country, could only carry short distances, and what had been mistaken for those reports had been big Dane guns, after all. The explosion of the two are far from dissimilar, or perhaps the 7-pr. had been in reality the one which Captain Aplin's column had left behind, and had been fired by the Ashantis with the specific object of deceit. What a mercy the troops at Esumeja had not been tempted to go out and reconnoitre that dangerous main road! It might have been a *ruse* on the part of the enemy to induce them to do so, in the belief that they could succour the desperate garrison. The natural surmise would have been that they were actually engaged, because, knowing they were extremely short of ammunition, it was a moral certainty that they would never have wasted ten shells on signals. Assuredly in such a case they would have been cut up. Caution is good, but perhaps one had given savage cunning credit for too much.

Once in possession of this all-important fact, Colonel Willcocks was not going to wait for anything, neither reinforcements, nor news from Lieutenant-Colonel Burroughs. All he cared about then was the salvation of our fellow-countrymen in the fort. There was now no room for any doubt; facts spoke plainly for themselves. The next morning Colonel Willcocks was going to push on at all costs, with practically no defence for his carriers, only one hundred odd soldiers and some more guns. We were to race back again and join him, and Captain Wilkinson, with Captain Wright, were to do so, too, from Prahsu, with A Company, 1st Bn. W.A.F.F. In only as many days as one could count upon one's two hands, a fresh garrison, with adequate supplies and ammunition, would have to be put into that fort, and the gallant starving little band there taken out. And this was duly done; for even if we had been crippled by mishap, like Lieutenant-Colonel Carter, the relief would have been carried through somehow.

All possible loads were temporarily left behind by us, to shorten our column, and to enable us to march light. There was no time now to peep into the forest at all ; the next day's march was stepping out in front, and almost a double in rear, but it had to be done. It turned out very well, for not a shot was fired at the flying column as it streaked along the greasy path and slipped through village after village. Converging forces put the enemy out. Lieutenant-Colonel Burroughs, as we subsequently ascertained, had been instructed in these despatches to collect all possible supplies in Bekwai, and to meet us at Dompoasi in two days' time. One doctor was left at Brufu Edru to attend to a wounded man with a fractured leg. Captain Eden's Yoruba company was dropped at Sheramasi to bridge the river there; whilst we proceeded on our way, until the Commandant was met, some three miles from his starting place.

It was found impossible to reach Sheramasi, so, crowded up in a small village, the combined force halted for the night. It was then we learnt in detail the important news that Captain Bishop had been left in command in Kumasi: he was not dead, as we had previously heard; that the six hundred soldiers who had come out were presumably on their way to the coast with the Governor; and that our threatening the enemy from the south must have greatly facilitated the garrison's flight. We also heard about the surprise at Dompoasi. I remember that night getting a glance at a book on Lord Wolseley's campaign of '73, and it was most interesting to see the similarity between his experiences and our own in regard to places, troops, and country. In fact, I read considerably longer than was required to induce sleep—a needless practice during those times of fatigue.

The following morning a telegram from the Secretary of State for the Colonies, wishing us all luck, and sympathising in the difficulties we were then encountering, was received, and pleased us all very much. The two Staff Officers, who had accompanied our convoy in order that they might "see a show," then returned disappointed to their duties. Nevertheless, they gave us breakfast, which was exceedingly kind of them and most opportune, as our provision box had, in the confusion of falling in, wandered away somewhere to the rear.

Captain Eden's company was picked up at Sheramasi, the water crossed by his newly made bridge, Brufu Edru

passed, the hill scaled, and Kwisa reached without
special incident of any kind. The Colonel's past misfortunes had now turned into "General's luck." The
Kwisa garrison was at once despatched to bring in the
one from Brufu Edru, which thenceforward ceased to be
a post, and returned late that evening, to remain and
make up a more suitable complement for the defence of
this dangerous place. That evening Lieutenant-Colonel
Burroughs' despatch, relating to his repulse at Kokofu,
came in. Four of his officers were down with fever,
and a similar number of ours were taken ill that night
with the same disease. It appeared to be an absolute
certainty that we should have a battle on the morrow at
Dompoasi. Accordingly, it had been arranged that we
should advance from the south side, and Lieutenant-
Colonel Burroughs, with three hundred men, and no
transport, was to attack it from the north. This form
of tactics the enemy could not abide, and never could
make out. The plan was again successful. In anticipation of fighting, Colonel Willcocks personally held a
short parade at sundown, and practised the men in
shouting so as to get their blood up, by sounding
the "Charge" with massed buglers, whilst the officers
drew their swords and cheered.

Then commenced a deluge, which not only spoiled
our dinner, cooking in the open, but also our night's
sleep, which had to be attempted in the gimcrack shelters
recently erected. Of rest there was absolutely none ; on
the contrary, we were more tired in the morning than we
had been over-night—by no means a good preparation
for a fight. I cannot congratulate that Public Works
official, either upon his knowledge of architecture or
upon his display of common sense. The officers'
shanty was like a row of loose boxes, no reservation

as to numbers having been made. The walls were of bamboo, and good enough. But the roof was of the same material, and, what was worse, it was flat, the interstices having been filled up with earth, nor was there so much as a covering of grass or leaves. The obvious result was that streams of water, with large lumps of mud to break the monotony, fell unceasingly upon one's bed. In the end the bed had to be rolled up, if one wished for a dry sleep next night, and, arrayed in a macintosh, one sat upon it in disgust. I am glad, for his own sake, the offender was not present to hear the remarks made, not only about his professional skill, but as to what some pugnacious sufferers would have liked to inflict upon his person. In fact, the language became so expressive, and reached such a pitch of indignation, that in self-defence the Colonel had to send round a mild protest to say we were disturbing him. However, we were full of "beans" and forgiveness by dawn, when we sallied out, and began preparations for the more tangible enemy we expected to engage forthwith. We had conquered a most harassing foe by most praiseworthy fortitude during the night, and we intended to try and do the same thing by day. We were all game.

CHAPTER XVII

BEKWAI BECOMES HEADQUARTERS

WITH every probability of severe opposition, there was a general desire to be in the van, where the chances and risks were always the greatest. The post of honour was given to Captain Melliss, who commanded the advance guard, led by F Company, 1st Bn. W.A.F.F. A special service officer was attached to these Hausas, so that each section might be under the special control of a white man. The "point" had already reached Fomena before the column was completely formed up waiting to go on. Fomena, which now no longer exists, contained a few houses and many gold holes. It was understood to be occupied by the enemy, but such did not turn out to be the case. This place had been a thriving town at one time, but had been so satisfactorily demolished in 1873 that it had never recovered the shock. Together with the order to advance, all being ready, came a pencilled note on a scrap of paper from the Commandant, stating that a native spy, sent out the night before, had just come in, and reported that the rebels were collected in force on our side of Dompoasi, awaiting us. So we looked to our firearms, warned our men, rubbed our eyes, and started away slowly, prepared for anything.

On we crawled, taking all possible care not to be ambushed, at intervals firing volleys into the bush because

we had no scouts ; and, I am glad to say, this was the
last occasion upon which we were compelled to do without these necessary flankers.   The constant expectation
of that ominous b—o—o—m, however, was not realised,
but another sound, ere long, caught our straining ears.
Do you hear that?   No, it was too faint to be certain
about.   Dompoasi could not be far now.   Yet there it
was again.   Could it be imagination playing one a trick?
No ; there was no longer any reason for doubt: it was
a bugle.   The information was sent back, not without
some feeling of surprise on our part.   Yet it proved to
be quite correct.   The enemy had again been scored off
in the same way, by the meeting of two forces, and after
their recent experiences in this very place, had forsaken
their intention, and gone to a war camp in the forest to
fight us at a later date.   There was the undergrowth all
cut away on our right, the *débris* of that formidable
stockade, and the path literally paved with empty cartridge cases.   Little wonder, in such a locality, and in
such dense bush, that the former column had fallen into
such a terrible trap.   We even moved for one moment
off the road, to look for the first time on one of the
enemy's huge entrenchments, which were soon to become
so familiar to most of us.   There was no jerry-building
there; solid, uncut trunks formed the walls of this stockade.
The great timbers lying about in disorder showed clearly
what labour must have been expended upon its construction.   Then we entered the village ; we first saw that
small portion of it which Captain Wilson had burnt,
and then advanced into the centre, passing through
Lieutenant-Colonel Burroughs' men, who had been
drawn up to receive us, the massed buglers sounding
shrill blasts of welcome.   The danger was past, and
we were glad of it.   Not a casualty could be afforded,

not a man thrown away, until our comrades were relieved. The formalities of this military reception were soon over, and we fell out in little groups to breakfast and to gossip. In graphic terms were related to us the two fights these troops had had : the first, successful, at this very place ; the second unsuccessful, at Kokofu. It was pleasant to feel that the first part of the concentration had then been effected, though one could not banish from one's mind the consciousness of all the misfortunes which had occurred in this town.

Once again we were off, with lighter hearts and a feeling of greater confidence. As we emerged from the village we saw the wreckage of the other great stockade, and more cartridge cases told us of the cruel experience our men had lately had there. We plodded steadily on ; another river, another swamp, were passed. At last we rounded the thousandth bend of the winding track, and beheld, to our astonishment, a large Union Jack. This was Essiankwanta ; it was under the sway of the king of Bekwai, and therefore friendly. Here we were to spend the night.

This is the only part of the main road which does not run through hostile country after the Prah is crossed. The district is in the extreme E.S.E. corner of the Dengiasi country, and from here there is a branch road straight into Bekwai, so that further risks could be thus avoided. In continuing our advance next day we had to choose between going by the main road, which we had hitherto followed, or adopting this alternative route to Bekwai direct. We decided to keep to the main road, and succeeded in doing so, although we encountered, some distance ahead, a most difficult bog, many hundred yards in length. By dint of the utmost efforts we got through it, but later on a little more rain made it absolutely impassable.

Although we had not fought, we were considered to have earned a "medical comfort" each, and this experiment was highly appreciated. The officers of the W.A.R. were very short of food, and had nothing to drink ; so they were particularly pleased. I remember having a short chat with one of them over a drink, which he enjoyed very much after his recent experiences of enforced teetotalism. He confided to me that he was of opinion that an armchair with a whisky-and-soda, in the Naval and Military Club, would be very pleasing after the mode of life he had been leading ; but, for all that, he never seemed to be in any hurry to alter his plans, and at the very moment at which I am writing this is still in the land which he then so heartily abused.

That night, owing to want of men and no reinforcements having come in from the old Kumasi garrison, Colonel Willcocks decided to temporarily evacuate Kwisa until the relief was effected, there being no fear of our prestige being lowered with Dompoasi taken, and the enemy in that immediate neighbourhood dispersed. Accordingly next morning, when we marched out for Bekwai, two of the less wearied companies of the W.A.R. went back to strengthen and bring in by double marches the Kwisa garrison to that place. We all went to bed feeling that we had every reason to congratulate ourselves on the day's work ; and although one of my Hausas, who in turning round unexpectedly with his rifle sloped over his shoulder had bayoneted me through the right ear, and made me better comprehend the enemy's dislike to these weapons, I was as thankful as any one.

The next march was as laborious, wet, and unpleasant as usual. We passed through a little village where Lord Wolseley's dead were interred after his biggest engagement ; and just beyond, where a by-road to Bekwai goes to the left and the main road bends to the right towards Esumeja, we came upon the spot where the battle of Amoaful took place. The place is now, and ever will be, marked by nature. So much of the bush was cut down that the forest will never again recover its extravagant growth of timber ; and tall, rank grass now fills up the original clearing, and gives the locality, in contradistinction to its surroundings, quite an open appearance. That conflict finally ended the enemy's main resistance in 1873 ; and our concluding struggle was to be at an almost identical distance from, but on the further side of, the same place, Kumasi.

Six Ashanti signal guns, from sentries in trees, were heard at various times that day, acquainting the enemy with our advance, and the time of our arrival at various points, but no more firing took place. On the 9th of July, in the late afternoon, our force marched through the narrow gate into the bamboo palisade which Lieutenant-Colonel Wilkinson had erected, and up the broad main street of straggling Bekwai. A hut near this entrance was reserved for the Commandant, outside which the guns were parked under the folds of the Union Jack, floating from an extemporised mast of bamboos. The officers and troops were told off to their crowded quarters ; for the makeshift barracks, which afterwards grew up in such profusion, were then scarce. The king of Bekwai met us on our arrival, and was not only greeted by Colonel Willcocks, but given a pecuniary reward—quite a fortune for a native. The hands of old friends were hastily shaken : we had ended our journey without a casualty. A runner, who was pro-mised fifty pounds if he got in, not even being asked to come back, was sent off to tell the garrison at Kumasi of our arrival, and that we were coming to their relief. He was never again heard of.

The next three days were very busy ones indeed. All laboured willingly from early morning till late at night, in preparation for the greatest effort in the campaign. Little or no rest was taken by any one. My company was, I think, most wearied of all at that time, and it certainly had the longest sick list. This was not so much due to the mileage covered by our marches, as to the slow pace, which undoubtedly kills more surely than the fast. To judge by the medical returns, there is no question that the Hausa is a sturdier man than the Yoruba, and can endure hardships longer. It is hard to draw comparisons, nevertheless, because both these races, in respect of endurance, were positively marvellous; and how they ever accomplished so admirably, and with such complete success, all that they did, will always be the wonder and admiration of their officers, who alone can fully appreciate it. When it was my turn to go round the sentries at night, after a long march, including perhaps a fight, knowing the men were of necessity underfed, it used to be my dread at first that I might find one of them asleep. Such an offence would, on active service, have been met with the severest punishment, and rightly so, however painful it would have been had one been detailed to award it. But I soon lost all nervousness on this score, and performed my duty with as light a heart as if I had been engaged upon it as a humdrum Orderly Officer in time of peace. The " Halt, who goes dere ? "—as they pronounced it— always came as regularly as it was followed by the word " Friend," or " Visiting rounds." Night duty was by far the most trying of all, under such conditions as we were in then ; and a night attack we subsequently made was, in my opinion, one of the most anxious experiences of the campaign. We have more highly developed nervous systems than the black man, but he has a superstitious dread of the darkness which we have not ; so no doubt, in our different ways, we both felt it unpleasant and equally disliked it.

Lieutenant-Colonel Wilkinson, the Inspector-General of the Gold Coast Forces, was recovering from an attack of fever, and was rather disappointed that he still had none of his men to command ; however, he was a host in himself, and all were glad to see him again, and so nearly well that he would not be cut out of the honour of taking his share in the relief—the reward of all those who had borne the brunt at the beginning, which was by far the worst period of all. We heard of the Kokofu repulse in detail : how Lieutenant Wilford, W.A.R., had been hit in the pouch by a bullet which had damaged some of the cartridges, but had done him no harm ; how two more helmets had been shot through, one nearly as badly as Captain Roupell's ; that behind the stockade was reported to be a river, on the far bank of which was a parapet and ditch, as a second line of defence to the war camp, and the town behind it ; and that an officer of high rank was so much impressed with the slenderness of his chances of surviving the campaign after these experiences, that he had made his will on his return from the action.

During this period it was discovered that the supply of two months' rations, required for the white men who were to remain in the fort after it was relieved, was insufficient. The officers of the W.A.R. were also, by then, left without food. To make up for these deficiencies, all officers' private stores were handed in, and the worst of the difficulty removed. This was the reason why, for some time afterwards, we were so short of provisions, and, during the trying days taken up with the actual relief, on half-rations, not to say at times positively hungry. For the same reasons, the soldiers and carriers necessarily existed, during this period, on a totally inadequate allowance of food.

During this halt Colonel Willcocks, with some of his staff, went to Esumeja to inspect that post, and he was in no way averse to the fact becoming known to the enemy. Whilst he was there, Captain Carlton, W.I.R., with two companies W.A.F.F., one weak company W.A.R., which had already suffered sixty casualties, a 75-m/m gun, the pioneers, some carriers with *machêtês*, and some of the Esumeja garrison, moved for some fifty to a hundred yards along the road to Kokofu, cutting the bush on each side, and finally building two flimsy stockades. His orders were, if possible, not to become engaged, certainly not seriously, and above all, not to incur the risk of casualties. This, as any one could see, was a feint, with the object of instilling into the enemy's mind the idea that we were again going to try and take that place. It was, however, hoped that when the Kokofu General sent this information to the Commander-in-Chief of the Ashanti army, the latter would, according to their excellent tactics, reinforce the threatened point ; such, later on, appeared to have been the case. The *ruse* was completely successful, and the enemy fell into the trap prepared even more readily than had been hoped. For not only was the right flank of our subsequent advance thus rendered safe from the attacks we should otherwise certainly have had, but the resistance from the main war camp on the Cape Coast road, when we did get to Kumasi, was largely reduced. Thus it came to pass

N

that the enemy gave us great assistance instead of
hindrance in the achievement of our chiefest object,
and were checkmated in their own wily favourite style.
" *Fas est et ab hoste doceri.*"

Those left at Bekwai were not idle.   The amount of
details, arrangements, checkings, estimates, stocktakings,
and what not, was immense.   Always running to and
fro, with never a spare moment, and yet at the close of
each of these days there seemed to be nothing to record.
On the evening of the 11th, the Commandant and all
the troops, except those who were to be left to garrison
Esumeja, returned at 7 p.m., not having had any
fighting.   Shortly afterwards, a sad little note reached
us from the fort, its brief wording showing the soldierly
pluck of the men who sent it, and the starved soldier
(selected for his condition and strength), who brought
it safely through after two days with his life in his
hand, well exemplifying the stuff of which the African
rank and file is composed.   The message ran as follows :
" Governor broke out seventeen days ago.   Garrison
rapidly diminishing by disease.   Can only last out a
few more days on very reduced rations.   Help us."
That night, six star shells were fired, to let them know
deliverance was at hand, and that we were coming ; but
we subsequently learned that they never saw them.
With a heart filled with compassion, one could scarce
refrain from thinking, as one watched those showers of
sparks falling in vivid brightness through the darkness,
as if from heaven itself, that they seemed like angel-
messengers, sent to comfort those within that living
tomb, and nerve the arm of those sent to deliver them.
At midnight, the last contingent of W.A.F.F. from
Northern Nigeria, the Kwisa garrison and its escort of
two companies W.A.R., came in amidst the cheers of

the townsfolk and soldiers. They had marched magnificently. They were the last troops Colonel Willcocks
was waiting for, and completed the force though
bringing it up to only the regulation strength of one
battalion ; but, with this handful of soldiers, the way
was to be forced through a rebel army of from thirty to
forty thousand " braves," entrenched to bar our way, and
annihilate us if they could.

A massed parade of all the troops, stretching from end
to end of the village, was held next day for the Commandant's inspection, and to impress the king of Bekwai,
who came in full barbaric state, with a gigantic scarlet
and gold umbrella (probably obtained from a caravan
from Tunis, by the look of it), and an ill-clad throng
of courtiers, wives, and warriors. A few of these last
finally came with us as scouts, but they were found to
to absolutely useless.

Meantime, nearly all the officers, British N.C.O.'s, and
troops, had come in from Esumeja, which, until after the
relief, could only be spared a garrison of a hundred
Lagos Hausas. Obuasi had fifty, Bekwai had only two
hundred men, and no posts were then held on the main
road between this latter place and Fumsu. The first
temporary promotions appeared in orders at this time
when Captains Melliss and Beddoes were given the
local rank of Major.

At sunset on the 12th, before we started, the "Officers'
call" was sounded, and in the dim light of the departing
day, under the Union Jack, outside the Commandant's
mud hut, might have been seen a silent, serious throng
of British officers and N.C.O.'s, in travel-stained khaki,
waiting for their final orders to set out on the hazardous
undertaking to participate in which they had manfully
toiled to reach this spot by this, the latest, day. It was

one of those solemn occasions when men stand face to face with death—a time the recollections of which linger vividly and long. The Colonel did not detain us more than a few moments, for much yet remained to be done by all. In a few brief sentences, he placed the situation rapidly before us. He made no secret of the fact that he expected very severe fighting. That, although the Governor and the majority of the garrison had left the fort, the Ashantis were still determined to take it, and there was no reason to doubt that the enemy were aware of the desperate plight of those still holding out. It was needless to appeal to British officers in a time of emergency when every one would do his level best. He pointed out, however, that this occasion was no ordinary one. We were engaged in a holy cause : the rescue of our fellow-countrymen was, for the time being, the sole object in view. The gravity of the situation was so keenly realised by all of us, that we merely saluted in silence, and dispersed with anxious hearts to see to the final duties which were still uncompleted. Every preparation had to be made ; no detail, however trivial it might appear, might be overlooked. Despite what we were to undergo on the morrow, every one was busily occupied until nearly midnight. The direction of the march was, even at that moment, a profound secret. The column had to be kept as short as possible, and only two carriers could be allowed to each officer. As only half-rations were available, the loads had to be made up with extra care ; and arrangements were made to serve out food and ammunition to the men for their immediate needs. There were, therefore, but a few hours for sleep at one's disposal when all was at last completed, before the bugle would sound reveille at 4 a.m., the summons for our start.

CHAPTER XVIII

THE RELIEF OF KUMASI

IN dripping darkness the wet, shivering troops fell in according to the order of march. As soon as the light admitted of it, the advance was sounded from rear to front, and there slowly moved out to accomplish the grand object of the campaign a force of two 75-m/m guns, four 7-pr. guns, six Maxims, a thousand rank and file, sixty white men (including civilian officials), and seventeen hundred carriers. To Captain Eden's company had been allotted the privilege of leading, on the ground that he had volunteered to remain in the fort after it had been relieved. We knew what marching with a large column meant in that country, an experience already heartily disliked, but what lay before us that day nobody imagined. None of the officers were very raw, most wore the ribbons of past campaigns, African and Indian in particular, but there was not one who did not agree afterwards that this was the most terrible day that he had ever spent. The rain fell in almost ceaseless torrents, the road was practically an unbroken swamp, and the fatigue and discomfort of that journey strained every muscle and nerve to breaking point. The Ordah river, in flood, had to be crossed by means of a felled tree ; and other streams of various sizes forded.   In order to arrive at the fort by the appointed date, it was imperative to make Pekki that night.   This was the last friendly village, and lay on the confines of the Ashanti territory.   Somewhat longer than the main road, this route, we then learned, had been selected both for strategic reasons and because a shorter extent of hostile country would have to be traversed.   The distance from Bekwai to Pekki was fifteen miles (leaving eleven more before Kumasi was reached), but it took the relief force nineteen and a half hours to get in, and the rear guard some two hours longer.   The few hammocks allowable in a column some three miles in length were reserved for the sick and wounded, so that one had to foot it both going and returning.   Some hours before our destination was gained, night came on.   Thenceforward, worn out, we struggled along, holding on to each other in the inky forest-darkness.   Nothing broke the death-like silence, save the dropping of water from the trees overhead and the squelch of filthy mud churned by three thousand feet.   Soaked with rain, the column was forced at times to wade waist-deep in water.   The exhausted carriers fell out by dozens, one even died ; others injured themselves and caused much delay. When a carrier dropped from sheer collapse, his load would be cheerfully picked up and shouldered by some soldier ; so that, wonderful to relate, not a single one was lost.   Frequently some jaded white man would fall asleep when a short halt was necessary to help the transport over a particularly bad spot.   In the small hours our immediate goal was reached, and, too fatigued either to undress or take food, we turned into the native huts to get a few hours' rest.   But even then sleep was

ONE OF THE DIFFICULTIES ENCOUNTERED BY THE RELIEF FORCE

CROSSING THE ORIAH RIVER ON A SUBMERGED TREE-TRUNK

not for all, for sentries had to be posted and picquets thrown out round the village.

Notwithstanding a sleepless night, passed in wet clothes and without shelter or proper food, the men never grumbled, but were as cheery in the morning as if they had been quartered in cantonments. Our march this day lay through the thick of the enemy's country, and every yard of bush had now to be searched by scouts cutting their way as they went, a process that reduced the pace of the column to a slow crawl. The weariness of this movement was added to by the constant strain on our nerves, which increased with every mile traversed. We never knew when we might not be ambushed, nor on what part of the long column fire might not be opened. Flankers would find an artificial entrenchment, but they could not be depended upon to obviate these two contingencies, for the foe, aware of their coming, might let them pass and await a favourable opportunity to entrap us. In consequence of the previous day's fatigue the column was not ordered to start till 8 a.m., and no bugles were sounded. These facts, added to our late arrival the night before, were quite providential, for the next village, Treda, a large fetish one, was completely surprised. Had the enemy heard of our movements, or had we set out as early as usual, the resistance, determined as it was, would have been stronger, and we should have suffered proportionately.

Before our advance guard had got clear of Pekki the enemy's scouts were encountered, and, long before the rear guard had filed out, an action had been fought and the village taken at the point of the bayonet by a brilliant charge conducted by the Yorubas and the S.L.F.P. Treda stands on the top of a slope, and the enemy held the ridge most tenaciously after their scouts had fallen back. They also fought stubbornly in the place itself, and at such close quarters, that one Ashanti came deliberately out three times and fired point-blank at an officer. Much amusement was afforded us during this fight by another of the officers rushing on towards the foe at the head of his company, brandishing a native *machêtê* as he had not time to get hold of his sword. But the whole affair only caused us some half-dozen casualties ; and these were sent back to Pekki after their wounds had been dressed. In the town we caught thirty sheep, which were indeed a god-send, and were duly eaten for dinner the same night. Amongst other loot, we found one of Lady Hodgson's boxes and Major Morris' saddle. As a protest against past mis-conduct and as a suggestion to the inhabitants to mend their manners in the future, Treda was burnt by the rear guard, the "ju-ju" house pulled down, and the sacred trees in the fetish grove felled ; but no sooner had we passed through than the enemy returned and sniped us from the rear with some effect, showing that the lesson was not immediately laid to heart. We found on our return journey that these people had subsequently retired into a war camp in the bush near by, whence they proceeded to attack the Pekki people in our absence, killing and wounding several of them. It is a noteworthy fact that never once did we engage the enemy, but that the sharp crack of rifles was distinctly audible amidst the deep boom of trade guns, and scarcely ever did we capture a village or a war camp without finding amongst the spoil Lee-Metfords, Martinis, Sniders, and muskets—clear proofs of the number they must have had in addition to their well-known Dane guns.

From this point onwards we were fighting at intervals throughout the day, which retarded us so much that, at 4 p.m., it was decided to spend the night in a village then taken after some resistance. This was another Ekwanta, and was less than half-way on the road from Pekki to Kumasi. In one of the huts we found a Gold Coast Hausa uniform, riddled with bullets, and in others marks that showed unmistakably that the inhabitants had shared in the attack upon the Governor's outgoing column. Again, in a tropical deluge, pitiless necessity compelled the troops and carriers to pass the night with no more shelter than a few leaves. Shortly after dark the guns were again fired as a signal to the fort, but we still got no response. On our arrival we ascertained that our fire next day was the first intimation they had had of our coming, but it was not until we were engaged in the final action that they allowed themselves to feel certain that relief had at last really arrived.

Late that evening, Colonel Willcocks, for the first time, confided to us all the plans he had formed for the crowning struggle before Kumasi. He told us that on the morrow, after an hour and a half's marching, we should reach a fetish stronghold where a fierce resistance might be looked for, but that the final battle would be fought at some stockades a few hundred yards from the fort. He intended, he added, to attack this entrenched position without encumbrance. With this end in view, a halt would be called at the last village, which would be rapidly fortified into a sort of *zariba* and defended by a certain proportion of the troops. In this enclosure all possible carriers and stores would be placed, while the fighting force would take the stockades, return for the transport, and then enter Kumasi ; by this means the risk of losing the precious loads of rice, ammunition, and stores would be reduced to a minimum.   In fact, so desperate did our situation appear, and so determined was Colonel Willcocks to reach the fort at all costs, that he gave orders that, if necessary, all soldiers or carriers, who might be killed, would have to be left where they fell.

At four o'clock the next morning reveille was sounded, and with the first streak of dawn the column got under way. Haversacks and water-bottles had to be filled before starting, for not a superfluous carrier was allowed that day with the fighting portion of the force. The march again resolved itself into a more or loss severe running encounter, though, to our surprise, the fetish town of which the Commandant had spoken, was not held. As we drew nearer to the capital, which stands on a low level, we had to wade for a mile or more through water one or two feet deep. Not infrequently we passed decomposing and headless corpses in the undergrowth, doubtless the relics of the garrison's final sortie. The march had been so much impeded that, by the time the last hamlet was reached, evening was approaching ; the wise plan proposed overnight could not, therefore, be carried out, and we went for the stockaded position hampered by all the paraphernalia of the column.

The final action was commenced about four o'clock by the enemy, before our scouts had located the stockades. At a point where the Cape Coast and Pekki roads converge towards Kumasi they had taken up a position on slighly rising ground, a circumstance that mercifully assisted in making most of their fire go harmlessly over our heads. Each approach was barred by massive entrenchments stretching across it far into the adjoining undergrowth and flanked by two breast-works of timber, from which concentrated cross-fire

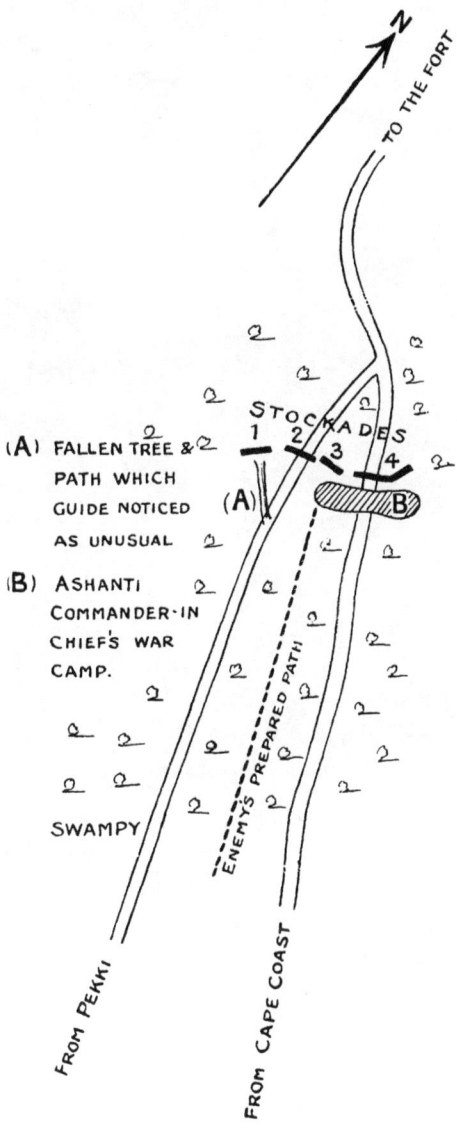

N

TO THE FORT

STOCKADES
1 2 3 4

(A) FALLEN TREE &
PATH WHICH
GUIDE NOTICED
AS UNUSUAL

(A)

(B)

(B) ASHANTI
COMMANDER-IN
CHIEF'S WAR
CAMP.

SWAMPY

ENEMY'S PREPARED PATH

FROM PEKKI

FROM CAPE COAST

PLAN OF THE FINAL ACTION OF THE RELIEF FORCE AT KUMASI

could be brought to bear. These formidable obstacles
had originally been intended to envelop and keep in
the garrison ; consequently, the war camps were on the
side facing us—a point in our favour. At first a heavy
fire from the bush was directed upon both flanks of the
rear guard, but the attack from the left was soon
successfully repulsed ; and that flank was left unhar-
rassed thenceforward. On the other side, however, the
roar of hostile musketry never ceased, the enemy
gradually advancing along the column by a track they
had specially prepared on the east side of the Pekki
road, [until the head of the line had reached the main
position, previously mentioned, where they joined their
comrades in making a final stand. At a point some
fifty yards from the stockades, the Ashantis had cut a
fresh path, diverging to the left, which gave the first
intimation to our guide that something unusual lay in
front. Major Melliss, who, at his own request, was
directing the scouts on the left of the road, and
Lieutenant Edwards, who with his men was similarly
employed on the right, had come out of the bush and
were conferring in the pathway as to what ought next
to be done. It was getting late, and the flankers were
so tired out that it was a question whether they might
not have to be called in, but the enemy anticipated the
decision by a terrific volley from their fortified position
in front, slightly wounding both these officers, and four
soldiers. Our leading men immediately took shelter
behind a fallen tree lying across the track. At this time
the stockades were invisible, their number unknown,
and the proximity of the specially large one on the
Cape Coast road was a complete surprise, this only
being discovered in the final charge which carried all
the four, as well as the war camp of the Ashanti Com-

mander-in-Chief. Lieutenant-Colonel Wilkinson, commanding the advance guard, then ordered up the guns,
which were massed in a semicircle a short distance in
rear of the fallen tree, whence they began to belch forth
destruction at the unseen foe, whilst the murderous
Maxims poured belt after belt of hailing lead into the
adjacent bush.   The scream of the shells, the sharp
tapping wh-i-r-r of the machine guns, and the dull
crash of the infantry volleys at intervals, created a
perfect *pandemonium*, while the ceaseless roar of Dane
guns continued with unabated fury on our front and
flanks.   It was enough to strike terror into most savages,
this duel at two-score yards, but neither side wavered
for an instant; and so the battle went on until night
began to lower the curtain of darkness upon this closing
scene of the drama.   None of these facts, however,
escaped the watchful eye of the Commandant, who at
that moment advanced and took up his position by the
guns, from whence to direct the progress of the fight.
As, apparently, no impression had been produced upon
the enemy by this hour and a half's rain of shells and
bullets, and ammunition had to be economised as much
as possible, the expected order to charge soon came.
Then was heard the shrill blast from massed buglers,
" Cease fire," and, to quote from despatches, " it was
obeyed as if on a field day."   The Colonel was changing
his tactics.

An unearthly silence intervened for a few seconds.
The enemy, wonderstruck, also instinctively followed
the same course; but only to redouble their fusillade
after a few moments.   The leading companies then
formed into line to the front and left flank, whilst three
more took up a position almost at right angles to them.
Then came the inspiriting notes of the " Charge."   The

men were already chafing like restless war-horses for
the shout that was to lead them on. Some had fallen,
and casualties were coming fast now, though hitherto
the very fact of our propinquity to the enemy had kept
down our losses considerably. Then with a cheer, the
whole of the advance guard, the Commandant's own
escort joining in, sprang into the bush, while an answering shout of savage rage pealed back from the stockades. Unfortunately, the dense undergrowth checked
the impetus, so the soldiers had to cut their way with
machêtês, chanting the while their deep-toned war-song
and ever drawing nearer to their prey. It was not
until our men rushed round and clambered over the
stockades that the enemy finally quitted them, leaving
in their haste many of their dead and wounded, which
unmistakably showed the panic in which they fled.
The troops behaved magnificently ; and in making this
statement it must be borne in mind that they knew they
were terribly outnumbered by the dreaded Ashantis ;
that they had hitherto had no big success, but had
suffered an almost unbroken series of reverses ; and
that they were all young soldiers. In this supreme
effort, one officer, at the head of his men, fell unconscious, sword in hand, at the foot of one of the stockades. His failing strength had given way in the
moment of victory. He was picked up and carried in,
apparently dead.

Any prolonged pursuit is impossible in the bush, so,
as daylight was fading, the troops were recalled at
once. The only thing that had to be done was to pull
down the stockade immediately across the Pekki road
to enable the transport to pass. Here a very gruesome
sight awaited us. A shell from one of the guns had
penetrated and done terrible execution, bespattering the

timbers with blood and shreds of human flesh. Its defenders themselves presented a loathsome spectacle. A pile of mangled forms, some still breathing, lay in confusion, many having fallen across one another, some disembowelled, another with the whole face blown off— all variously mutilated. Limbs had been carried yards away into the bush beyond, and the ground was slippery with blood.

It was most fortunate the battle was over so soon, for, as it was, the rear guard did not get in till after dark, and the risk and confusion would have been much worse had it been later. When all was over, Colonel Willcocks collected those officers and troops nearest him into a body and advanced at their head along the broad road in front. It would be impossible to express the delight we felt when, the last stockade taken, we emerged into the open and saw Kumasi ahead of us. At this point the route was down a slight incline, and the throng of white and black soldiers, advancing in triumph, with measured tread and flashing bayonets, was a sight not one of us will ever forget. But what a scene of desolation and death lay before us! True, acres of forest had been cleared, but the tall, rank grass, uncut for months, grew in extravagant profusion everywhere, in places almost hiding the ruins of the once populous villages. What a sickening stench came from all sides! Right and left, foul gases from putrefying corpses, left by their comrades, poisoned the evening air. Then a start. Yes, with eyes uplifted, straining to catch a glimpse of the fort, one stumbled against something in the path; it was a body from which the vultures had picked off half the flesh—many more lay near. After the roar of the past two hours all seemed so quiet. On, on we went, till the painful silence chilled the heart of every man, and a great dread, which he dared not utter, entered into his soul. Were we indeed too late? No, round a bend in the road, and there stood the fort, in bold relief against the sunset, while the faint notes of a distant bugle sounded the "General salute." In an instant the air was rent with wild cheers, and our buglers sent far and wide the joyous notes of our greeting to those who had so long waited for it; who had well-nigh given up hope, but yet stood staunchly by their country's flag, fulfilling yet again England's expectation that all her sons would do their duty.

Then the gate opened, and out came Captain Bishop, Mr. Ralph, and Dr. Hay, followed by such few of the brave, starved little garrison as yet had strength to walk. Only the day before all hope seemed gone; nothing for them to do but sally forth to almost certain death—perhaps by torture. Unwillingly one turned one's eyes from this happy sight. What was that glow some half-mile further on? That was no setting sun, sinking in crimson glory; no, it was the enemy, showing by yet another act their wanton hatred. They had fired the Basel Mission, and a company had to be despatched at the double to drive them off.

The poor famished garrison was in too deplorable a condition to make any great military display, but the happiness shown by all, white and black alike, was ample recompense for what we had gone through. The terrible strain of anxiety, together with fatigue and short rations, had told heavily upon all, so that greetings between rescuers and rescued and cheers for the Queen and Colonel Willcocks were soon over. Then the Commandant, for the first time during that memorable day, relinquished personal command and with his column entered the fort which he had relieved on the very date that he had promised.

CHAPTER XIX

THE SIEGE

IT is necessary at this point to turn back and detail the series of events which had brought the garrison of Kumasi to the pass in which we found them on the 15th of July.

The Governor of the Gold Coast, accompanied by Lady Hodgson, left Accra on the 13th of March, 1900, to make a tour of inspection of the Colony, which was to embrace a visit to Kumasi, a place that had not yet been visited by him as H.B.M.'s representative. On his way up country he was met at all the villages with every demonstration of friendliness, and when he arrived at the fort on the 25th he was not only greeted by all the officials and local missionaries, but by a very large number of Ashanti kings who turned out in state to receive him. A triumphal arch had been erected for the occasion, and a gorgeous pageant organised to do him honour ; the ceremonies were duly enacted, all the chieftains passing in procession before him. In a word, the political horizon appeared unclouded ; no breath of wind gave warning of the coming storm.

There is no doubt, however, that at this time not only was discontent with their status as our dependents rife among the Ashantis, but a more or less organised rebellion was on foot, needing only a spark to set it going. Several days passed quietly, during which Sir Frederic Hodgson held several palavers with the chiefs about various state matters. Little by little the eyes of H.E.'s retainers, accustomed as they were to savage ways, descried certain indications that all was not right, and it was, therefore, decided to supplement the garrison of two hundred native soldiers by troops from the coast. Accordingly, a wire was despatched asking for reinforcements, which arrived on April the 18th.

Captain Armitage, of the Gold Coast Constabulary, the Governor's private secretary, and Captain Leggett of the same force, were detailed about this time to take a small party of soldiers to a neighbouring village for the purpose of bringing in the Golden Stool. This object, though of trumpery value in itself, was regarded by the natives with considerable veneration, for, in former days, it had been used as the throne of the king, who was president of their council of chiefs, and it was, *ipso facto*, the sign of supreme temporal authority. The party sent to claim it was fired on, and, after a fight in which both Captains Armitage and Leggett were wounded, forced to retire without having accomplished its mission.

It was clear that rebellion was intended, though its nature and extent were not realised at the moment. The native chiefs were sounded, and, happily, several influential ones decided to throw in their lot with us, the most important being the kings of Mampon, Juabin, Aguna, Nsuta, and Nkwanta. Through thick and thin these brave fellows stuck to us, sorely tried though their loyalty was by all that happened subsequently.

The storm-cloud was not long in breaking, for on

o

April the 25th the Basel Mission servants were set upon,
and several of them were killed by the malcontents.
The missionaries fled to the fort for protection, and
were admitted. Elated by this minor success, the
Ashantis attacked and captured the villages in which
the traders and friendly natives lived, together with the
cantonments and outlying buildings. Some desultory
fighting occurred, but, fortunately, the attack was not
pushed home, the enemy contenting himself with setting
fire to the captured villages and cantonments. Driven
from their homes, the unhappy refugees, to the number
of some three thousand five hundred, with two hundred
children, came crowding round the fort, essaying in
their terror to scale its walls and batter in its door. It
was beyond the capacity of the fort to accommodate
a tithe of these luckless creatures, but to afford them
some protection the troops were marched down from
the barracks, and drawn in a cordon round them.

Now, for the first time, the garrison realised that it
was besieged—isolated from civilisation. Measures
were forthwith taken to ensure safety, and to help the
refugees. The fort gate was finally closed, and a rope
ladder let down from one of the bastions. Thus,
entrance and egress were confined to a single individual
at a time, and the danger of a rush obviated. Round
the walls booths were erected to shelter the friendlies
who, huddled together, were exposed to all the in-
clemencies of the weather. Sanitary arrangements, not
the least necessary of precautions, were made by Dr.
Chalmers. Thus passed some wretched days and worse
nights, for sleep was constantly interrupted by bogus
alarms—the rebels being in possession during these four
days of all the buildings except the fort, many of which
they fortified and loop-holed.

ROUGH HAND SKETCH. (FROM MEMORY) OF KUMASI

(SHOWING STOCKADES TAKEN DURING IT'S RELIEF)

To Cape Coast

To Pekki

WAR CAMP

STOCKADE

To Accra

WAR CAMP

STOCKADE

SWAMP

Craters

SWAMP

1, 2, 3, BURNT HAUSA & FANTI VILLAGES

ASHANTI SYNDICATE LTD HOUSE

GOLGOTHA (WHERE HUMAN SACRIFICES WERE OFFERED IN THOUSANDS ANNUALLY & THE SACRED FETISH GROVE ONCE STOOD

PREMPEH'S PALACE

BURNT NATIVE VILLAGE

ROAD BY WHICH THE GOVERNOR ESCAPED

SMALL STOCKADE

PARADE GROUND

BASTION & GATE (WITH GUNS)

BASTION (WITH GUNS) RESIDENCY

FORT

WELL

MAGAZINE

UNDER THESE DOUBLE LINES WERE COVERED BARRACKS WITH BANQUETTES TO DEFEND THE LOOPHOLES

BASTION (WITH GUNS)

POST OFFICE

LIEUT GREERS GRAVE

BAMBOO FENCE ENCLOSING GRAVES OF CAPTS MIDDLEMIST & MAGUIRE

JAIL (BURNT)

HOSPITAL DOCTORS QUARTERS

KITCHEN

OFFICER'S QUARTERS

CANTONMENTS (BURNT)

BURNT VILLAGE

BASEL MISSION (BURNT)

WEYAN MISSION (BURNT)

STOCKADE

WAR CAMP

BANTAMA

STOCKADE

WAR CAMP

INTIMIDU

To Berekup

NOTE.

IN BETWEEN THESE PATHS OTHER TRACKS, SMALLER WAR CAMPS & BARRICADES EXISTED. THE WHOLE OF THIS AREA WAS ONCE A CLEARING. BUT WAS NOW DENSELY OVERGROWN WITH ELEPHANT GRASS

PRIMEVAL FOREST & SWAMPS SURROUNDED ON EVERY SIDE THE LOCALITY SHOWN IN THE DIAGRAM. THE OPEN SPACE IS ABOUT ½ OF A MILE SQUARE

PLAN OF KUMASI

On the 29th a determined attack was made on the Residency, the enemy advancing boldly across the open, and fighting long and stubbornly. Captain Marshall, with his two hundred and fifty native troops and the friendly Ashanti levies, was equal to the occasion, and taught them such a lesson that they never again tried fighting the white man in the open. A hundred and thirty Ashanti corpses were found, and buried—how many were carried off by their friends will never be known. At sundown, after the foe had received this drubbing, Captain Aplin came in with his crippled column, but without food or much ammunition. Welcome as troops were, they added a strain to the commissariat that it was little able to bear, especially in view of the fact that the prospect of any effectual relief was hazy in the extreme.

Aided by these troops from Lagos, the outlying official buildings were reoccupied, and the friendlies housed in shanties a little further from the fort. It is a matter of sincere congratulation that the former structures were not destroyed, for they had been erected by the Government at considerable expense. Some little relaxation from toil and anxiety was afforded by these measures, but time dragged on wearily till May 15th, when Major Morris arrived with his force. He, too, was short of food and ammunition, and the dangers of the situation were eloquently borne in on the beleaguered garrison.

The enemy, shirking the offensive, busily occupied himself in building stockades to bar every outlet from Kumasi, sniping meanwhile such foragers and units as ventured too far afield. Many attempts were made to take their entrenchments, but they always failed because it was impossible to push the attacks home owing to lack of ammunition. The soldiers, too, became demoralised by the non-success of the operations, by their know-ledge of the want of warlike material, and of food.

After each repulsed sortie—notably so after Captain Maguire had been killed at Bantama—the Queen-mother at Ejesu used to send trade gin as a reward to the war camps by which many of her warriors became intoxicated. On such occasions the orgies were kept up with *verve* and *esprit*, the Ashantis drumming and shouting till all hours of the night, the noise running from one camp to another round the complete circle of investment. I reproduce here a sample of the enliven-ing conversation that would be kept up between two war camps, as it was overheard:

Camp A. to Camp B. "We are like the mighty bull that prowls about the forest; what are you?"

Camp B. to Camp A. "We also are as strong as that great bull."

Camp A. "Are you ready?"

Camp B. "Yes, we are."

Camp A. "Then man your stockade."

With screams and yells B. would fly to carry out this behest, and A., if not too much overcome with the fumes of trade gin, might do likewise. This game would be passed on and taken up by other camps, with anti-phonal iteration, till too frequent rehearsals blunted their enthusiasm, and induced sleep.

No news came in from the outside world except in-formation cooked up by charlatan spies and native *canards* of the wildest description. These statements were so extraordinary and contradictory that no reliance could be placed on them, no plan of action formed, no steps taken. Some affirmed as gospel truth that Cape Coast roads were full of ships with soldiers, others that troops were concentrating at Bekwai; again, some trivial detail would be described in graphic language, such as that an officer's tent had been pitched in one war camp, or a white man's head been brought into another. Of our column and preparations no authentic information was ever received, in spite of all the runners we despatched ; as a matter of fact, Sir F. Hodgson first heard Colonel Willcocks' name when he reached the coast on July 10th.

Provisions, which had been carefully husbanded, and systematically served out, were running perilously low. Rations consisted of one and a half " dog-biscuits " and five ounces of preserved meat per diem. Five ponies that Major Morris had brought in with his force, and a few cows that were kept at the Residency, were killed and eaten. Native traders sold a few luxuries at fabulous prices while they lasted, for example :

A spoonful of whisky, 2s.

A 7-lb. tin of flour, 6s.

A box of matches, 2s.

A small tin of beef, £2 16s.

Straitened as the garrison was, the poor refugees were in far worse plight, for they had no reserve of food, and foraging was hardly possible. They died at the rate of thirty or forty a day ; their comrades, too weak to bury them, leaving them where they fell.

When only three and a half days' rations were left, it was obvious that something *must* be done, and the Governor called a council-of-war. It was then and there decided that as many as could put foot to the ground should make a dash for it, whilst a garrison of three Europeans with a hundred rank and file should be left behind. It was admittedly a council of despair, but what else could be effected ? As for those left behind, the fort was held to be pretty secure against attack (as a matter of fact it was not), and twenty-three days'

rations could be left them. Relief, it was argued, would
surely be at hand by then, and the fort was a valuable
structure. For the rest, they must certainly all starve if
they remained where they were, so it seemed better to
fight and march whilst they had strength, and before all
the food was exhausted. Major Morris, being senior
military officer, was to command the sortie, and he
naturally cast about for the line of least resistance along
which to make his attempt. The rebels were known to
be expecting them to go down the Cape Coast road, and
were in force there; consequently, he chose the route
through Potasi and Terrabum to Ekwanta, in the
Dengiasi country, whence the coast could be reached
through the Denkera territory. Not only could friendly
country be most quickly reached this way, but it was
blocked by the smallest stockade of the whole cordon.
The line of route was kept a profound secret, and not
revealed till 10 p.m. on the day before the sortie. An
attempt was made to provide bullet-proof hammocks
for the Governor and ladies; sheets of corrugated iron
were experimented with to this end, but it was found
that not only did slugs go through them like paper, but
the starving carriers could not support the great weight
they entailed.

At five a.m. on Saturday, June 23rd, in a thick mist,
the column fell in. It consisted of the following
Europeans : Sir Frederic and Lady Hodgson; Acting
Commissioner and Commandant, Major Morris; Cap-
tains Marshall and Digan, Special Service Officers;
Inspector-General, Captain Aplin; Travelling Commis-
sioner, Captain Armitage; Inspector, Captain Parmeter;
Assistant-Inspectors, Captains Leggett and Berthon,
Gold Coast Constabulary; Assistant-Inspectors, Captains
Cochrane and Read, Lagos Constabulary; Medical

Officers Garland, Chalmers, Tweedy, Graham, Gold Coast Colony, and Macfarlane, of Lagos ; Telegraph Clerk-in-charge Branch, Messrs. David and Grundy, of the Ashanti Syndicate ; Rev. and Mrs. Ramseyer, Rev. and Mrs. Jost, Rev. and Mrs. Haasis, and Mr. Weller, Basel missionaries. With them were six hundred rank and file, with one hundred and fifty rounds per man, seven hundred carriers, and some one thousand refugees.

Captain Leggett was ahead with the few men of the vanguard, followed by Captain Armitage in charge of the advance guard. Then the main body, with the carriers and hammocks for the Governor and ladies, the two latter surrounded by strong escorts, whilst Captain Aplin commanded the rear guard. The refugees were to follow behind all, and Captain Aplin was instructed not to let them approach too closely.

Aided by the mist and a feint made by the garrison of the fort to direct the enemy's attention to the main road, the column was not engaged till the Potasi breast-work was reached. This was taken after a short fight, though, in a turning movement to outflank it, Captain Leggett was mortally wounded, four men killed, and nine other casualties suffered. The central portion of the stockade was partly pulled down to enable the hammocks to pass, and the general forward movement to continue with as little loss of time as possible.

All through that day the column was constantly attacked, and in one of these onslaughts Captain Marshall was seriously wounded in the head. The wretched friendlies, defenceless as they were, were perpetually being fired into by the enemy, and Captain Aplin's rear guard had no more unpleasant or arduous duty to perform than that of repulsing the panic-stricken rushes of these poor starved unfortunates, who, being unarmed, were the most harassed of all. Numbers of soldiers, carriers, and refugees fell out from exhaustion, and had to be left to their fate ; nearly all the loads were thrown away by the worn-out porters, and the hammock-boys found themselves unable to support their burdens. Mrs. Ramseyer, who was lame, was carried for some portion of the journey by soldiers, who were stronger than the non-combatant natives. The rate of progress was so various in different portions of the column, that large gaps were constantly occurring ; units were thus isolated from each other at one moment, and inextricably mixed up at another. Rain fell most of the time, making the road heavy and slippery ; the only compensation for which was that the enemy's charges of powder being damp, frequently missed fire.

Terrabum, eighteen miles from Kumasi, was reached with the loss of six soldiers killed and several slightly wounded. Here the night was spent ; the crowding of some two thousand human beings into a small village, in a tropical deluge, not tending much to ease the anxious minds and aching limbs of the Europeans. Owing to the loads having been lost, there were no dry clothes for any one to put on ; one officer, I know, was extremely grateful for a table-cloth to sleep in. To afford some protection the soldiers were posted round the camp in the form of a square ; though had the Ashantis attacked in the darkness, they might have wrought awful havoc.

The next day was a repetition of the former one— rain, muddy roads, dying soldiers, carriers, and refugees, attacks by the enemy, constant anxiety, and discomfort. Masiasu, some twelve miles further on, was reached, and the night passed there. Thus one day succeeded another. On the 28th, Captain Marshall breathed his last, and was buried in his hammock at the roadside, whilst Captain Leggett succumbed to his wounds the next day, and was interred at Takarasi. The loss of both these officers was acutely felt by all, for the personal esteem in which they were held was only equalled by the admiration felt for their devotion and bravery. The ladies bore their trials with wonderful pluck : owing to the hammock-boys breaking down, they had to tramp with the rest along the flooded, miry track, and endure all the privations of that terrible march.

At last Ekwanta was reached, and, being in friendly country, a two days' rest was called to recuperate the worn, half-famished frames of both white and black men. Want of food had been one of the greatest of the trials, for, though there was a tiny stock of provisions to start with, much had been thrown away by the carriers : as for the refugees, they had had to live on what they could pick up in the bush. From Ekwanta a letter was sent to the Officer Commanding the relief column, telling him of the sortie, the route the column was taking, and that a small garrison had been left in the fort at Kumasi.

On resuming this hurried march, which resulted in the deaths of many of the severely wounded, the worst obstacle to contend with was the Offin river. Swollen by rains, the stream had become a torrent, and overflowed its banks to such an extent that the country round was waist-deep in water. Soon after this the force was divided into two parts to enable food to be obtained more easily, for it was now entirely dependent on what it could pick up.

Three weeks after the exodus from Kumasi, half-starved, wearied, and travel-stained, the decimated column reached the coast, and never, I ween, were eyes more rejoiced with a sight than were theirs with the blue waves breaking on the shore.

Now to return to the three officers who had been detailed to remain behind. They were Captain Bishop, Gold Coast Constabulary; Assistant Inspector Mr. Ralph, Lagos Constabulary; and Dr. Hay, Medical Officer, Gold Coast Colony. These Europeans, with one hundred and fifteen decrepit Hausas, were left to hold the fort until relief should come or—the end. Scarce more than a score of these soldiers were fit for active duty; Dr. Hay was ill with fever; and on the morning of the general exit was carried in a hammock from his quarters into the fort.

The firing of the outgoing portion of the garrison had hardly ceased before the Ashantis from the Bantama war camp came out to see if the evacuation had been complete. The enemy's appearance was met with a fusillade from the Maxims, which quickly undeceived them, and, after firing a few shots, they withdrew. The little party that remained in the Residency had much to do at first, and, as the men were weak and likely to become more so, it set to work as quickly as possible.

One of the first duties was to tell off the men to their positions in the bastions and other points of defence in the fort, for no attempt could be made to hold the outlying buildings. The soldiers who were to man the guns were told to sleep beside them, whilst others were posted at the loop-holes in the walls, and on the verandah, this last being protected with sheets of corrugated iron and bales of stuff. Stock was taken of the ammunition, which showed that there were only a hundred and twenty rounds per carbine, with a reserve of fifty. There was a considerable supply of .45 cartridges, but as they did not fit our rifles, they were of little use. The rations were estimated and divided up according to the number of days (twenty-three) for which they were intended to last, and a daily parade for this issue ordered. A most disgusting but necessary task next lay before the defenders. In close proximity to the fort-walls were some thousand shelters. From a military point of view their continuance was impossible, for not only did they obscure the field of fire, but they would afford excellent cover from view to the enemy. Sanitary reasons for their demolition were even more pressing. The herding of masses of refugees in them had led to the accumulation of quantities of filth and *débris* of every kind, which the poor creatures had been far too weak to remove. The stench was unbearable, and the exhalations from the putrefying mess highly dangerous to health. The work of clearance was taken in hand at once, but proved considerably greater than had been anticipated. Closer inspection revealed a most revolting condition of affairs —human bodies in various stages of decomposition, decaying offal, and pitiable, starved victims who were just alive and no more. The rain, moreover, had rendered the wood and grass of which the booths were made so sodden that all attempts at burning them failed till June 27th, when a big blaze purged the air, and enabled the Residency windows to be opened on the windward side—the first time for many days.

Sickness began to tell its tale from the first day, on which three of the gallant band breathed their last. The rate of mortality mounted higher and higher, and, as if there were not enough troubles, smallpox broke out. Each case of this disease had to be isolated in a hut outside the walls, and Dr. Hay, still ill, found his hands more than full. The daily issue of rations was a sorry sight : discipline alone prevented the famished soldiers from scrambling greedily for food ; not infrequently a man would drop dead in the act of taking his share. Every day at sunrise and sundown the gate was opened for a mournful little procession bearing the bodies of the victims to a neighbouring trench for burial. Apathetic despair settled down over the natives, not a few of whom ended their sufferings with their own hand.

Of rumours there were plenty, but whether reliable or not there were no means of judging. A biting pang of disappointment was experienced by every heart when a report, that a relief force was at Esumeja, and would rescue them in five days after the Governor's departure, turned out to be untrue. Stories of spreading rebellion and repulses of the white man's troops came in, in many instances with only too much probability of their authenticity. Not one word from the men who were straining every nerve to help them ever reached the besieged in spite of many a runner despatched with news.

"Hope deferred maketh the heart sick," and, as the weary days dragged on, even the white men's cheerfulness, kept up to encourage the black, became a hard struggle. The uncomplaining, stolid fortitude of the rank and file made these little deceptions more difficult to maintain, and the hollowness of the mockery became more and more apparent as the same answers were returned day after day to the same questions. Rations were reduced at last to a cupful of linseed meal and a 2-inch cube of preserved meat a day, and now and

again it would be discovered with chill horror that the
contents of some carefully cherished tin of provisions
had gone mouldy. A few women traders occasionally
hawked their wares outside the fort, and got astounding
prices for them. A bit of cocoa, worth a farthing, cost
15s.; plantains were 1s. 6d. each; and a small pine-
apple fetched 15s. The men received 3s. daily in place
of half a biscuit when these ran short, and this ready
cash was willingly bartered for edible leaves. There
was no standard of exchange: money had no equivalent
value in food-stuffs.

Luckily, the enemy made no attack during the whole
period, though the little force were harassed with constant dread that one might be essayed, knowing full
well that their depleted, sickly ranks could offer but
little resistance. At night the Ashantis could be heard
prowling around the fort, and the darkness was often
lit up with flames from some building or shanty that
they had set on fire. Not for a single day were
guard and sentry duty relaxed, even though the invalid
soldiery could scarcely carry their arms. In desperation
Captain Bishop offered £100 to any man who would
take a message. Several volunteers made ineffectual
attempts, but, finally, an orderly got through, though
those who sent him never knew whether he had succeeded or been massacred, for no reply came back.

Three dreary, heart-breaking weeks wore slowly by.
Rations were now at their last ebb, two-thirds of the
troops were lying in the trench outside, and death in its
most horrid forms stared these brave fellows in the face.
When the food had all gone it was arranged that they
should cut their way out in the darkness, each man for
himself. The three white men, each with a dose of
poison, would stick together, and never, come what

might, would they fall alive into the hands of the savages. But the end was not yet! On July 14th reports were brought in that firing had been heard—a tale too sweet to the ear to be allowed. So firmly, however, did an old native officer adhere to his belief that, in the evening, three shells were fired in answer. Next morning Captain Bishop himself thought he heard three volleys, but not till half-past four were they all assured that they had not been forgotten, and that the long arm of the Empire was being stretched out through the African bush to help her sore-stricken servants. Then a tremendous, continuous roar of guns and rifles told with iron mouth and thundering voice the tale that the relief column was having its last desperate fight for their salvation—a fact emphasised by shells bursting round the fort. Whilst their comrades outside were in mortal struggle in that duel for the supremacy of the black man or the white, the three imprisoned officers opened one of their last medical comforts—a half-bottle of champagne—and drank success to the issue. It was a touching fact, that at the eleventh hour of hardship, so heroically borne, whilst their officers were gazing through their field-glasses and the rank and file straining their eyes in the direction of the battlefield, the flickering flame of life in some poor bodies went out, the effort to live till the supreme moment having proved too much for them. Then a shell went screaming over the topmost pinnacle of the fort's roof, whilst others burst in various places; then were heard ringing cheers of victory as the troops carried the barrier between themselves and their compatriots at the bayonet's point. The beleaguered garrison fired a Maxim in reply, but its rattling note of welcome was drowned in the din of the conflict that was raging. At a distance, Ashantis fled in direst terror ; they had fought well, but the bitter dregs of the cup of failure were theirs to taste at last. The distant notes of " the Halt " were heard, which the two buglers in the fort were soon answering with might and main, braying out the " General salute " in noisy greeting time after time.

Finally, at six o'clock, when the day was waning in a flood of scarlet light, the head of the relief column came winding round the bend of the road, at the point called " Golgotha," Colonel Willcocks and his staff in front ; the dying glories of the sinking sun lit up the white and black faces of that joyous throng and danced with delight upon a sea of flashing steel. Then those of the garrison who were able rushed through the open door of the fort and, with deep emotion, welcomed their rescuers, joining them in hearty cheers for the Queen, whom both had served so faithfully and well.

CHAPTER XX

A DAY IN THE AUGEAN STABLES

BEFORE finally shaking down after the relief was a *fait accompli*, and when the finding of beds and the like made such a course possible, a prearranged signal of five star shells was fired, to let those on the look-out at Esumeja know that we had successfully effected our object. Then we reoccupied the outlying quarters, and, packed very closely, slept the sleep of weariness and satisfaction.

We were to stay one day before returning, but it was not to rest. This was out of the question ; there was too much to be done. It happened to be the anniversary of my birthday ; it certainly was one of the most eventful ones I have ever spent, and one of the busiest. Not only did the surrounding ground speak for itself as to the rigours of the siege, but so did the very houses in which we were quartered. These had been occupied by the enemy ; they were partially filled with rubbish, and the walls pierced with numerous bullet-holes. It was from such points of cover that the enemy used to take snap-shots at the inmates of the fort.

About 8 a.m. a column of four hundred was sent out to destroy the stockades we had taken the evening before, cut away the bush between them, and burn the camps. The one in which the Ashanti Commander-in-Chief's headquarters had been situated, contained over a thousand "war palaver" huts and shelters, each with bamboo camp-beds, and outside some of them the rebels had made garden-seats of the same material, and other luxuries of a similar kind. Our men found that, in accordance with their custom, the enemy had carefully removed all their dead during the night, only a forearm having been overlooked in the darkness. We then saw the method of the investment for the first time. It consisted of large entrenchments, barricading all the roads and tracks, each with a camp in rear of it. In the bush between these were similar stockades, to complete the fortified *enceinte*, and afford flank defence. All these links were joined by a wide path, cut from one point to the other round the entire circumference, so that as soon as one position was attacked, it was reinforced by those to right and left. We had, therefore, every right to think that our surmises of the previous day were correct, and that we must have been opposed by thousands and not hundreds ; the way in which we were subsequently allowed to pass unmolested being proof of the disorganisation of the enemy, and the severe lesson they must have received at our hands. It was curious how slowly they rallied after a repulse, and how hard they found it to carry on an action when we adopted unexpected tactics, instead of fighting them in the way they had anticipated and had taken every precaution to meet.

Meantime, the remainder of the troops and all the carriers were engaged in trying to remedy, as far as time would admit of it, the shocking insanitary condition of the place, whilst the Staff and other officials were

P

looking into the matter of stores, European and native provisions, big and small arm ammunition, and medical comforts and dressings, which were to be left behind with the relieving garrison. The labourers worked in relays with every available *machêtê* in use, and not only escorted, but aided, by the rest of the soldiers. The elephant-grass had grown almost up to the fort's walls, and made the approach, even to the watercourse, extremely dangerous. All this, of necessity, had to be cut down. The further the work progressed, the more terrible became the disclosures, telling mutely the horrors of the past few months' experiences. The overpowering smell of decaying flesh became, after a while, almost unbearable. Skeletons and corpses in all stages of decomposition, many headless, were met with. These had almost all died of starvation, and not by the enemy's hand. At first, bodies had been buried, but latterly their compatriots had become too weak to render them this needful service. The wretched victims had either just been able to crawl a few yards into the jungle, to hide the sufferings of their last moments, or, unable to do this, had died on their way thither in the open ; whilst some had ended their misery in the huts, the other inmates being incapable of removing the remains, or of quitting the place themselves. Time forbade our burying the multitude of bodies we found, and so they had at last to be burned in heaps. We knew the original native friendly population had numbered nearly four thousand, and that a quarter of them were supposed to have died of want and disease ; a similar number had attempted to break out, and the majority had been slaughtered. Many had accompanied the Governor in his escape, but had mostly been killed, or fallen out from weakness and been left to their fate, as had also been the case with the wounded soldiers and stragglers. Scarce as many scores were left where once hundreds had been congregated; their condition was deplorable in the extreme, and they were dying fast, even that day. Out of the hundred and fifteen men who had remained with Captain Bishop in the fort, most had been left behind because they were too sick and weak to travel. A mere handful were capable of hobbling any distance; and most of the remainder, of whom numbers had died quite recently, were compelled to stay where they were; although, whenever possible, arrangements were made for them to be removed with us on the morrow, on stretchers or in hammocks. This fact is evidence of how impossible it would have been for this little band to make its escape, not to mention that almost every capable carrier had gone away with the original garrison.

It is easy to believe that the doctors were not idlers that day, with the refugees, the details of the old garrison, some thirty casualties from the fight of the day before, and some more white men ill with fever, all of whom had to be attended to; nor is it difficult to concur in Colonel Willcocks' opinion, that the little party we had found was quite inadequate to hold the fort against the foe, had they again attacked it in force.

The Ashantis had burned all the cantonments, and all the friendly villages, but had carefully left undamaged Prempeh's old palace; so we burned this structure for them, and it was about the only congenial duty we performed throughout that unpleasant day. Near the officers' quarters, and by the Basel Mission, were found some beautiful English roses in full bloom; and how sweet was their scent in comparison with the pervading, penetrating odour of decay in which we had been living! Kumasi [1] (the place of death) could not have been a more suitable name for the capital of this cruel race.

One disquieting discovery of that day was the loss of a few sacks of rice, some of which only were recovered. The rest were generously made up by the men who had not yet consumed their narrow commons. Two or three carriers, who had pillaged these stores, and one gentleman caught red-handed drinking a bottle of medical champagne, were flogged ; and this produced a salutary effect, inasmuch as such thefts were henceforward very rare.

The order bugle was sounded shortly after " Retreat," when the distasteful work we had been engaged upon had to be discontinued. It had, however, been sufficiently completed for the immediate necessities of the case. We then learnt that reveille was again to be at 4 a.m., and that the coveted post of leading the column out next morning had been given to F Company, 1st W.A.F.F. This was a much-desired billet, as a tremendous lot of opposition was expected. We also found that we had absolutely no meat or drink left for the return journey, and the P.M.O., in the goodness of his heart, gave each white man a small piece of cold bacon, and a bottle of brandy amongst four, out of his slender resources. Ink and paper cannot describe what this windfall meant to us.

The fort was a handsome square stone building, with turrets at the four corners, containing barrack accom-

---

[1] The suffix "asi" denotes, in Ashanti, "the place of," or "under the shadow of." Thus Sheramasi means "the place of slavery," and Dompoasi "under the shadow of dogs," the presiding fetish-demons of that place. Many of the sources from which names in this country are derived, have a religious significance.

modation, store rooms, a post-office, and a well. The
loopholed walls were possibly a trifle too low for
absolute safety, but quite enough protection against a
savage enemy. Just above the only gate was a two-
storied house, used for the accommodation of the
Europeans and the Resident's quarters. The sole outlet was closed by a bullet-proof shutter, travelling on
small wheels in grooves into the wall. Round the first
story ran a balcony, and the rooms were excellent, with
French windows, and comfortable furniture. The floor
above was less commodious, and was usually untenanted.
The whole of this portion was roofed with corrugated
iron, and well-fitted up inside. Quick-firing guns were
mounted on the circular bastions at the four angles, and
from a short distance it did not look unlike some of the
fortifications one might see in Southern Europe, which
combine defensive with residential requirements. It certainly seemed a Paradise to us then; and from this point
of view we were perhaps a little sorry we were so soon
to leave it. The other surrounding buildings were also
excellent, water-tight bungalows, with broad verandahs :
in fact, this was the only up-country place upon which
much money and labour had been spent. In consequence, it had these advantages. The circular clearing,
too, in which this station was situated, some three-
quarters of a mile in diameter, was a relief to the forest,
and, after its monotony, appeared quite like open
country.

We had little time for gossip with our three newly-
made friends, but we heard that a final parade for the
inspection of the troops had been held ; that it had
unmistakably shown the impossibility of any concentrated attempt to cut a way out ; and, in consequence,
it had been decided, after a consultation, that, when all

the rations were expended, the garrison should sally out at night, each man for himself. The white men thought of taking with them a previously prepared dose of poison, so as to end their lives if they were taken by the enemy, and avoid a lingering death by torture. We were also told how circumstances at first had led them to feel assured of relief within a few days, and how subsequently, like a wet cloud of depression, instructions had been received as to what was to be done in the event of the fort having to be evacuated, such as the destruction of ammunition, rendering useless all the guns, burying the treasure, and so on.

After supper, as I walked from the fort to where I was going to sleep, in what had been the doctor's quarters, thoughts of the terrible tragedies which had been enacted on the scene which lay before me kept coming vividly before my mind. The white walls of the fort gleamed in the light of the new moon; all looked peaceful, even charming; but beyond, the tree-tops were lit up by the fires in distant war camps. It was a playground of spectres. Kumasi was beautiful, a strange paradox of fascination and repulsion, a Delilah of the forest, mate of savage might; drunken for countless generations with the blood of a myriad victims; a place accursed, where ghastly memories shudder in the gloom. Had any gaping arena of Imperial Rome beheld more horrors than this ghostly sepulchre? But its hour had struck—

The light of day saw the troops collecting (for once quite a simple matter) in the broad open space around the fort, which had been so much increased the day before. The garrison left behind, in command of

Captain (now local Major) Eden, consisted of three officers, one doctor, two British N.C.O.'s, one hundred and fifty men, 2nd Bn. W.A.F.F., and a few Gold Coast Constabulary gunners, with fifty-four days' rations, and an ample supply of ammunition. The road selected for our return was the one by which we had come. With such a number of sick and wounded, no more fighting than necessary was wished for; and this was very rightly considered the best line of retirement, with the object we had in view. The column was longer than ever, and the straggling worse than before. Owing to the enormous number of invalids, wounded, refugees, women, and children, and the fact that the old garrison were mostly carried on stretchers or in hammocks, only a few being able to limp slowly along, the pace was so slow that there was no chance of reaching friendly country that day. Fortunately, this splendid opportunity of attacking a very weak force was not taken advantage of by the scattered enemy. The first night was spent at the half-way house, just on the Kumasi side of the one in which we had slept on our way up. The villages on this road, to reduce opposition next time we used it, were destroyed. All possible crops were cut down, but there was not then time to thoroughly finish the punitive work, by hunting for farms in the neighbouring bush. A burning camp is quite an effective sight, but the roofs get damp in the rains, and the process is lengthy. The huts are so easily thatched, that setting fire to the roof alone is a futile form of punishment; so the walls also have to be razed, and this is what takes the time. However, the soldiers liked the work very well, dodging about amongst the blazing, falling shanties; and they were so energetic that a smouldering pile of ruins soon represented what had previously been a quaint little African stronghold. It was most noticeable how much rifle ammunition the enemy had got hidden away in their dwellings, and the crash of destruction was always accompanied by a *feu-de-joie* of sharp explosions from cartridges.

Pekki was safely reached the next evening, time having been available to complete the demolition of truculent Treda, which, in the hurry on the way up the rear guard had not finished quite satisfactorily. At Pekki the night was spent, and in accordance with instructions the king had prepared a market, to enable the now starving force to get a more substantial supper than usual. At this place the unwieldy caravan was divided into two parts. A flying column, under the personal command of Colonel Willcocks, was to go right through next day into Bekwai, so as to be ready for some more work. The second, with all the casualties and cripples, under Lieutenant-Colonel Burroughs, was to take two days over the next fifteen miles into camp.

The people of Pekki were much relieved and pleased to hear of our success, and incipient distrust in the white man's prowess was entirely removed; in fact, he went up many pegs in their estimation. This was also the case with Bekwai, and with all the other Chieftains, so that in result the recruiting of native levies became quite brisk.

It was late the following afternoon before those of us in the first contingent got in; and simultaneously there arrived Major (local Lieutenant-Colonel) Morland, commanding the 1st Bn., W.A.F.F., who had just come from Hausaland to take up the post of Officer Commanding the Lines of Communication. He had with him some more Special Service Officers, and a convoy of supplies. We then formed up into three sides of a square, and Colonel Willcocks, in a few gracious words, thanked the troops and complimented them upon what they had accomplished ; then, after again cheering the Queen and our Commandant, the fatigued soldiers were dismissed, and went off to seek the rest they needed so badly.

For the next day or two it was impossible to continue active operations; no reinforcements had arrived, and the white and black men were completely done up for a short time. The past few days of exposure and want had decimated the relief force; coughs, colds in the chest, sore throats, and fever, were universal, and a dismally long list of invalidings showed what hardships our experiences had entailed. The worst part of all was that no one could be spared, as reinforcements had not yet come to fill up vacancies, and barely enough men remained with whom to carry on operations which could ill brook delay.

CHAPTER XXI .

THE STORMING OF KOKOFU

ONLY a couple of days of comparative inaction, and then the dangerous foe who harassed Bekwai and our right flank had to be taken in hand. Until this source of danger was removed, little could be done in the way of completing the campaign, which would now be entirely of a punitive character, and devoted to the stamping out of the rebellion.

Bekwai was not productive of anything like an adequate supply of food for its then large population, but it did one good to see the way in which the men appreciated what they got, with never a word of discontent. They knew that everything possible was being done for them. The rations for seven days which we had received would have made no more than two full ones, or a short allowance for three. So away went two thousand empty carriers with an escort by the Obuasi road for more stores; and most of the remainder of the troops were detailed to form the force for our next move in this war game.

Early on Sunday morning, the 22nd inst., three 75 m/m guns, two 7-prs., and six companies, to be brought up to eight hundred infantry by a draft from the Esumeja garrison, fell in under the command of

Lieutenant-Colonel Morland, with orders to make a reconnaissance in force towards Kokofu, and if possible to attack and destroy it. It was a compact fighting body of men, with no bulky transport; each white man had but one carrier to take some food and a blanket, in case the night had to be spent at our destination. Every one, from previous experience acquired there, anticipated a very warm outing. Major Melliss, recognised by all as one of the most dashing officers in the Ashanti Field Force, was given charge of the all-important advance guard, and my Hausa company had the honour of leading the attack. Some men of the W.A.R. were also detailed to scout the bush in line with the "point." The road as far as Esumeja was known to be practically safe, so off we started for that place, no precious time being wasted with needless precautions. We had barely got clear of Bekwai, when boom was heard a distant shot in the bush, followed by another further on. The natural conclusion was that these were signal guns fired by the enemy, and that all would be ready for us when we arrived.

However, as it turned out, they must in reality have been Bekwais, or hunters, because one could hardly believe such a warning would have been lightly treated, in fact neglected, by such a careful foe as the one we were then measuring swords with. It was regrettable, but could not be helped, so we hurried on, and without further mishap than a thigh-deep wetting, reached Esumeja in safety. Through this village we went, and then halted at the foot of the fortified mound, on which was built the rest-house, and where the garrison was quartered. Then the ranks were closed up, arms were piled, and as we were, we sat down for a little breakfast to " buck us up " for what was coming.

There were but few arrangements requiring completion, so that it was not long before the officers were
assembled, briefly told the plan of the movement,
instructed as to any special duties which might be
required of them, and informed as to the supposed
details of the hostile position.   Then we were sent back
to rejoin our units, the scouts extended, and the column
moved slowly and cautiously on.   It was only a few
yards from Esumeja where a previous force had
sustained casualties ; and only two days before some
of the garrison, who had ventured a short distance out
of the laager, had been picked off by the enemy ;
moreover it was less than a mile to the stockade itself,
so that an attack was momentarily expected.   At last a
small village, which had been burnt by Captain Hall,
was sighted, reconnoitred, and found empty.   Here the
troops halted, and a few sentries were thrown out.
Lieutenant-Colonel Morland then came up, and held a
short council of war with Major Melliss and one or two
of his other officers.   A suggestion which had been
made as to the possibility of cutting an entirely new
road for ourselves into the forest and round into the
town, thus avoiding and outflanking the first entrenchment, was obviously impossible in this dense bush.   The
question was, what was to be done?   Major Melliss was
then ordered, with F (Hausa) Company 1st Bn. W.A.F.F.,
to go on, and immediately the stockade was seen, to rush
it with cold steel, not wasting any time in firing.   This
was really the cause of the completeness of the surprise.
The risk that the company might possibly be annihilated was justified by the occasion.   The place must
be taken, a third repulse could not be thought of for
an instant.   Lieutenant-Colonel Morland's further instructions were that, once the stockade was taken, the

company should only proceed as far as the river bank beyond it, along which it was to extend, and hold it so as to cover the advance of the guns. Then an organised attack would be made on the formidable parapet and ditch which were reported to be on the further side of the water, protecting the war camp. The dead and wounded were, in due course, to be picked up by the hospital in rear. The company was enthusiastic when the news was whispered to them. The buglers and drummers advanced to the head, the native guide simultaneously retired to the rear, and the scouts, who were no longer needed, were called in.

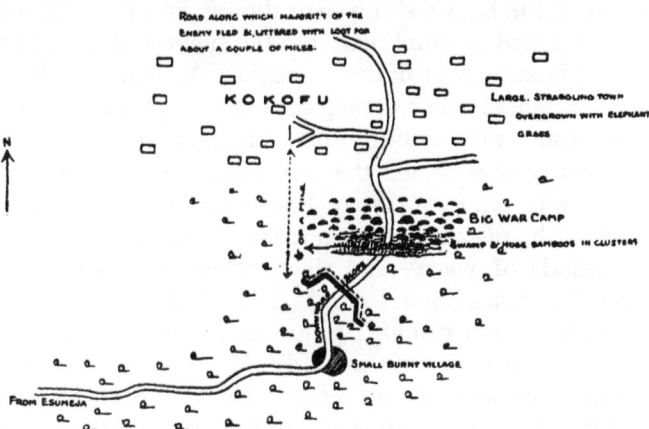

Then the Hausa company closed up in fours, the most the path admitted of, and moved stealthily out of the village along the road to Kokofu. Scarcely a couple of hundred yards had been traversed, when the crouching, almost crawling "point" halted, and signalled that something had been seen. Yes, there it was, round the next sharp bend of the road, not thirty yards away, a great six-foot stockade, right across the path, and extending an unknown distance into the bush on either side. It was in the usual favourite position, half way down a gentle slope, to compensate for the enemy's high fire, and to get the object on the top at a murderously close range. But this time that decline was to aid us. We had no intention of becoming their target, and the impetus of a charge could be got up quicker down hill. Down went the whispered order, " Stockade just ahead : prepare to charge." With set faces, the men crowded together as closely as was possible, each gripped his rifle more tightly than before, and bent forward for the final dash. Once again the inspiriting notes of the bugles shrilly rent the air, and the ruffle of drums rolled solemnly out into the silent forest. Then with a hoarse shout of determination, the Hausas, like a pack of bloodhounds, sprang full tilt at the position. In an instant the leading white men were scaling the timbers, over swarmed the rest, but, lo and behold, the place was empty! What had happened? Like the roar of the distant ocean came the confused murmur of thousands of voices, and like rabbits from a warren, countless black figures surged forth from everywhere. Unaware of our coming, the guard for the stockade had gone to feed with their comrades in the war camp, and not even the sentries had remained at their posts to keep watch. But now they were rushing up to meet us, and from front and flanks they opened a heavy fire ; it was no time to halt. We must dash on, no matter what lay before us ; a check would mean disaster. The shouting mob of glittering bayonets rolled on, and the sheen of the white men's swords showed them clearly our intentions. The enemy in front, after a few more desultory shots, wavered, turned, and fled, hotly followed by our men whom they had dared to hold in contempt. The

AN ASHANTI STOCKADE AFTER BOMBARDMENT

river was no depth, and there was no parapet; the enemy were gaining on us. Come on, come on! Already shouting had winded one somewhat, and the men were also pumped. A few of them in this plight even let off their rifles from their hips, at forms firing at them from the bush, as they struggled on in the mire. Then we were in the darkness caused by giant clumps of bamboos. Ah, the path was firmer then, the pace quickened wonderfully. Another turn, and there was Kokofu.

From almost every house, running for their lives, went nude Ashantis. The sight only maddened our men the more; in a moment their strength revived, and they were after them again with renewed vigour. One of the enemy, who had rashly stayed his flight to fire at a white man, was clubbed over the head with a soldier's rifle-butt. Another turned a complete somer-sault, shot through the back as he ran. A third was overtaken by a fleet-footed soldier, who sent his bayonet through his body; and thus blind excitement carried on the race of carnage. Already some thirty corpses lay along the pathway of this fierce onslaught, and more were to be found. Then the further extremity of the town was reached. Was the company closely followed up behind by the rest of the column? Was the risk of being cut off imminent? Discretion demanded prudence. The officers, with uplifted swords, turned about and halted the victorious tide of men, who well might have borne them off their feet; but discipline checked them as nought else could have done. A crowded vista of eager faces gazed at one reproachfully for an instant; then, with rifles raised above their heads, they implored leave to press on in pursuit, it was not too late to swell the slaughter, and terrify yet

more the stubborn foe. Yes, half the company might
go on, the other must remain in case of any unexpected
development. This sanction was received with a gratified
yell of satisfaction, and away bounded the delighted
men to whom it had been given. The track was strewn
with household goods of every kind in disordered profusion ; brass-studded chairs of chiefs, robes of others,
pillows, bedding, cooking pots, a medley of barbaric
property. Their abandonment might aid escape, but
it could not check the onward course of those behind.
Some more casualties were added to the list ; even
guns had been thrown away, the clearest proof of
panic with this warlike race of hunters. But it was
useless to go on for ever, and at length nothing was to
be seen, besides which there was too much danger of
some trap being run into. Bugler, sound the " Retire."
With the alacrity of trained obedience, the soldiers
turned, and we marched back. Then those who wished,
picked up any souvenir from the collection before them
on the way. By the time we got back, the main body
had come in without a casualty, and two companies, which
had gone right and left into the bush by the war camp,
had not only stopped the snipers, but completed the
rout in those directions. Picquets and sentries had been
thrown out round the town ; some soldiers were eating
the food that the enemy had cooked for them ; and
piles of loot were being dragged out of the houses, in
which quantities of loaded guns, rifles (including some
of our own carbines), powder barrels, and the like, were
discovered. Parties were patrolling down the various
roads by which the terror-stricken inhabitants had
fled, collecting further trophies. Thus the busy work
went on ; but being tired, I sat down, while Dan
Leno, with beaming face and dancing eyes, having

found the carrier who had brought the load of food and blankets, produced some refreshment. Some soldiers of the W.A.R. had discovered one of the enemy's war-dance costumes, a sort of straw kilt and cocks-comb headdress of the same material, and were *pirouetting* and dancing under the leadership of one attired in it. Others, riding on the shoulders of their fellows, waving their short swords, were carried round in a circle, their excited comrades shouting some song of triumph, whilst the rest joined in characteristic buffooneries.

But time was pressing, the work of destruction had still to be done. Various company calls, and the "Fall in" were heard. Then the town was methodically razed, and a collection of over two hundred captured guns was burnt. It was a great day. The proud Kokofu army of some six thousand warriors, which had terrified our allies, dangerously threatened our lines of communication, and already repulsed two of our columns, was completely routed and scattered to the four winds of heaven. In one week, to the day, the enemy had suffered two crushing defeats in two of their strongest positions; and the effect upon the two rival white and black commanders was illustrative of the feelings of their respective commands. Colonel Willcocks was reported to have been so delighted, when the news reached him, that he actually threw his helmet up into the air and cheered, whilst the Kokofu General was so depressed by his reverse that he blew out his own brains.

The appearance of the returning troops was less dignified than their advance. Scarce a white or a black man was not loaded with some token : all were laughing and talking, and at intervals singing some

Q

victorious chant. F Company, which had led the way
in so well, was ordered to head the procession back
again ; and an advance despatch was sent on to the
Commandant. At the burnt village the column was
again halted, but this time for food, to allow time for
the demolition of the stockade and the burning of the
war camp. Then was discovered the real nature of this
entrenchment, which was bespattered with bullet marks.
It was some three hundred yards in length, the usual six
feet in height, and of similar thickness. It had also
long arms for flanking fire. The defenders of the
stockade had built a continuous leaf and grass-roofed
shelter, with seats at intervals, to protect themselves
from the sun and rain. The path in front, down which
we had charged without noticing anything, had been
obstacled against a rush by sharpened stakes sunk into
the ground, which were quite enough to have lamed for
life any barefooted soldier ; but the rope with a bell
attached to it, which was tied across the path at night
to give warning of any approach, had not been put into
position. In our haste we had avoided one of the
nastiest traps the enemy ever prepared for us : to one
side of the road an inviting gap had been left in the
stockade, which insinuatingly suggested itself in preference to scaling the high timbers, particularly so under a
hot fire. On the enemy's side of this was found to have
been dug a very deep pit with vertical sides, precluding
any attempt to get out again, and at the bottom of it
were more pointed stakes, upon which the victims would
inevitably have been impaled. Kegs of powder had also
been put in some of the roofs, so that, if we fired these
domiciles, some of the charges would have blown up ;
as a matter of fact, one of these rough and ready mines
succeeded in damaging a few men and one officer.

The Esumeja garrison, on our return there, could scarcely believe that the success had been so complete and so sudden. As we passed the first sentry of the guard, one of our Hausas said to him, " Kokofu *babu, ya kare*" (the Hausa for " Kokofu is no more, it is finished "); and I remember the beam of delighted relief which lit up his face, for the poor fellow had been present at two previous repulses.

Bekwai was reached as dark was setting in, and here we found, to our surprise, the whole of the garrison drawn up to receive us, and the Commandant in person with all his Staff, at the head of his body-guard. Each unit of our column was welcomed with cheers, and presented arms. Finally, when the remainder had been dismissed, the Hausa company, which had behaved grandly, and with the utmost dash, was ordered to stand fast. Then Colonel Willcocks came and congratulated them, shook hands with and thanked all the white men ; and after three cheers had been given for the Commandant, under the leadership of Major Melliss, we fell out and marched off to quarters. That night we again got an issue of medical comforts, which was even more welcome and beneficial than usual, as we had had a prolonged strain, and nearly sixteen hours' hard going and excitement.

CHAPTER XXII

ORGANISED PUNITIVE MEASURES

THE stamping out of the insurrection could now be taken in hand in a thorough and systematic way. Captain Wright was sent to join the remainder of his company at Obuasi, where some three thousand Denkera levies had been collected, to take charge of them, and superintend the cutting down of the crops in the Adansi country to the south and south-west. They were gradually to work their way up, so as to be able to follow in the wake of the advancing army, when the time was ripe for it to move on. Meantime the Akim levies were similarly acting on the eastern flank of this region of sedition, under the guidance of Captains Wilcox and Benson ; whilst yet a third body of levies, under Major Cramer, was guarding the Upper Prah district. Captains Stallard and Tighe, with Dr. Hay, were sent with a company, W.A.R., to reoccupy Kwisa, and thus enable the main road to be reopened as the line of communication. Convoys moved backwards and forwards along the entire route with mechanical regularity, bringing up supplies of all sorts, but those north for miles around. These bodies were compact little fighting forces, which took out large numbers of un-laden carriers. When a suitable place was found the troops surrounded it, whilst the carriers looted it ; then another spot would be visited, and so on, until every man had a load, when a return would be made and the results divided up amongst the garrison.

The remnants of the re-concentrated Adansi army, which had not already gone northwards to join the Kokofus and Ashantis, were reported to be in a war camp in the bush, east of Dompoasi. It was imperative to clear them out before the Adansi country could be subdued, the telegraph opened up between Fumsu and Kwisa, and the lines of communication up to Bekwai rendered at all safe. Consequently, on July 26th, a flying column of four hundred W.A.F.F., one 75 m/m and the 7-pr. gun of the W.I.R., to be joined by the Kwisa company for the fight, was despatched under the command of Major Beddoes, to find the enemy, and do this piece of work. This they duly completed, the force being back again by the last day of the month. Dompoasi was reached without any trouble, but from there they had to strike into the bush by almost unknown roads, where, owing to the ignorance of the guide, much difficulty was encountered. A prisoner was luckily caught on the 27th, and he consented to lead them to where the enemy were, under their king, on condition his life was spared. On the 30th, after having followed traces of the foe for two days, an advance was made to Yankoma, on the direct route from Insuaim to Kokofu. Amongst other discoveries, our men found at one place the looted rations of a wretched miner who had been murdered there. The column had barely started on the before-mentioned date when it was

attacked, the enemy holding a series of positions in
the undergrowth, from which they were with difficulty
forced, one after another, by companies in extended
order. Quite early in the day Major Beddoes was
severely wounded in the thigh, and Captain Greer
(Royal Warwickshire Regiment), a Special Service
Officer, assumed command. A couple of miles further
on the rebels were again met with, this time holding the
bank of a stream. The Maxims were at once opened
upon them with great execution, putting them rapidly to
flight ; the trail of blood and numbers of corpses testi-
fying to the losses they had sustained. Close in rear of
this spot was found a scarce-completed stockade of some
three hundred yards in length, but it was not held.
Somewhat further on the force was again severely
attacked on all sides, and the rear guard was at one
time enveloped. Despite the guns, the foe advanced
boldly to within a few yards of our men, and once
attempted to rush the 7-pr., which might have been
lost, but for the steady and excellent volleys poured into
the enemy by the detachment of the W.I.R. which was
serving this gun. It was here that Lieutenant Philips,
R.A., and Lieutenant Swabey, W.I.R., were severely hit,
whilst Lieutenant (local Captain) Monck-Mason and
Colour-Sergeant Blair, both W.A.F.F., were slightly
wounded. Then Captain Neal, Lagos Hausa Force,
with a company of W.A.F.F., worked round the
enemy's flank, and forced them to retire. It was
4 p.m. when the Adansis made a last stand to cover
their war camp, and they were not finally driven back
until nearly dark.

It transpired that the rebels were informed of the recent
advance of Major Cramer's levies, which were then a
day's journey distant from them, coming from the

south-east. The enemy were, therefore, not only anxious to repulse our force, so that they might fall upon this other one, which they could have beaten with ease, but had actually been fighting a splendid rear guard action, so as to cover the retreat of their women, children, and property. Their families and effects had been collected in this camp for safety, as the Adansis were unaware that the white man knew of its existence, and had been quite sceptical as to his ability to find it out. Their final dispersion in the encounter which has just been narrated, was again due to a charge, by which the village in rear of their camp was taken. Here were found many dead, some actually lying in heaps. It was long after dark before the wounded were got into a place of safety, and the force was able to rest. However, the job allotted to them had been well done, though at the cost of five white men wounded, three of whom had at once to be invalided home, and forty black soldiers killed and wounded. The large hospital train prohibited pursuit, which would probably have been not only risky, but unproductive of much good ; and so next day the column started on its return journey to headquarters.

Meantime at Bekwai the list of sick and invalided steadily increased ; and henceforward to every south-ward-bound convoy there were added hammocks with the unfortunate white and black victims of the climate and hostilities. The kits of those who died were sold by auction at enormous prices. I remember one box, which contained three cakes of soap, fetched 27s., and a broken box of twenty-five cheroots, two guineas. Special Service Officers continued to arrive in driblets, to fill the many vacancies.

It was at this time that the hearts of all were cheered

by some good news from home. A telegram from Her Majesty to Colonel Willcocks was read by him to us all on a garrison parade, congratulating him and those under his command on the relief of Kumasi. Then, to every one's delight, came the information that our Commandant's distinguished services had not only been appreciated, but rewarded. From the Commander-in-Chief arrived a wire, stating that he had been promoted to the rank of Brevet-Colonel in the army; and one from the Secretary of State for the Colonies, that he had been raised to the dignity of a K.C.M.G. Finally, a eulogistic telegram came from Mr. Chamberlain to Colonel Sir James Willcocks, and Lieutenant-Colonel Morland, about the fall of the great war camp at Kokofu. The receipt of these messages caused great enthusiasm amongst all ranks, every one being especially proud of Her Majesty's personal recognition of the services of the Ashanti Field Force, and most glad that its popular Commandant had received the honours he so richly deserved.

Late on the following day, the 31st of July, a runner arrived from Pekki, stating that his town was going to be attacked in force by the Ashantis the next evening, as a punishment for the assistance they had rendered to the white men. Major Melliss was accordingly ordered to proceed thither the following morning, with two guns, my Hausa company with its Maxim, a column of carriers under a Transport Officer, and a doctor, to garrison the place temporarily, and repulse the assault if it were made. We were to remain there a day or two, putting the·place in a state of defence, when we would be joined by, and proceed with, a force under Lieutenant-Colonel Burroughs, which was to complete the relief of Kumasi by doubling its garrison and supply of stores.   As the Commandant laughingly said : " But you will be back here again by the 12th, though not for grouse-shooting."   It was arranged that, when we left Pekki, our place was to be taken by Captain Wright's company and the Denkera levies.   These latter worthies, under their king, had then completed their work in the Adansi country, and in a day or two's time would be ready to begin depredations in Ashanti, north of the Bekwai territory.   But it was subsequently found that their operations in this country were very slow, and shortly became suspended.   A handful of plucky Ashantis could check this army of cowards with the utmost ease, and in the end they did nothing of any value, until once again a movement of headquarters northwards cleared the way for them.   The little guard for Pekki started off for a cheerful Bank Holiday next morning, and tramped the same old fifteen miles again, but with much greater comfort.   The rains had temporarily abated, and the track had been greatly improved . by the kings of Bekwai and Pekki, who had received orders to this effect some little time before.   The native bridge over the Ordah River was positively alarming from the flimsiness of its construction.   It swayed so violently that balance alone was difficult, and when the heavy millimètre was crossing, although there was no other weight on the structure at the time, one was filled with misgivings for the safety of the gun.   The groans and cracks it gave were ominous in the extreme ; however, mishap was avoided.   When we eventually got to our destination about 4.30 p.m., having heard terrible yarns from village chiefs on the way, I saw, for the very first time, a village of West Africans really glad to see one.   Their faces lit up with pleasure as they crowded out to meet us, and when they saw us cutting down their banana crops, which grew up to the very huts, though mystified by the white man's tactics in preferring to see his foe, they willingly helped to destroy their sources of sustenance. They knew it was, somehow or other, for the best, and would work out for their good. Every house was filled with Pekki warriors, with their long trade guns, but they appeared to have taken no steps for defence, except to send out a few scouts. Their war-chief put his house at our disposal, and we were very fairly comfortable, especially after we had erected a palm-leaf shelter in the courtyard, under which to bathe and feed. After having detailed a strong in-lying picquet, with carefully posted sentries, we were disappointed to find that no attack came. It would have been nice for once to have had the positions changed, and for us to be the ones attacked. What a hot time the enemy would have had! But they appeared to know it also, for as soon as our arrival was signalled to them, they gave up the idea. The Pekki force was good enough for them to assail, although it was behind cover, but disciplined, well-armed troops, directed by white men, were not. When we inquired how it was that the exact time of this attack had been known with such precision, we heard that the rebels had captured and sadly maltreated a Pekki native, and that he had overheard them talking over their camp-fires, and arranging their plans. The information appeared to be as perfectly genuine as the man's escape had been wonderful.

The rest of our short stay was spent in making hasty fortifications, building a rough bamboo barrack for the soldiers who were to replace us, stockading a portion of the perimeter of the rambling town by thus joining up the houses, and the like. The Transport Officer took

enormous pride in a fowl-house and sheep-pen which
he had made to receive the live stock portion of the
supplies which the king had been ordered to bring in.
Out of his boast, however, a joke was coined that he
had actually built a hen-house in three days with only
three hundred carriers at his disposal ! It was whilst
here that my company, for the very first time since the
commencement of the campaign, received an issue of
meat. It was perforce only a small piece each, enough
to give a taste to their diet of rice, plantains, and koko-
yams, but their delight and gratitude were quite
touching. We white men managed to raise a couple
of fowls, which were a corresponding luxury to us.
During our last day the natives, who were out fetching
materials for the palisade, found a poor starving and
wounded Lagos Hausa, who, having been compelled to
fall out, had been left behind in the Governor's retreat.
From June 23rd, therefore, until the 3rd of August, the
poor wretch had miraculously managed to hide himself
in the bush, infested as it was by the enemy, and had
lived upon roots that he had found by night. He was
then only eleven miles from Kumasi, but had all this
time been crawling and trying to get into friendly
country, where he might eventually find some white
officer. We felt a strong temptation to sally forth
and destroy a war camp, mostly composed of the
ousted Treda people, who were still full of fight and
revenge, as we soon found out. This stronghold, some
nine miles distant, also threatened the road along which
we were to proceed ; but our orders were otherwise, so
it had to be left for a later date, when more reinforcements would have arrived, and time was not so pressing.
As it happened, the excursion thither was to be a
disappointment, and the subject of it, Major Montanaro,

R.A., a Special Service Officer, who was to join us next day with the troops from Bekwai. It was considered necessary to utilise this same route to Kumasi the second time, as the main road was still too dangerous for anything in the nature of a convoy.

The late afternoon of the 4th saw the advent of Lieutenant-Colonel Burroughs and his men. With him was a freshly-arrived half battalion C.A.R., with their Sikhs, under command of Lieutenant (local Major) Cobbe, I.S.C. There were also two more 75-m/m guns and two 7-prs. We were to go on the next day with them, thus bringing up the total strength of the infantry to seven hundred and fifty men.

It did one good to see the tall Sikhs again, and hear once more their Oriental language. They instinctively inspired confidence, although we did not know at that moment what severe fighting was immediately ahead of us. Pekki was, for the second time, swamped with troops and carriers, and its accommodation strained to the utmost limit, but we were now accustomed to such finishes to our marches. All were soon quartered, the loads piled in orderly heaps for the morrow, and those rice bags, which were more trouble to us than babies to their mothers, put securely into water-tight huts, out of the falling rain.

Lieutenant-Colonel Burroughs' instructions sounded like a programme involving plenty of work. It appeared that, owing to the misty weather, the prearranged signals to show that all was well, had not been seen from the fort for two successive Sundays, and that there was a disquieting native rumour in circulation, that the enraged Ashantis had again attacked the garrison. Therefore, this column was to double its numbers, bringing them up to three hundred soldiers and ten white men, leave a large increase of supplies, destroy all the stockades round Kumasi, and fight its way down the main road ; thus opening it up for the first time. This scheme, if accomplished, would have finally removed all anxiety about the isolated fort, and have enabled the country south of it to be cleared of the rebels, until the moment arrived for headquarters to advance thither. From the hostile capital alone could the termination of the war be satisfactorily directed and carried out, since there was as much territory to the north requiring subjugation as had already been traversed up to the present. We were to endeavour to do the whole of the remainder of the march to Kumasi in one day, and we were not sorry to hear it, as, thanks to our own precautions, there was not an atom of shelter from the rain all the way.

CHAPTER XXIII

THE RELIEF COMPLETED

THE grey dawn saw Pekki again open to attack, provided that the enemy did not delay and thereby lose their opportunity. But they had their plans, and it turned out to be our column they were after. At first we got along very well; and then our old Treda foes, who had tracked us down from their bush camp, let us have a hot fire from an ambush. Not long after they had been shaken off, we met our old friend of former fights, " Ping-ping," with his double-barrelled ·220 rifle. He had brought down a company or two to harry us, and kept up this game incessantly, until the last village before Kumasi. This man personally shot one carrier dead, and, curiously enough, during the whole day they only attacked the transport and hospital, from which no effective fire could be returned. However, just after their last ambuscade, they received such a smart lesson that they gave up these tactics for good and all. Their method was at last spotted. They lay behind their tree or other cover, let the head of the column go by, and then let off a few furious volleys into the unlucky carriers, of whom all the killed and wounded happened to be those carrying the white men's loads. After this they would hurry along a previously prepared path to another place further on and play off the same *ruse* again. Howbeit, before the last of these traps, they had been seen running parallel with the column, till they passed the advance guard, not more than a few yards away in the bush. Consequently, as soon as we heard the unmistakable "b-o-o-m" of their deep-sounding volley in rear, we immediately prepared for their return journey past us, determined, at the risk of expending a little ammunition, to stop this most dangerous practice once and for all. Major Montanaro had a gun crammed full of case shot, and the infantry were ready with a carefully aimed volley. Lastly, a Maxim was sighted and arranged for " rapid traversing fire." Soon came an excited shout " They're coming ! " and then were not the biters themselves bitten ! The terrific explosion of the big gun into their midst was instantly followed by several well-directed volleys, section by section, up the line, each firing when the other had finished. Then came the sound of the furious little Maxim, whirring and cracking as it swung horizontally from right to left, and pouring a ceaseless stream of bullets on to the little track amongst the naked murderers who madly raced along it. It cost a few cartridges, but it was a cheap experiment as it drove home its moral wonderfully successfully.

Upon our arrival at the fort about 6 p.m., we found the garrison well, only one officer being down with fever, and, of course, all the rumours about the enemy having made a concentrated attack proved quite false. All that the rebels had done had been to snipe from the outlying buildings, and, with the coolest bravado, to streak across the open within range. When fired at, they dropped down flat, only to spring up and run on until fired at again. And, as a matter of fact, it had been rather a diversion for the imprisoned white men.

The next morning I started with rather a stroke of luck, for whilst standing on the verandah of the upper story of the house in which we had slept, talking to a superior officer, somebody, in cleaning his rifle, which happened to be loaded, let it off, the bullet passing just over our heads into the wall and covering us with dust. Shortly after this it was time for the day's work to begin. The question was whether the remaining stockades were held at all ; and if so, whether the enemy were at this late stage of the campaign in force ; and finally, how we were to divide up the work so as to give each his fair share. It could not have been foreseen that we should meet with so much opposition round Kumasi itself, or larger supplies of ammunition would have been issued. From a rough plan, sent up from the coast by the officer who had been in command during the siege, there appeared to be four more large entrenchments beyond those which we had taken when we entered at the time of the relief, and the small one which the outgoing garrison had destroyed. Therefore it was decided that two columns each of three hundred men, should sally out and take on a couple a-piece. In the morning, the one under Major Melliss was to go and destroy the stockade on the Bantama road, whilst the other under Major Cobbe was to advance against the one on the Kintampo road. After lunch, arrangements were to be made regarding the other two, which barred the Ejesu and Accra roads.

In accordance with this plan, Major Melliss' column, which consisted of three companies W.A.F.F., and a 75-m/m gun, fell in at 10 a.m. ; and Major Cobbe, who had under him two companies C.A.R., with the Sikhs,

KUMASI FORT

From the N.H., showing the Residency to the right

one company W.A.R., and a 75-m/m gun, was to parade his men an hour later. Both were to be followed by a gang of unladen carriers, who were to carry out the work of demolition.

Therefore, we inspected our men at our leisure ; and at ten o'clock the first of these two little forces started off with my company in front. At first, all went well. We passed the burnt Basel Mission and rounded the bend of the road without seeing any sign of life. The same thing, by the way, subsequently happened to Major Cobbe at the burnt Wesleyan Mission ; and he, like us, also began to think that there was going to be no opposition. Nevertheless, we advanced rather gingerly. The tall elephant-grass, which surrounds Kumasi on all sides, was so thick that it was not worth our while to make an attempt to penetrate it, as the undertaking would not only have been slow and arduous, but would also have had to have been carried out under the fire of the enemy at close range, which would have made it very costly. Major Melliss, in consequence, trusted to his " point." Suddenly that useful eye of the column became somewhat agitated and excited, and the news was sent back that the village of Bantama had been sighted just ahead, with the enemy running out of it. This was instantly confirmed by the report of two sentries' guns, and again a moment later, as we advanced, by the sight of the still burning fires which had just been hastily quitted. The track wound irregularly through the village and then divided. By all means, we thought, let us follow the one by which the rebels had escaped. Certainly it looked all right, for there was a mildewed umbrella stuck up by the roadside—whatever that might mean, probably some " ju-ju "—and again, in the middle of the path, that unmistakable token of

R

war, a large vulture pegged out spread-eagle fashion. One more turn to the left in this serpentine advance, and there was the stockade at the foot of a slope some eighty yards distant—a massive entrenchment of timber at right angles to our path, which broadened out at that point. How many hundred yards it extended into the bush on either side, goodness only knew! Was it held or not, that was the question. Surely it could not be another surprise like Kokofu? The running savages and the signal guns negatived such an idea for the moment.

To test the reliability of appearances, the order was given to bring up a Maxim. But before the gun carriers had got their loads off their heads, a deafening salvo of Dane guns, accompanied by flashes and clouds of smoke, came from the black sullen obstruction. Several of the carriers fell wounded by this rain of slugs, and the rest fled precipitately. But, despite this desertion and the heavy fire, the little weapon was soon unlimbered.

Already half a belt of ammunition had been expended ; but of what use were rifle bullets against a six-foot thickness of tree-trunks, carefully built up with timber, earth and stones? The enemy were firing on our flanks ; perhaps they were trying their enveloping game and working their way round to cut us off if they could. We decided to give them a few volleys, and then see if a way could be cut into the bush ; inside it might be less thick. They got their few volleys, but the jungle grass was impenetrable. Perhaps they were behind flanking stockades after all. Down went the order for the millimètre, and up trundled the great gun, ready mounted on its wheeled carriage. It took up its position on the crest of the slope, and Sergeant Desborough, R.A., began hurling great 12lb. shells at the target. But we

had to be careful of our own engine of death, for the recoil
was so strong that one stood a good chance of being
knocked down by it and getting a leg broken. It was
strange : the enemy's fire was getting worse instead of
better. As far as could be seen the shells were doing
no good. Surely the enemy must be firing 7-prs. at us
themselves! "Look out," was heard, "for that tall tree
on the enemy's right rear of the stockade, the one with
the falling creepers down it ! They are firing rifles from
it." Whistle ! Phut ! No doubt about it. "Colour-
Sergeant," was the next command, "turn the Maxim on
the tree!" Unfortunately, in turning the gun round
half-left, Colour-Sergeant Foster was severely wounded
by a bullet in the left shoulder, but we knew nothing
about it. He said not a word, but sent such a shower
of lead back in reply that the fire from the tree ceased.
"Ping-ping" and his fellow marksmen had climbed
down. The noise was deafening, and the fire so heavy
that every white man belonging to the leading company
had been hit, in addition to many of the rank and file.
Around the gun and the Maxim lay prostrate many
members of the teams. Dead and dying were heaped
together in piteous plight, but for the moment they had to
be left as they were. Under the circumstances, a turning
movement was scarcely practicable; and certainly it was
not good enough at that range. The place was beginning
to look like a butcher's shambles ; and to stay where we
were was only throwing valuable lives away. So the
order came from Major Melliss, as we had expected it
would, "Mass the buglers ! Form up F Company ! I'm
going to charge !" For a moment the buglers stood
waiting the word to blow. It was only the first
company, which was then kneeling and facing outwards,
which was causing the delay, as with it the assault itself

was to be made. At that very moment, whilst these three brave youngsters stood rigidly in line under a galling fire, little bugler Moma was shot in the head. The blood began streaming down his face ; but no thought of giving in entered his mind. He was determined to do his duty when the word was given ; and what was more, unarmed as he was, he was going to charge, too, and do his best to be the first in the coming race of death.

Those moments of waiting seemed like hours. At last, drawing his sword, Major Melliss, who always commanded his columns from the front, gave the order, "Sound away !" Once again the familiar notes of the "Charge" pierced the din ; and in an instant every man scented blood with distended nostrils. Like panthers, the Hausas made one wild spring forward ; and down the slope they rushed, jostling each other in their eagerness. Major Melliss, with his usual recklessness for his own safety, was already yards ahead of all. But this spectacle did not terrify the stubborn defenders of that stockade, which had already repulsed the white man and his soldiers. Then, for the first time, when only a few strides from those shell-torn timbers, we saw that they were loop-holed. No wonder the hostile fire had not been high that day ! And through them we saw not only the barrels of trade guns, vomiting forth fire, lead, and smoke, but also the fierce black faces of the men behind them. One European put his rifle through one of these loop-holes at that moment and forestalled his dusky antagonist. By now the first white man was on top. Another clambered up after him, but a third slipped back ; the place was wet with blood. Over went a fourth with a frantic jump, and then an officer dropped the eight feet on the other side, landing on the

ground, and almost instantaneously running his sword
through one of the enemy. By this time bayonets
began to bristle over, but even then many of the foe
would not budge. A short hand-to-hand fight took
place, fierce while it lasted ; and cold steel did its work.
At last the rout began. Here one white man proved
too fleet a foot even for a naked savage, and his sword
pinked him, bringing him to earth. Over there was
another officer chasing an ill-clad warrior. "Shoot him ! "
shouted the first ; but back came the breathless answer,
" I can't ; my revolver's empty ! "

Every minute the brave Ashantis were getting more
and more outnumbered. Reluctantly at last they turned
and fled, hotly pursued by white and black ; and every
yard added to their losses. Hard astern scudded Bugler
Moma, his face plastered with blood, but his treasured
bugle still in one hand, running as fast as his little legs
would carry him. Some one had helped him over the
stockade, and now he was making up for lost time.
Round to the right bore the race. What a gruesome
sight that swarthy face was ! The man had been run
through, and lay writhing in agony, until a second
stroke mercifully put him out of his pain. The turn had
revealed the war camp. What an enormous one it was !
Already the last of its garrison were disappearing pell-
mell into the forest and down any track that afforded a
chance of escape.

It had been a long run and a hard tussle ; and now
further progress would have been as futile as it was
impossible. So the " Retire" was sounded, followed by
the " Assembly." Panting and gasping each man
checked his headlong career, and dragged himself back
again. Captain Eden's company, keeping well together,
came up at that moment at a steady double. It was

under orders to proceed up the road as far as Intimidu, a hamlet just beyond, which was to be burnt; and then they were to rejoin us. In the meantime the war camp had to be destroyed. The troops lined its outskirts, whilst the carriers cut down and burnt the huts. Another party returned with an escort to pull down the stockade. It turned out to be nearly three hundred yards long, solid as a parapet and crescent-shaped, which explained why the cross fire from it caught us so badly. Now that the excitement was over, we noticed that Colour-Sergeant Foster's khaki jacket was soaked through and that he was faint from loss of blood: but this was by no means the only field-dressing Dr. Thomson had to apply! That mound of timber had been bought dear with the price of precious lives however few the moments the bargain had taken to clinch!

At last the great tongues of flame that leaped up to meet the rays of the scorching sun assured us that our work of destruction was accomplished. The Yoruba company had returned and reported the same satisfactory information about Intimidu. We therefore turned about and retraced our steps. Along the path lay traces of the fight covered with swarms of flies. Three of them, we afterwards heard, were big chiefs. The trenches were blood-stained and black with the contents of upset powder barrels. Slowly the little force wended its way up the undulation, down which it had come so quickly but a few minutes before, and halted in Bantama. This sacred village, favourite scene for centuries of human sacrifice, we paused to raze to the ground: and fire soon parched the ground that had oftentimes drunk blood.

On our left flank Major Cobbe was obviously engaged heavily: another stern action was in progress. The millimètre, Maxims, rifles, and thundering Dane guns plainly showed this to be the case. Then from some neighbouring tree were distinctly heard the sharp reports of "Ping-ping," this De Wet of Ashanti. Evidently he had only left one fight, unharmed as usual, to hurry across and join in the other. Could not we make a flank movement through the intervening bush, render assistance, and perhaps cut off the enemy? It was very tempting, but the very thought was madness. Our own soldiers would be the first to fire into us, ignorant that we were coming to their aid. So, with Bantama reduced to ashes and our orders fully carried out, we returned to the fort. There we found Lieutenant-Colonel Burroughs, who seemed much surprised at the great amount of firing he had heard, and at that which was still going on, and wondering at the fierceness of the enemy's opposition and their large numbers.

It was trying and tantalising work to take a little lunch, while listening to the continued heavy firing. It was late, too, before it ceased. At last, just before dark, Major Cobbe's column came in, with many wounded in hammocks, on stretchers and in blankets tied to poles. They had had a very stiff show indeed. The first two signal shots—from guns tied to wedges in the path, and pulled by strings—had slightly wounded Major Cobbe and Colour-Sergeant Rose at the outset. After a prolonged fight the former in person had finally turned the right of the position, with two companies C.A.R., but losing heavily owing to the thick grass and consequent slow progress. Meanwhile, the W.A.R. company in front had engaged the stockade, of similar proportions to the one we had rushed, but horse-shoe in form. Thus our men had been almost completely surrounded by a circle of hostile fire. When the movement had at length been completed, the enemy, who had in the meantime suffered heavily, were charged simultaneously from the front and flanks: whereupon they broke and fled. Then the large war camp had been looted, and much food had been found in it. Afterwards our men had burnt it and pulled down the stockade. The millimètre gun and Maxims had again failed to oust the foe, who had only been turned out at the point of the bayonet after a fight of nearly two hours' duration. But, as must ever be the case in the forest, the enemy had made good their retreat, leaving, however, many things behind them,—including some more of our carbines and ammunition.

A good many unfortunate carriers had been hit in these two engagements; and the attacks upon these two stockades had been costly both in life and ammunition. The casualties for the day had been half-a-dozen white men wounded, Major Cobbe and Colour-Sergeant Foster severely; and although the slugs were extracted the next day from their wounds, they had to be left behind in the fort when we returned to Bekwai. Seventeen Sikhs had been killed or wounded out of fifty, who had gone into action that day for the first time in West Africa. These, together with the native rank and file, brought up the roll to a total of just under seventy—a very large proportion of the small number of men who had taken part in these two operations. It was a pitiful sight to see the last column coming in; but, as Major Cobbe remarked to Lieutenant-Colonel Burroughs, who was much pained when he saw what a reduction had been made in the small Sikh contingent: "Well, sir, I am glad to say it has been a success; and, of course, one must have casualties."

The remainder of the day was spent in visiting the

wounded and hearing the details of the encounter in which one had not taken part oneself. I ended up, I remember, by sitting in the brilliant moonlight in the room of a wounded officer, feeling at peace even with " Ping-ping," having been generously given, amongst other things, some real Egyptian cigarettes, by the *khitmagar* of the C.A.R. mess, whose members, having so recently arrived, were still in possession of a few luxuries.

CHAPTER XXIV

THE NIGHT ATTACK

WITH the exception of replenishing the men's supplies of ammunition, giving them rations, cleaning guns and rifles and burying the dead (the Sikhs, in accordance with their religion, burned theirs), no other orders were issued. The experience of the day before had opened every one's eyes in an unexpected manner, and much serious conversation took place, with the result that a consultation was held in the fort; and out of it came one of the most novel and important actions of the campaign. What was the best course to pursue under the circumstances was the question which was occupying everybody's mind. Two more big entrenched positions had to be destroyed, if possible, before we started upon the perilous march before us down the main road, which was infested by the enemy, and where stockades and camps were known to exist. We had left Bekwai with only three hundred rounds per man; and it was out of the question to draw on the ammunition which we had just put into the magazine of the fort for the use of its isolated garrison. This fact alone precluded the idea of taking these two stockades in the same way that we had captured the other two the day before. But, on the other hand, our orders were most emphatic; and we had to be back again at headquarters by a fixed date. Matters finally resolved themselves into this :—we had either to make an assault upon the remaining stockades and return by the safer road through Pekki, or to leave them and go back by the main road—the route mapped out in our instructions. Either of these plans was unsatisfactory, inasmuch as each left half our programme not carried out. Then it occurred to somebody that the moon rose early and was almost full by eight o'clock. Why not try a night attack? Certainly we should have to rely upon cold steel alone to do the work in such a venture and not fire a shot, for there was no other way of capturing such fortifications without expenditure of ammunition. Of course, with superstitious black soldiers it was extremely risky and hardly advisable to penetrate into the fastnesses of the forest in such a dim light, as a panic would mean disaster. Night work, also, is under any circumstances always most trying and exhausting to troops. But in this case matters were rather different. The object of assault could be located in the day time almost to a yard, thereby reducing to a minimum the danger of losing the way. Also no dependence need be placed on ignorant native guides, as the place was quite close and the full moon was so propitious. Finally, it would be eminently undesirable and inexpedient to leave Kumasi again practically in a state of siege. Without a doubt, all things considered, the undertaking appeared worth while. Attempts could not be made upon both stockades simultaneously; and these tactics, although they might pay once in a way, would not bear repetition. Which one ought we to select, was the next question. Though equally formidable, the rules of sound strategy

nevertheless pointed out plainly to any thoughtful
tactician that the one on the Accra-Kumasi road was
the more suitable for our purpose :—firstly, because it
adjoined the main road to Cape Coast down which we
intended to go (and if this hostile army could be driven
out, our exposed flank would by this movement be
rendered much safer); and secondly, because this
stockade, if captured, would isolate the remaining one
on the Ejesu road, as we had taken only four-and-
twenty hours before the one on the Kintampo road,
which had supported its other flank.   In all probability,
then, if we were successful, the Ashantis would of their
own accord abandon this, the last remaining stronghold
of their original line of investment, as both the adjoining
camps would have fallen into our hands.   It turned out
afterwards, by the way, when Kumasi was next visited
for the purpose of permanent occupation, that our con-
jecture had been well founded.   We had, therefore,
though not conscious of it at the time, carried out our
orders to the letter in face of the greatest difficulties, as
it had seemed utterly impossible to complete our task
with the ammunition in our possession.

As the result of this decision, Captain Loch, W.A.R.,
was sent out about midday to reconnoitre the position.
It was a most hazardous undertaking, but could not
have been better carried out.   His men, by creeping
through the tall grass like cats and at times climbing
high trees to look round, succeeded in reaching a large
cotton tree within some seventy yards of the enemy's
entrenchment.   At that point, the road took a turn to
the left, sloping, as usual, gently downwards ; and there
lay the stockade across the path, with a war camp in
rear of it.   At that moment the hum of innumerable
voices was heard, and the hostile scouts were encoun-

tered for the first time. But it made little difference
then that our soldiers had at last been seen, as their
mission had been accomplished : so they retired rapidly
without casualties, leaving the foe under the impression
that they had thought better of it and did not wish for
any repetition of yesterday's fighting, anyhow for some
time to come. To make assurance doubly sure, Captain
Loch, who had not been idle, had made a careful sketch
of the approach, in which no detail was omitted.

Long before this company returned every officer had
guessed what was in the wind, but it was not until
5 p.m. that our suppositions were officially confirmed.
At that hour the order bugle collected us all outside
Lieutenant-Colonel Burroughs' quarters, when he explained to us the details of the evening's work. We
were to fall in at 8 p.m., so as to deliver the attack
between 9 and 10 o'clock. The moon would then be at
its zenith, and we hoped, with luck, to be back again in
time to get some rest that night. Lieutenant-Colonel
Burroughs informed us that he intended to go with the
force in person. Some Maxims were to follow in rear,
just in front of the hospital and unladened carriers, the
latter being intended for the usual work of destruction,
but no big guns were to be taken. It was useless to
employ a large column, which could not be satisfactorily
handled at such a time ; in fact, the smaller and more
compact it was the better. Only five hundred men
were selected to go, and the honour of leading the
assault was given to Captain Loch's company, weak
though it was at the time, as a reward for the excellent
reconnaissance of the morning. My company, with
Major Melliss—always a good man in an emergency—
was to follow immediately in their rear.

These two companies were to be the storming party,

while those in our rear were to move to the flanks when
once the stockade had been surmounted, so as to guard
against attack from the adjacent war camp or any
return of the enemy, or so as to try and cover a retreat
in case of mishap. It was an impressive little conclave
whilst it lasted. Lieutenant-Colonel Burroughs and
every officer who was to take part for the first time in
such an undertaking, in such a difficult country, felt
keenly the anxiety inseparable from it. No one dared
to think what failure might mean, but we knew that
success would finally end the siege of Kumasi, and
complete the relief. We broke up silently and went slowly
away in twos and threes to warn our companies. The
news was received with acclamation by the men, and
Captain Loch's company went so far as to indulge
majestically in a saraband in the exuberance of their
spirits at being permitted to lead.

Major Melliss and I had an early meal, at which I
remember we drank a pint bottle of medical champagne
which had been presented to us, for we agreed that it
might be the last dinner, so we might just as well have
the best we could get! Poor Colour-Sergeant Foster,
who, with his arm in a sling, had just recovered from
the influence of chloroform after his operation, was
much upset when he heard the news and was told that
he could not possibly accompany us. The idea of
losing the chance of a fight, after the distinguished
services which his regiment, the Devonshire, had
rendered in South Africa, was not at all a pleasing
prospect to him; but, plead as he might, it was
obviously impossible for him to go in the state in which
he then was. However, in the end, this gallant N.C.O.
has abundant cause to hold his head high amongst
his fellows, for his name has been specially brought to

notice for the excellent services he has rendered during this war.

Dan Leno was instructed to prepare a little cold supper for us on our return, and then, having tightened our belts, pulled down our chin-straps, and unbuckled our sword-scabbards for fear of tripping over them in the excitement and darkness, we sallied forth for a last look round the company, which was by this time assembling outside, previous to marching to the place of parade outside the fort's gate. Already the company of the C.A.R. was moving in that direction, and we could hear the subdued, but none the less determined paean they were chanting.

A little while before the moon had been slightly clouded over, but at that moment she shed forth her pale cold light in tropical brightness, exaggerating the shadows in contrast until they appeared to be of unnatural blackness. Like sprites of another world, from all directions came the units of this phantom column, seeming to spring from out of the murky forest itself as they made their noiseless way into the white light from the heavens. Silently they fell in in their allotted positions, and the hushed tread of bare feet made the scene quite uncanny. Down the line was softly passed the word that all was ready. Once again each white man whispered the orders to his men : " No smoking, no talking, no noise, no firing, bayonet only, follow me." At that moment the sound of singing broke the tense silence. Mother of mercy! was all chance of surprise doomed ? Were all our plans to be foiled in the hour of their execution ? From the motley mob of Mendi carriers arose a song of encouragement and victory. The music rose and swelled, until a fear seized every heart that an answering shout of fetish

fury would come from the very camp we were bound
for. In an instant we were in their midst, beating them
with the flats of our swords across their naked shoulders
and quieting them with no measured language. At
length the noise was quelled, and the order was given to
advance. Then the bugle from the fort, as if nothing
unusual were occurring, sounded the " Last Post."

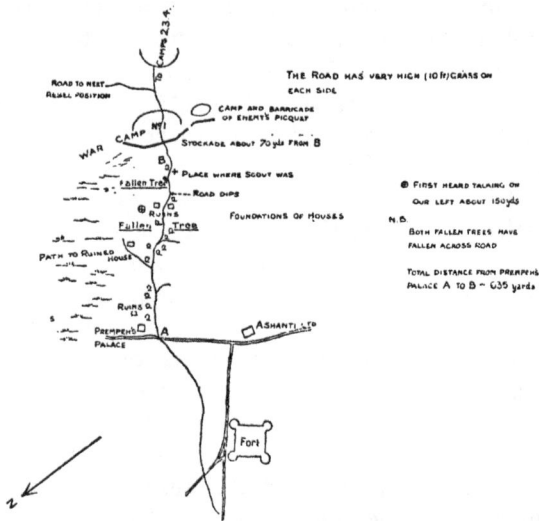

At first the pace was good, but soon we had to
slacken, although we were all the time on a downward
grade. Prempeh's palace was passed, after which the
road became a tortuous track. Every yard we found
the tall grass thicker, and here and there an occasional
fallen tree would cause a momentary check, whilst now
and then some stately forest king would temporarily
obscure the moon, rendering the next few paces doubly
dark. It was " jumpy " work indeed. Was that rustling
noise some hostile scout, or only the night wind sighing

in the branches overhead and rocking the rank vegetation ? At last we came in sight of the great cotton tree
at the final bend. There we halted and crouched down
for an instant, whilst the two leading companies formed
into fours and closed up. Now F Company was ready.
The stick was passed up to Captain Loch—the prearranged signal for the silent charge, which was to be
carried through without cheer or bugle. The plan was
that we were to extend on the broadest possible front
along the dim barricade, which lowered across our path
just round the turn of the track, sullenly blocking our
way. Then we were to swarm over it, and dash into
the rebels with a yell of triumph. How faint was the
light under the pall of overhanging leaves ! What
fantastic shadows the struggling moonbeams made as
they forced their way through on to the path beneath !
What an impressive sight those silent kneeling soldiers
were, with never a sound to betray their presence to
the sleeping foe, not a stone's throw distant. The glint
of some white man's naked sabre or the gleam of
a bayonet—that was all. But the time for the advance
had come.

Ah ! at last something had roused the drowsy
sentries. Bang ! bang ! went the two signal guns, the
echoes ringing again and again through that hushed
fastness of the forest. We involuntarily started at this
sudden outrage on the stillness of the slumbering
night. In the twinkling of an eye, the black timbers
were lit up with a lurid flare of flame ; then a rolling
cloud of smoke obscured the vista down the wooded
glade, followed by the dull crashing boom of a heavy
volley which woke the camp behind and let loose a
whirlwind of slugs and leaves into our stationary troops.
Lieutenant Greer, of the W.I.R., who, at his special

s

request, was in front of the leading four on his Captain's right, fell riddled with lead from that cruel fusillade : and yet, lying in a pool of his own life's blood, faint and hardly conscious, the gallant subaltern's only thought was of his duty, as he feebly waved his sword towards the foe, murmuring, "Charge!" He was right—it was useless to continue our noiseless approach. Stern duty forbade us even to pick up our wounded comrade; he had to be left where he had fallen so bravely, until picked up by the hospital. The moment was critical in the extreme. The shock of the sight of their fallen officer had momentarily staggered his men, and a backward tremor was perceptible up the column, like the receding wash of the tide : but it was only to culminate in the crest of a mighty wave, which, surging on with irresistible force, was to carry all before it and burst with the violence of revenge over every obstacle. With a savage shout of rage came the word "Charge!" which was repeated in the same breath by all the Europeans near. The former stealthy creeping gave place to an impulsive rush that brooked no opposition ; shimmering swords waved forward bristling bayonets, and the flood of fury was launched indeed. Plans to perdition! The Hausas would not be restrained, and the mingled mass pressed on, led by white men. The stockade was scaled, no one knew how ; it seemed as if cleared with a stride by that stampede. What a sight awaited one! There, through the war camp's centre, ran a road, inundated with terror-stricken demons, as they fled in panic from their huts, struggling to force a passage down that living lane. Swords and bayonets could not be pulled out quick enough to be plunged afresh into another body. Compensation for a comrade's death was indeed being exacted, and there stood an officer in the path alone, his arm so tired that his sword was lowered a moment whilst he emptied his revolver into the human whirlpool around him. The air was rent with shouts and groans ; the earth was strewn with corpses and reeking with blood. The headlong race continued to right and left, and down the road. Would this camp never end ?   Already we had passed through three, and yet there was a fourth beyond. Exhaustion forced a halt at last ; by then the enemy had disappeared in such mad disorganisation that there was little fear that they would rally. The only danger was the possibility of a counter-attack from the adjacent Ashantis on our left. We did not then know that so complete had been the panic, that they too had fled in disorder, never to return.

So we halted our men and turned about. Had the pursuit been continued, probably little more could have been accomplished ; and much yet remained to be done in the camps. We instinctively rubbed our eyes to recall our senses. Had we really gone to bed after all ?   Was it some hideous nightmare, or had we dreamt that we had been in hell awhile ?   No, it was no rude awakening ; it was bloody war in all its strange stern reality. Was it glorious, or was it repulsive ?   Perhaps a little of both, one thought, as one looked first into the exulting face of some soldier, intoxicated with victory, and then at some corpse, weltering in its gore.

A cordon of soldiers was then, as usual, thrown out round the furthermost camp, and after we had carefully counted our various commands to see that nobody was missing, we set fire to it. It burned with wonderful brilliance and gave forth the intensest heat. Once the flames were unquenchably alight and greedily devouring everything around, to the accompaniment of an intermittent fusillade of exploding cartridges, we made our way to the next and treated it in a similar fashion, and so on, until the last and largest was reached, the one nearest to the now demolished stockade. Here a broad path ran to one flank, connecting it with the adjoining war camp—part of the system of investment ; and opposite to it was another, which we exploited, finding a big flanking stockade, with a small camp for the picquet.

In one of the houses, which was entered casually, we found a child asleep. It had been left behind, and had not been roused by the noise. The terrified little one, when awakened in that scene of destruction, clung to a white man for protection, forgetful of the fact that her guardian was supposed to be her bitter foe, and was finally conducted by him to a place of safety. Afterwards, a grateful, though unconscious return was made in the form of some valuable information.

The *bizarre* sights in the glare of that conflagration will ever live in one's memory. What targets we should have made, had the enemy returned to the comparative outer darkness of the forest and sniped at those who had so inconsiderately spoiled their night's repose ! The ashen face of the European in his helmet, the dark, stern Sikh in his turban, and the ebony blackness of the African soldier in his scarlet or black fez, made a striking combination, as they worked like a machine in the same cause and for the same Queen, under circumstances of excitement and apparent disorder. But had they not all been trained by the same methods, had they not all confidence in their officers, who were made of the same stuff all the world over—offspring of the one Empire whose greatness they have built up at divers times and in different climes?

Thus, in about an hour, their adversaries had destroyed what had taken the Ashantis weeks to construct. The killed and wounded, numerically few in comparison with the fights by daylight with these determined Kumasis, the flower of the rebel army, had already been removed to the fort and were being attended to. Thither we now followed them. After a short eulogistic speech from Lieutenant-Colonel Burroughs, every one returned to quarters just before 11 p.m., to rest before marching out at 8 a.m. on the morrow. For the work accomplished, and for the moral effect upon the foe, the night's venture had been successful beyond all hopes, but we were filled with a feeling of regret at the loss of a gallant comrade. Lieutenant Greer was buried by his company the next morning near the north-west bastion of the fort, in the presence of all the white men left in garrison, but not till after our force had marched out, so that full military honours could be accorded to him without any fear that the volleys fired over his grave should attract the rebels to the main road which we had followed.

So we went to bed at last with a sense of fatigue and depression; for was any stockade worth a white man's life?

CHAPTER XXV

A T the appointed hour on the 8th of August our column paraded, having, owing to our economy, enough ammunition to make it possible, if necessary, to force the passage of the Kumasi-Cape Coast road, upon which we expected heavy fighting. The last body of troops which had passed over it was that under Captain Aplin in April, since which time this road had been absolutely closed. Our column, though much reduced through various causes since it had entered Kumasi, was a more compact fighting unit, as it had comparatively little transport. All the wounded who were unfit for duty had been left in the fort, together with sufficient men to double the garrison. We did not then, of course, know the full effect of the previous night's work ; progress in consequence had to be slow, and no precaution could be neglected. Not long after the start, the scouts of the W.A.R., who were again reconnoitring, sighted the big stockade at Karsi, where the Lagos contingent had had such a hot time ; but it turned out, to our surprise, to be deserted. So, in passing, we destroyed it, together with the usual adjacent war camp, without interference.

From that point onward we found that all the camps

were on the Kumasi side of the various entrenchments.
There was no doubt whatever from their appearance
that without exception they had been planned to repulse
any relief forces for the fort, which the enemy had
evidently surmised would be sure to choose the direct
main road, the state of which, however, was after all no
better than that of any of the others. We were certainly
disappointed to discover that we had to wade all the rivers
on this route, just in the same way as we had to do on
the less frequented approach through Pekki. Until we
got quite close to Esumeja, most of the villages had
either been burnt or were falling to pieces. We passed
many camps, ambuscades, and light stockades ; and all
the telegraph wires for the first few miles had been
removed ; but never a single Ashanti was seen. Only
once did the " point " open fire, and it proved only to be
upon a few natives carrying Dane guns, who immediately
fled and were not, I think, damaged. It is by no means
unlikely they were really friendly Denkeras, but they
were certainly not wearing their scarlet armlets ; and we
did not then know that any levies were in advance of
Esumeja. One of the barricades we destroyed was most
splendidly arranged, and was quite invisible to any one
coming up the path. It was a few yards from the
precipitous bank of a waist-deep river, over which was a
rude bridge of a couple of tree-trunks, which had
previously been partially cut through in such a way that,
when the first of our men set foot upon it, it collapsed
entirely. The opposite bank, consisting of some hundreds of yards of swamp, was enfiladed, so that, if the
leading men of any upward-bound party had crossed
the water and scaled the almost vertical bank on
the Kumasi side, they would have found themselves
quite unexpectedly at a range of some ten yards from

the enemy, whilst those in rear of them would have been crowded up in comparative confusion in the river and the bog, also under heavy fire.

However, to our astonishment, the first and the most dangerous day passed off safely, with only one incident of note. The scouts captured a young girl, who had hidden herself in the undergrowth to wait until we should have passed. She, too, was brought into Bekwai. Nevertheless, we learnt some useful intelligence from her, which made our progress more rapid. She had been sent out, like many other of the women, to get supplies for the army at Ejesu, where the Queen-mother was ; and it appeared that this august lady had been so much upset by the night attack, that she had collected all her warriors for a big war palaver, to decide upon what was best to be done now that the siege of Kumasi had been raised, and to discuss further what the white man would be up to next after his erratic and unexpected behaviour of the previous evening. Then for the first time we understood why our advance had been unopposed, and realised that, had it not been for this council, we should have found every place, including the villages, occupied in force to oppose our march.

We spent a wretched night with little or no shelter ; but before noon the next day reached Esumeja without any trouble. Here we breakfasted, and an advance despatch was sent in to headquarters. As a consequence, our hard fighting and the successful execution of our instructions ended in a procession into Bekwai, the entrance of which was lined with troops formed up to receive us. This method of showing approbation was only accorded on special occasions, as there was too much real work to be done to fatigue the men with merely ceremonial parades. We appreciated the honour, and

F (HAUSA) COMPANY, I BN. W.A.F.F. LEADING THE COLUMN INTO BEKWAI

cheered the Commandant in return, as warmly as we ourselves were greeted. Best of all, we each got in the evening a ration of fresh meat and another round of medical comforts. We then found that the wire had been put up as far as Bekwai, and that the main road through Kwisa was again being used by troops and convoys. Details of the Governor's flight had also been received during our absence, including some painful particulars of that disastrous retreat :—how Captains Marshall and Leggett had been mortally wounded and had subsequently died, and how much valuable *matériel* had had to be abandoned on the way. Then we understood for the first time how it was that we had found ·303 carbines in almost every position we had captured, and why so many had been used against us in our late encounters with the enemy. But, on the other hand, there was one piece of most gratifying news: Her Majesty had not forgotten us in her opening speech to Parliament. Perhaps the worst intelligence of all was that no Indian or Soudanese troops could be spared, which meant that we should have to go on as best we could with the war-worn African regiments we already had. Another weak half-battalion of the W.A.R., under the command of Captain Leveson, had arrived during our absence ; and shortly afterwards, on the 14th inst., the transport *Dwarka* from Berbera, landed ten British officers and four hundred and eighty-one men of the C.A.R., with some Sikh N.C.O.'s from Somaliland, the whole being under the command of Captain (local Lieutenant-Colonel) Brake, D.S.O., R.A. These completed the complement allowed to the Ashanti Field Force, and brought up the total strength of troops available for punitive columns to one thousand eight hundred.

The same day upon which this last reinforcement arrived in the colony a column left for the Sacred Lake, under the command of Major (local Lieutenant-Colonel) Henstock, W.I.R., Chief Staff Officer, who had joined the Commandant just before headquarters had advanced into the hostile country; and on the following day another set out for the same destination under Lieutenant-Colonel Wilkinson. These forces, taking different routes, were to join hands in the neighbourhood of the sacred fetish lake called Bosomakwe, where large numbers of Ashantis and Kokofus were reported to have concentrated. It was known to be a particularly rich tract of country, productive of a large part of the supplies upon which the enemy depended, including abundance of fish. Furthermore, no troops had hitherto penetrated so far in that direction so as to clear it of insurgents. It was this trip which at last convinced every one that the idea of starving out the rebellion was almost impossible. In fact, all this disaffected land was one vast indestructible farm.

Lieutenant-Colonel Henstock's instructions were to proceed to Dompoasi, and there to strike into the bush and work his way, *viâ* Dadiasi, up to the Accra-Kumasi road, thus approaching the rendezvous from the south; whilst Lieutenant-Colonel Wilkinson, moving through Kokofu, was making for the same road further north and then marching down south. But this excellent plan of closing upon the enemy from both sides—a move which always entirely upset their calculations—did not come off, owing to the absence of roads, and to the useless men bearing the misnomer of "guides." The former column reached Dadiasi, whence it was compelled to retrace its steps, after having made fruitless efforts to carry out its orders. However, it made such rapid progress, that by forced marches it overtook the other column just in time, although it had been compelled to utilise practically the same line of advance which they had employed.

After five and four days respectively, without encountering any opposition, the lake was reached, after a journey through dense bush and over paths which were so overgrown in places as to be almost indistinguishable. Most of the villages had been destroyed *en route*, including Ahurai, where some gold-miners had been attacked at the outbreak of hostilities. Native rumours of hidden stockades again proved false, and once more discomfort and fatigue were unproductive of any reward. Howbeit, having ascended the highest hill on the western side of the lake, from which point it was first seen, the discovery was made that the whole neighbourhood was rich in farms and villages. Crackling Maxims, and blasting volleys, announced the arrival of our men to the hamlet beneath, which nestled at the foot of the slope near the foreshore; and the reply from a few trade guns showed that the enemy were at home. This exchange of courtesies was followed by a charge on our part; but they did not wait to receive their uninvited guests. The cool pluck and determination of one of the rebels caused great amusement, not unmixed with admiration. Sitting astride a floating log, he paddled himself within range of the unwelcome visitors and opened fire with his long gun; but, seeing his efforts were futile, he slowly turned round and retired in the same curious manner—a most absurd mixture of dignity and comedy.

Darkness prohibited further operations that day; so it was decided to bivouac in this filthy little fishing kraal, in which the Mendi soldiers had already started an exciting hog-hunt.

The lake was about eight miles long by some five in width, and made a lovely picture in the sunset, with its distant girdle of violet hills, topped with crimson and gold, and its immediate fringe of silver sand and verdant vegetation. The view itself was worth a tramp to reach it; and without doubt it was finer than anything else which greeted the tired eyes of the troops throughout this long, dreary campaign. But it was not only a feast to gaze upon; it was more practical and commonplace at the same time. The plashing, rippling waters were full of fish, as shown by the scores of pelicans fishing with greedy beaks. Needless to say, nobody had any tackle; but by dredging the water's edge with mosquito curtains, every one was enabled to obtain a change of diet. Unlike most West African fish, these, though brightly coloured and curiously shaped, were good eating.

The next day the two columns set out on a two days' reconnoitring excursion, in which they encountered no opposition, finally rejoining forces on the northern side, after passing through over thirty villages and thousands of acres of cultivation. This tour completed and the local "ju-ju" outraged beyond redemption, the return journey was commenced, and for some distance there was no sign of obstruction; but there seemed every prospect of a fight at Ejemum, on the main road, just north of Esumeja, where the enemy were reported to have built an entrenched war camp. When the combined columns reached Kokofu, they met Lieutenant-Colonel Brake, with his newly-arrived troops, and from his report the aforementioned rumour seemed a certainty. His force had been sent out from headquarters the previous day to assist the troops returning from the lake by covering their exposed flank, and to inform them of this fresh concentration of the rebels. When they had accomplished the matter in hand, they were ordered to proceed along a little known road where they would probably succeed in "getting a show," which was naturally enough their special wish. So Lieutenant-Colonels Henstock and Wilkinson, although having borne the heat and burden of ten days' marching and disappointment, were delighted to make this *détour* on their way back, and, buoyed up with fresh hope, started away forthwith. More stringent precautions than ever were taken, and five hours were occupied in marching the next four miles; but when the spot was reached, there were no enemy, no war camp, no stockade to be seen! Nothing but chagrin, drenching rain, without shelter awaited them. It was too late to do anything then; so the troops settled down in the open to rest, whilst the white men did their best to make themselves comfortable under inverted hammocks and stretchers supported by four sticks.

It was a disconsolate crew that marched into Bekwai next evening, the 24th; and it was not much comforted by the news brought in a few hours later from Lieutenant-Colonel Brake. The information was as follows :—That his body of troops, disappointed at having lost the opportunity at Ejemum, were none the less anxious not to return without doing something; so they had proceeded, in accordance with their orders, towards the town of Djarchi—situated between Kumasi and Kokofu to the east of the main road, and in the district which they had been sent out to clear—where an unsubstantiated report stated that the enemy might be. The road selected had never been much frequented; in fact, the enemy, it was afterwards learned, were unaware of the fact that the white man knew of its existence, and in consequence considered themselves in a place of safety, which accounted for their relaxed precautions. Lieutenant-Colonel Brake left Kokofu at the same time that the other columns departed for Ejemum, and at first found every place deserted; but on arrival at the village of Odum, about 1¼ miles from Djarchi, he suddenly came upon the rebels in force and completely surprised them. The leading company instantly charged and continued on its way until it got right into the big town beyond, despite erratic hostile fire from the bush which they did not reply to. We suffered only one slight casualty, whereas an appreciable number of the enemy were killed, the remainder fleeing in disorder to Ejesu, which was only five hours' march further on. Djarchi itself was not only crammed full of loot, but the enemy's line of retreat was also strewn with it. In order to collect this, the night was spent there, and the return of the jubilant troops postponed a day.

Midday of the 25th saw the arrival of the now delighted flying column of the C.A.R. They had razed Djarchi to the ground and ascertained that the enemy had been commanded by Chief Opoku, brother of the Ashanti Commander-in-Chief, who had been killed in the fight. They were loaded with spoil, which was the first valuable stuff we had so far obtained. This was piled up in the centre of the stockade at Bekwai, and made an imposing show. The king of Kokofu's private iron boxes, containing much official English correspondence, lay amongst Union Jacks, elephants' tails, and other emblems of royalty, together with gold ornaments, gold dust, and English money to the value of some £200. In addition there was also an amusing diary by an educated black man, numbers of brass-nailed, vellum-backed chairs, which are given to Ashanti chiefs as part of their regalia, robes, guns, ammunition, drums, horns, and the like, together with sheep and poultry.

Prisoners brought in by the troops and the levies were by this time becoming numerous, and much valuable information was got from them. One chief told us how one of the white miners had been done to death by the rebels ; and another that two hundred Ashantis had been killed in the final action on July 15th with the relief column. A third informed us that the night attack had accounted for a very long list of casualties amongst the enemy, who were Kumasis and for the most part belonged to the Queen-mother's personal army.

The return of these last three columns had sufficiently cleared the way so far up country, and now all was ready, from a tactical point of view, for a general and strategic move on the rebel capital. A company C.A.R. was first despatched to the Sacred Lake to support Major Cramer's levies, which had been told off, like locusts, to eat up that district and at the same time check any attempt on the part of the enemy to trek in that direction—a not improbable move upon their part, seeing that they would be hemmed in on all other sides, except the north, as soon as the Field Force began to advance. Lieutenant-Colonel Wilkinson, the Inspector-General, with his Acting-Adjutant, Captain Haslewood, were ordered down to Accra to reorganise and recruit the remnant of the Gold Coast force, which would be necessary before that body could again take over military control of the colony. It was also decided that inconvenient Bekwai should no longer remain a post, but that all the stores there should be removed to Esumeja, as the whole main road up to Kumasi would shortly be open to convoys. The method of transport also was to be changed ; and henceforth the carriers were to work upon the principle of meeting half-way between depôts, when, the loads having been handed over, each party would return to its own station.

CHAPTER XXVI

LIFE IN BEKWAI

WHEN one column came in from a convoy or fighting expedition another usually went out at once. The troops available were so few in number for the amount of work that had to be done, that it was compulsory to strain them to almost breaking-point. The art indeed was to know when was the proper time to release the tension. The natural consequence was, that one sometimes got a day or two's rest, but this term must not be taken to mean idleness. On the contrary, these were busy days, except for the cessation of the physical fatigue of marching.

One commonly woke a little later than usual, with the pleasant knowledge that there were no loads to be made up, no hustle to fall in the column, no orders involving immediate bustle. Languidly stretching and turning over, one's eye caught sight of a cup of cocoa, stone-cold, with some half-dozen dead flies floating in it. Black boys never think—they do their duties mechanically—at least when they have been sufficiently drummed into them. One is "called," and simultaneously the cocoa is put on a box beside one. The boy never thinks of waiting an instant to see if one is fully awake, and thereby saving himself the trouble of making a fresh brew later.

"Dan Leno!" (*piano*).

No reply.

"Dan Leno!" (*forte*).

Still no answer.

"Dan Leno!" (*fortissimo*).

"Sar!"

That was comforting; training has really had some effect after all! Only three attempts, and then success! It was indeed gratifying. It was enough to soften the hardest of hearts. At length he arrives.

"I want some more cocoa"—with the utmost gentleness.

"Look'um, Massa, he live."

"You never waited to wake me, you little owl; so go and get some more. It's cold."

"Me self no savvy Massa sleep"—and he retires with the cup to fetch another.

Shortly he comes into view, but he is deliberately sipping the fresh cocoa out of the spoon to see if it is good; and, what is worse, when he has had enough he wipes it on the leg of his trousers, one of which is tucked up, and the other let down to its full length, *à la mode du nègre!* Wrath takes the place of gentleness, but it has to be choked down. "Rushes of blood," as they are termed in West Africa, do not pay. Such undue emotions exhaust nervous energy for the day, and at the commencement of it, at any rate, are certainly an error of judgment. One must reserve oneself for sterner duties than upbraiding or assaulting niggers. Besides, to have given Dan Leno his deserts for this would only have meant his total disappearance till nightfall, and all his work would have had to be done with

T

one's own hands! So one gulps down one's indignation, warns him of what will happen to him next time, asks for a clean spoon, and makes the best of necessity. At last up one gets and crawls out of the leaky compartment assigned to each officer in a horrid native hut; and then a rapid toilet. This is usually interrupted, and often painful. When one happens to be minus a razor-strop, such a thing can't be bought at Bekwai for love or money, and most of those belonging to one's friends are either mildewed or useless, so that shaving is daily torture. However, half a beard is less contrary to the Queen's regulations than a whole one; so one endures the agony from a red-tape sense of duty.

It always fell to my lot to do the catering for my little mess and to attend to the household duties. As I have said before, I had no trained cook, and this additional work was by no means a sinecure. The other members had the usual indifferent health common in the climate, which I also shared; and I had had no training whatsoever in domestic economics. The result was that my management was not considered a success, and the popular members dined out whenever they got the chance. But in self-defence I maintained that bully beef could not be made palatable; nor was I in possession of any condiment whatsoever by which to deceive an epicure as to its presence, want of nutrition, and lack of flavour. Bricks cannot be made without straw, tradition asserts (although baked clay is, I believe, the usual modern process); but the simile is good enough to illustrate the impossibility of making savoury dishes out of Yankee canned meats. It would be easier to make a blind man think that one was hairy by the application of goat skins than to deceive any British officer into the belief that he was having a really luxurious dinner out of Government rations. However, we did very hard work on the results; and now it is all remembered as a gastronomic bad dream, when we sit round little tables with shaded lights, and play with *hors d'œuvres* and savouries, sip iced champagne, and interchange badinage with pretty women. Such are the extremes of a soldier's life, and we like them both in their proper place. Each is a change from the other; and, so long as neither lasts too long, we can not only tolerate them, but become complacently resigned to either or both. Have not world-renowned caterers found that peace manœuvres made too great demands on their ability? How much more difficult, then, must it have been for the inexperienced officer, with no London near and no facilities to aid him—to say nothing of the fact that he was engaged all the time in actual operations in the field against a savage foe, who, to add to the difficulties, had chosen Africa for his home.

The good officer, whether particularly humane by disposition or not, never worries his men on service; they have quite enough work to do without the non-sensical trivialities of barrack-life, in addition to their guards and other routine duties. Consequently, instructional parades were most unusual. But men require attention, and returns, among other things, must be attended to, so that the morning was usually filled with endless details—whilst one's boy seized the golden opportunity to wash one's clothes, which somehow seemed to take him the best part of the day and to use up an enormous amount of a very scanty stock of soap. Then the military commission sat occasionally for the trial of captured rebels, who, having usually been caught red-handed, generally found it difficult to disprove their guilt; and the result was sometimes the unpleasant spectacle of a public execution by hanging on an extemporised gallows near the market-place.

In order that life might not become too monotonous, there was always a Field Officer and Captain of the day. Amongst other responsibilities, they had to turn out the guards and visit the sentries, both by day and night. The performance of these latter duties ruined the junior's chances of a good night's rest, as he had to go his rounds first, between "Last Post," about 10 p.m. and midnight, and again between twelve o'clock and reveille, usually 5 a.m. The occasional arrival of home letters or papers relieved the tedium by their unexpectedness, but Reuter's much-appreciated Service somewhat took the edge off the excitement of the more or less stale news. To read in some journal a terrible account of the massacre of Embassies at Peking fell flat when we all knew long before that such had never occurred. In an eminently practical life, such as ours was at that time, it caused us a certain grim amusement to have tragedy thus converted into comedy every other mail.

Our occupations during the daytime were generally very much alike, consisting principally of sitting or reclining in the particular shed which constituted one's quarter and reading or resting. Some amusement, and trouble, too, was occasionally forthcoming—such as at the time when the king of Denkera reached Pekki. He hugely overestimated his own importance, and once positively refused to take orders from the officer in charge of his levies, stating that he would only consent to do so from the Commandant in person. The latter, however, "dressed him down" so decidedly that he never was insubordinate to any white man again! Not in the least anticipating the snub, his black Majesty had arrived at headquarters in great state. He was lying

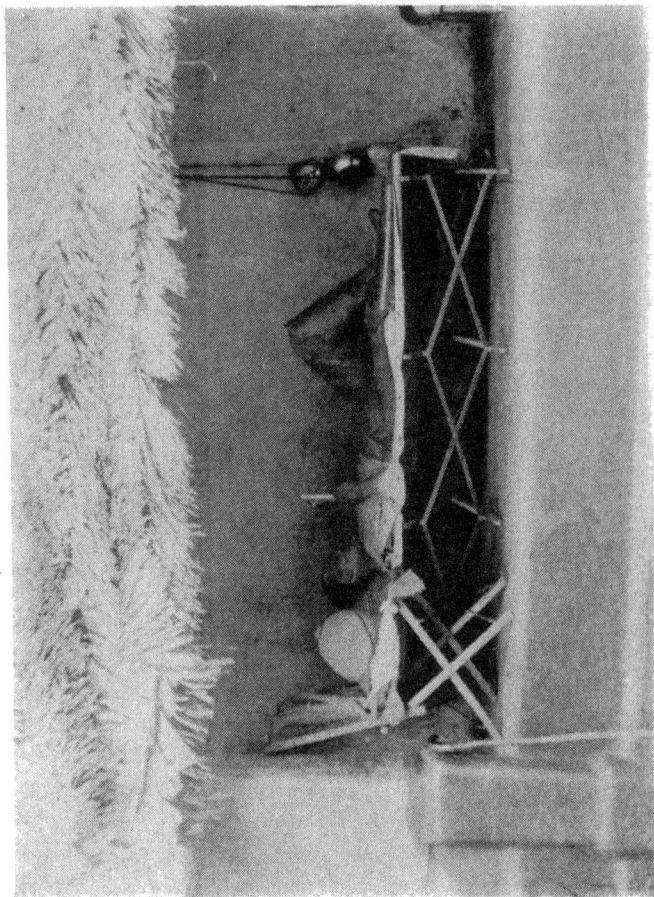

A LETTER FROM HOME

magnificently on a litter, chewing tobacco under the shade of a great umbrella. Musicians were beating drums adorned with human bones, and played on horns and carved elephants' tusks converted into flutes. Wives and " braves " completed the *cortège*, which they thought impressive ; but somehow with us it missed fire.

There were also pathetic passages in these dull days of waiting, such as the sale by auction of some deceased officer's kit. On these occasions everything, so badly needed then by all of us, was sold, with the exception of personal effects, such as private documents, jewellery, sword and the like, which were sent home, together with the amount realised by the sale of the other property. The prices paid would scarcely be credited by those who have never been similarly situated. Almost daily visits, too, were paid to the hospital, where white comrades lay sick or dying and black subordinates were stricken down by the many diseases rampant during this campaign. I shall never forget my own miserable time in the European hospital here. The building was walled with bamboos and roofed with leaves ; and necessity had moreover placed it in such close proximity to the main guard, that bugle calls and noise were almost incessant, both by day and night. Caterpillars, dirt and vermin fell constantly from the new roof on to the bed, which required eternal shifting during a downpour of rain, owing to the leakages above it. At other times the heat was very great ; and the flies by day and the mosquitoes by night made the conditions of sickness anything but inviting. Even the frequent visits of kind friends taxed one's strength. Therefore, it is not difficult to believe that removal into hospital was avoided by every possible device, most of us preferring to suffer quietly in our quarters. The melancholy part of it all was that nobody knew who would be the next victim. One of the saddest cases in the war was that of Lieutenant Payne of the Gold Coast Constabulary. He only reached headquarters on August 22nd, having just arrived in West Africa for the first time. He had formerly served in the Malay States, and I remember how he at first maintained that this climate was not much worse than where he had been, and that the pay and leave amply compensated for any difference there might be. We always dreaded to hear such remarks ; they were, of course, the fruit of inexperience and often sounded like the words of fate. This officer contracted fever during his upward journey, and three days after his arrival he was dead. He was laid to rest in a grave next to Lieutenant Brounlie's with full military honours in the presence of the Commandant and all the white men—another entry on the long roll of gallant soldiers whose names have swelled the host of victims in this pitiless part of Her Majesty's dominions, the last portion of the globe which may be said to be still incompletely explored and partitioned up.

At sundown there was usually a congregation of the white men outside the Staff office, from which orders were issued and where Reuter's telegrams were posted. Here we met to hear the news of all kinds, which usually led to an adjournment to somebody's quarters for refreshment. The commonest beverage was a "doctor" —Swiss milk, filtered water, and Government rum, all "swizzled" up together with a three-pronged stick. More ambitious people called their other concoctions "cocktails," but, as most of the ingredients required to make these American inventions palatable were absent, they were not successes. Wiser persons simply took a whisky-and-soda, the latter made with a sparklet.

The term " soda " never caused any disappointment or misunderstanding, as never a bottle of this aerated water, to my knowledge, left the coast during this campaign. A long drink, rather than a strong one, is what the tropical sunset mostly suggests, as it is more refreshing and more needed, after the hours one has endured with a parched throat and with one's tongue cleaving to the roof of one's mouth.   Conversation at these times was very much *sui generis*—principally " shop."

Dinner, for convenience, was usually undertaken in twos and threes.   Sometimes, however, one was tempted to invite guests. Such hospitalities had to be exceptional, because, as it was, one's rations were barely sufficient for oneself. The evening commonly selected for such enter-tainments was one on which there was a free issue of meat, and, better still, one on which medical comforts were also provided. On such occasions, the host drew not only his own, but also his guests' meat and drink, and served it up to them later, much to his black cook's disapproval at the increase in his work.   Those invited had to bring their own chairs, knives, forks, and spoons, so that about all they got was the pleasure of fresh society, with possibly some trifling little luxury which had been sent up from the coast.   The Base Transport Officer was a man to be on good terms with at that time ! The red-letter days were those when one was included in a Commandant's dinner party, as he always dispensed hospitality most generously.   At such times everything was provided, except that occasionally one had to bring the wherewithal to eat with and drink out of.   The fare always included items which were parti-cularly appreciated from their rarity, such as bread, a bush turkey, and a pudding.   Change is everything, and this is one reason why these were more enjoyed by us than any out-of-season delicacies which can be obtained in London at the haunts of wealthy *bon vivants*. There was no electric light, no flowers, and no music ; but they were not missed, any more than the white starched shirt or swallow-tailed coat.

There was, however, one form of duty which was never popular but always a weary grind—being detailed as escort to a convoy. Going down country with un-ladened carriers was not so bad, but the coming up was a trial. The usual stages of the Cape Coast-Kumasi marches had to be done each day. Alone, with a hammock and one's own dozen carriers, they were fairly easy distances ; but with a column of two thousand it was inexpressibly tiring work to already fatigued white men, when, even though occasionally there might chance to be one hammock between several Europeans, it was next to impossible to make any use of it. The whipping-in rear guard was, without comparison, the most arduous post of any. There was nothing to interest one, except to see what new buildings had been erected at the various depôts, and how the repairs to the road had progressed, until Prahsu was reached—the furthermost point at which any luxuries could be obtained and the termination of one's journey. One would notice such things as that the irregular company of pioneers had made a short cut from Bekwai to Essiankwanta : that the roofs of the huts at Dompoasi had been thoughtfully removed, to cover shelters for the troops at Kwisa : that the levies had, without orders, burnt most of the villages on the lines of communication, which might have been utilised for short halts : that the Monsi hill remained as formidable as ever, and the swamp between Sherabroso and Sheramasi got steadily worse from the constant traffic through it : and really one's interest in these matters was quite disproportionate to their importance! In fact, there was little worthy of note, except the excellent bridge which the Public Works official had constructed at Fumsu. This clearly shows, without further detail or comment, that this part of active service *régime* was as unproductive of incident and excitement as the time of rest at headquarters. It was, therefore, a pleasure when the move to Kumasi was announced, which possibly meant more fighting and certainly less of these two last-named forms of diversion. So one gladly said, though perhaps a little unappreciatively, farewell to muddy Bekwai, where some had lived and laughed, and others bled and died—the place which had helped to support the "white man's burden," and seen the black man suffer. But it was goodbye for ever ; our departure was for that shameful charnel-house, the ill-famed capital, Kumasi.

CONCLUSION

REMOVAL OF HEADQUARTERS TO KUMASI AND
FINAL OPERATIONS

LARGE quantities of stores, and shells innumerable for the 75-m/m guns, having been collected at Bekwai in anticipation of the general and final advance, all the Adansi country to the south, and Kokofu to the east, having been conquered and traversed so satisfactorily that the lines of communication up to the furthermost depôt were safe, and no particular grounds existing for anxiety as to the clearing out of the enemy between the southern boundary of the Ashanti territories and their capital, it was decided to move the whole of the Headquarters Staff and the advanced base to Kumasi, the subsidiary point between it and Kwisa being placed at Esumeja.

It was indeed a big undertaking, but at this stage of the campaign imperative, inasmuch as Bekwai was no longer a suitable or desirable centre from which to operate. It was necessary, therefore, to get men, guns, and stores into the heart of Ashanti proper, and punish that country in a similar manner to that in which the domains of their insurgent allies had been treated. It would then be possible to penetrate in a northern direction, until all had been subdued as far as the peaceful Northern Territories, with which once more communication would be opened up. There were yet posts in those regions, and by now they must be, without doubt, in need of supplies. The general plan was to send all the stores, carriers, and troops *viâ* Pekki, as had been done on both previous occasions, which would reduce the chance of attack and loss to a minimum and simultaneously for a fighting column, hampered with the smallest possible transport, to proceed by the road through Kokofu, eastward of the main road, to attack and take Ejesu. The two flanks cleared, it was rightly surmised that the main road would be finally open ; as was afterwards found to be correct. Lieutenant-Colonel Brake, the latest arrival, had not hitherto had much chance of any fighting, with its consequent opportunities. He was, therefore, to command the column, which would probably meet with resistance. Ejesu was the most important fetish town in Ashanti. It was practically, since the white man had put himself so much *en évidence* at Kumasi, the capital ; and it was the residence of the Queen-mother, Ya Ashantiwah, and headquarters of the remnant of the rebel army. A fight here, and a good one, was considered a certainty, and general opinion concurred that it would be the last one of the war. The spirit of resistance was fast dying out, and another decisive defeat was expected to finally crush it, consequently there was considerable anxiety displayed by every one to go by this road ; and when the orders concerning these details came out, there was much heart-burning, and—as far as was consistent with discipline—a little quiet grumbling. The cruel irony of fate again asserted itself on this occasion, and I well remember Lieutenant Burton's exultation, when he announced the fact that he had been taken off the transport and attached to Lieutenant-Colonel Brake's column. Lieutenant Burton was, I think, the junior officer of the Ashanti Field Force. He had had no previous experience whatsoever, and at that time had only a few weeks' militia service. This last year has been a record one for young officers, many of whom, in South Africa, Ashanti, and China, have earned a medal almost immediately after they joined their regiments. Lieutenant Burton's military career, however, was destined to be short, though far from ignoble, for, four days later, this gallant young officer fell, shot through the heart, at the head of his men, in his first and last charge.

With the exception of the troops on the lines of communication at Esumeja and Kwisa, Fumsu and Prahsu being garrisoned by some of the late inmates of the besieged fort who were rapidly becoming fit again, and those already at Kumasi, the whole of the force was to advance, and five thousand carriers were required to effect this movement. The news was very welcome to every one; there was not a soul who was not heartily sick of dull, dirty Bekwai, where an epidemic of small-pox was so rife that a dozen or more victims were being buried daily. The longing to get a change from the dense dark forest to the cleared surroundings of the cantonments at Kumasi was very strong in us all; and the remembrance of the superior quarters there was particularly refreshing after weeks of evil-smelling, incommodious native huts, which were undoubtedly responsible for the sore throats and debilitated condition of the Europeans.

On the 28th of August, Lieutenant-Colonel Burroughs left for Pekki, which was temporarily to be used as a half-way depôt, with a column of seven hundred and fifty men, and some three thousand loads of rice ammunition, and baggage. He reached his destination the same night, after another day of intense fatigue, which in this climate seems inseparable from a long train of stores and soldiers; and this one extended well over three miles. The hard-worked carriers were to return to Bekwai on the 29th, so as to be ready to march out again at dawn on the 30th, with the second column, under the Commandant in person.

On this day, whilst the carriers were thus employed, and the troops at Pekki, in consequence, compelled to halt, Major Montanaro took half of them out to attack the enemy's war camp at Ampiebamie, which from its close proximity had threatened Pekki so long, and completely checked the ardour for looting of the Denkera levies. However, the place was found to be evacuated, and the burning of it, and the bush camps on the way, was all the satisfaction got out of this trip. For those left at Bekwai, it was a quiet day, and the opportunity was taken by the Commandant to again inspect the W.A.F.F. The Provost-Marshal had to see the station cleaned up, in addition to his other unpleasant duties. There was no doubt that the second rains were well started. We never had a fine day, and the roads kept getting worse than ever.

The 29th saw the departure eastwards of Lieutenant-Colonel Brake's fighting and punitive column, of three hundred and fifty men 2nd Bn. C.A.R., three hundred and fifty 2nd Bn. W.A.F.F., one hundred W.A.R., and forty S.L.F.P., with two guns, and the smallest encumbrance possible in the way of carriers. Two very pregnant facts also became known that day: first, that some of the Kokofus had asked the king of Akim to intercede for peace on their behalf, and, also the first Ashanti flag of truce came in from the Djarchi district, which had so lately been surprised. The bearer, although he looked a mountebank, was quite genuine. ,He was completely clad in white, even his skin being painted that colour, and carried an enormous white flag. He was graciously received, but sent back with the very necessary information that chiefs must come in themselves, slaves not being accepted as intermediaries.

On the 30th, Colonel Sir James Willcocks, with even a larger column than Lieutenant-Colonel Burroughs, set out for and reached Pekki, from whence to Kumasi the combined forces would move in fighting formation, all loads that could not be transported being left behind with a small garrison. The Commandant and his enormous column arrived at Kumasi at 6 p.m. on the 31st, having left Pekki at 6 a.m. The distance traversed was not twelve miles, and the terrible condition of the roads can be easily imagined from this fact alone. The following morning, the troops were sent out to demolish any remaining stockades, none of which, it was found, were held any longer by the enemy. It was discovered, however, that they were much more numerous than was ever supposed, forming a continuous cordon round the perimeter of the clearing in which the fort, outlying buildings, missions, and friendly villages stood. These entrenchments were built in the bush and out of sight, in addition to those barricading all the roads and tracks. The enormous amount of labour this network of fortifications must have involved testifies to the determination of the rebels to take the fort.

Excellent news now came in from Lieutenant-Colonel Brake. Ejesu, some ten miles to the east of Kumasi, had been found to be held by the enemy, and stockaded, though less substantially so than some of those formerly encountered. The column had taken over two days to reach this town. The first night was spent in a bush encampment in heavy rain, and the second was passed at Osoasi. At 10 a.m. on the third day the scouts sighted the breastwork across the path. It was found to have the usual flanking portions, extending for some fifty yards into the undergrowth on either side. The milli-mètre guns had done great execution in demolishing the obstacle, thanks to Major Montanaro's discoveries from recent experiments; and this was the first time in the campaign that they had actually breached a stockade. Captain Gordon's company C.A.R. was sent into the bush on the left to turn the position, and Captain Greer's com-pany W.A.F.F. executed a similar manœuvre to the right, whilst yet another company W.A.F.F. made a frontal charge through the breach, by which time the turning movement had sufficiently developed to enable both of these other companies to join in the rush with the bayonet, away into the town and after the retreating enemy. The rebels were estimated at three thousand five hundred, and about two thousand of them were picked men of the Queen's bodyguard. Their losses were re-ported to have been heavy, and several chiefs were found among the slain. That evening, September the 1st, Lieutenant-Colonel Brake heard the good news that in his surprise of Djarchi of the previous week an important Ashanti general, brother of the Commander-in-Chief, had fallen in the action at that place. Much loot was found in the town, although it was apparent that much had been removed according to custom, and secreted in the fast-nesses of the forest, where it could not be traced. Many Lee-Metfords, Martinis, Sniders, and Dane guns were taken, together with a quantity of ammunition. The enemy fled to Ofinsu, about fifteen miles north of Kumasi. Our casualty roll was again heavy, particularly so, considering the fight had only been in progress one hour. One British officer killed, Lieutenant-Colonel Brake and one British N.C.O. slightly wounded, and of the rank and file, one was killed, three dangerously wounded, seventeen severely, and nine slightly. That same evening Major Montanaro massed all the guns at Kumasi, and had an extreme range bombardment in the direction in which the enemy were, but the effect of the firing was never known.

The next few days were spent in completing the destruction of the enemy's stockades, while reconnaissances in force were made along the Kintampo, Bantama, and Ekwanta roads. It was then fairly certain that all the insurgents who might possibly offer further resistance were to the northward of headquarters, but the general opinion was that the fighting was over, and that those who had escaped intended to hide themselves in preference to running any risk of capital punishment if they gave themselves up. Numerous flags of truce kept coming in, and many chiefs surrendered. In fact, Queen Ya Ashantiwah, the most important rebel leader who had, beyond comparison, the biggest following, sent envoys tendering her submission, which she stated was due to want of food and internal dissension in her war camp. The Commandant gave her four days in which to prove the truth of her message by coming in person. This period was regarded by him as an armistice, during which we made no aggressive movements. However, late on the 18th, shortly before the limit of time expired, instead of the Queen, there came an insolent reply that she would fight to the end.

Colonel Sir James Willcocks was determined to crush this rising once for all, and punish the ringleaders in particular. It was obviously unfair that the Ashantis, who were the instigators of the rebellion, should not have their country overrun, when this had been done to the territories of their allies. A gallows was constructed, but until it was ready a few executions were carried out by firing parties, at a few yards' distance from the trees to which the criminals were tied. On September 6th information was received of probable trouble on the western boundary, whither numbers of the enemy were reported to have fled for safety. A party of one hundred Hausas from the base was ordered to proceed thither to deal with the emergency, either by blocking their way of escape or preventing any attempt at concentration.

The surrendered chieftains, who were kept under a guard, all told the same story, which was, that they had had, for the first time, a fair try at regaining their independence, but that they had been beaten by the white man ; and that the patrolling columns which were incessantly at work, had taught them the lesson of their inferiority in the way of all others most distasteful to the native, and that it would ever be remembered.

The greatest tragedy of this expedition became known on September 8th, through a letter from a native clerk who was with the Akim levies, which had been raised and commanded by Captains Wilcox and Benson. These levies had worked up our right flank of advance from the south, in the same manner as the Denkeras had done on the west. The Akims were as cowardly, and as terrified of the brave Ashantis, as all the other neighbouring races ; in fact, the only work that these people were fit for seemed to be to follow in the track of suc-

U

cessful troops, living in deserted villages, or cutting crops and eating up the produce. Three thousand Akim levies had been ordered to co-operate with Lieutenant-Colonel Brake's column, by blocking the north-east and easterly roads, along which the enemy might retreat from Ejesu. These instructions were delayed, and they attacked this fetish town on the 29th, prior to the arrival of the troops. The levies fled to Odumasi as soon as the Ashantis opened fire upon them; and Captain Benson fell, deserted by his cowardly followers. It is a pathetic fact, that in a letter he sent home on July 31st, shortly before his death, he had expressed in no measured terms his poor opinion of the men under his command, and had stated that if he were ever required to take them into action he would do so without confidence and with the supremest misgiving. To quote his own words: "If it comes to a real show after all, Heaven help us! Three-quarters of my protective army are arrant cowards, and all undisciplined, and quite impossible to hold."

The general misunderstanding, which has been widely disseminated to the public by some daily papers, as to what native levies really are, is too serious a blunder to remain uncontroverted. They have absolutely nothing to do with, nor must they be confounded with, the regiments which constitute H.M.'s West African troops, who are soldiers, as in India, with British officers, modern weapons, uniforms, and the like. A native levy is *toute autre chose*. It is a motley mob of undisciplined, semi-naked scallywags, who are armed with trade guns, slugs, and powder. Their pay is what they loot, the kings who supply them usually hoping to eventually get a grant of land in return for their loyalty and services. A native soldier would consider himself insulted if he thought that such a comparison or mistake could be made for a moment between himself and these irregulars. The African private's training, drill, and duties are identical with those of the British Tommy ; his orders are given him in English, and his knowledge of our language is probably superior to that of most Indian or Egyptian soldiers, in support of which, I may say that the British officers in West Africa are rarely able to speak the language of their men, which they generally do in the two other armies to which I have just referred. Interpreters are only, as a rule, necessary for unusual occurrences, such as prolonged investigations and the like.

Immediately the news of Captains Benson's and Wilcox's disaster reached headquarters, a column of three hundred and fifty men, with one 75-m/m gun, under Captain Reeve, Leinster Regiment, a Special Service Officer, set out to Captain Wilcox's assistance, and was away ten days. Their destination was Odumasi, proceeding from Bompata and Abetifi, and returning by Agogo and Juabin. This force marched fifty miles, but was unable to come up with Captain Wilcox, as he had retired fifty miles further to the east. They had no fighting, the enemy having gone north. The only Ashantis they encountered displayed white flags, but they ascertained the fact that all the country east and south of the Kumasi-Mampon road was free from rebels, and desirous of peace. The spot where Captain Benson's action had been fought was strewn with headless bodies, baggage, ammunition boxes, rifles, and such like, clear evidence of the disordered flight, and the chaos which must have reigned amongst the levies. We learned that this deplorable encounter had commenced about 11 a.m., and that the levies imme-

diately bolted.   Then, with a few trained volunteers,
the white men hastily entrenched themselves, and held
out until the late afternoon; when, their ammunition
having run short, they were compelled to retire.
Captain Benson's remains were given Christian burial
by the Basel missionaries. About a fortnight later,
owing to information received from a captured chief,
Captain Jones, W.A.R., with his company, was sent out,
and found the lost specie, which had been hidden near
Adedientem. £1,500 was thus recovered.   September
10th brought better news; the telegraph had been
opened the previous day to the coast, and the whole
main road, from thence to Kumasi, became a safe line
of communication.   Over eight thousand more levies
had offered their services, and this had a cheerful ring
about it, suggesting an early finish and return home for
us.   It would be difficult, and after all, rather un-
interesting to most readers, if any attempt were made
to give the names of the various rebel chieftains who at
this period surrendered unconditionally; however, the
chief of Kumasi, Kwaku Dumfi (chief fetish man to
Prempeh), and the chief of Antoa, Kwaku Mensa (who
commanded the advance guard), came in.   They would
have been dangerous people had they remained at large.
King Inkanza of Adansi, who broke his treaty with
Captain Hall in the early part of the campaign, also
offered his surrender, but was told that he must do so
unconditionally.

Another column, under the command of Major
Melliss, then came in, after a five days' reconnaissance
in the west and south-west districts, it having gone by
the same road the Governor and besieged garrison had
chosen, when they broke out on the 23rd of June.   The
enemy had likewise deserted these parts, and the only

punitive work which had been done was destroying sources of food by cutting the crops, a measure common to many operations of this kind. Proceeding along the Ekwanta road, without any attempt to search the adjoining bush, ninety-eight headless skeletons had been counted, a painful testimony to the number of soldiers and sutlers who had succumbed to starvation, hardship, and the enemy's slugs during that retreat.

The day before, Captain Donald Stewart, the British Resident in Kumasi, who had been on leave in England, arrived in the Gold Coast. His services were badly needed, owing to his unique knowledge of the Ashantis and their country. To him was handed over, on his arrival, the political work, particularly later on the arrangement of the terms and conditions of peace, regarding which he was supposed to have had special instructions from the Secretary of State for the Colonies. He duly reached headquarters on the 20th.

All optimistic hopes that the struggle was over, and that a retrograde move southwards would soon be permitted for many, were now dissipated. Information came in that to the north the most reckless spirits had again concentrated, and intended to make another stand for their independence. Steps to counteract this movement had at once to be taken. Owing to some Denkera levies having been fired into whilst scouting on the Ejesu road, Lieutenant-Colonel Burroughs was sent out in that direction with two 75-m/m guns, one 7-pr., three companies W.A.R., and one company C.A.R., and followed by five hundred Akim and five hundred Denkera levies. On the 16th there was a big review of the seventeen hundred troops and nine guns in the garrison. Major Montanaro again experimented with the millimètre gun upon a stockade, similar in every detail to those constructed by the enemy. Some misunderstanding of this powerful modern weapon had existed, and its execution had hitherto been rather disappointing. It was then discovered, however, that with the very large 18-lb. double common shell, and its proportionately large bursting charge, the range had to be estimated at double its real distance. This was particularly important, as in this forest two hundred yards was, as a rule, the longest possible. The sixth shot completely smashed the 6 feet high by 6 feet thick barricade, which had been built as solidly as possible with tree trunks, rammed earth, and stones. The imprisoned chiefs, who were invited to the performance, were profoundly impressed and astonished. The way in which information is obtained by the natives is really marvellous, and there is little doubt that this feat was, in due course, reported to the enemy in the field ; for never again had a stockade to be taken, and the hostile tactics were completely altered to their old ones of bush fighting, behind only natural cover.

A flying column of five hundred rank and file left headquarters on the 20th, under the command of (now local) Major Holford, so as to reopen the road to Kintampo, which meant a march of over a hundred miles to the north, and enabled that post to be once more placed in telegraphic communication, which had been interrupted south of Nkoranza. Its destination was safely reached on October 1st, and a hundred men were left behind to reinforce the place. A goodly number of burnt villages were found, which were perhaps the handiwork of Major Morris' column ; and as they had done this work, there was not much shelter to be got. They had no fighting, but some more surrenders were made. It was during this outing that a hitherto unknown sickness broke out among the

Europeans, somewhat resembling mumps. It was put down to the damp; and certainly the amount of water, both above and below, was then as plentiful as it had been in the first rains.

The day after Major Holford's column had left, another one, double its strength, set out, under Major Montanaro. This large body of men, with guns, rationed for twenty-eight days, was to penetrate into the north-western country, where, if any more fighting was to come, it might be expected. In fact, opposition was considered certain, inasmuch as the enemy had sent in an impudent message that they would not only not surrender, but that if troops came in that direction, they would be attacked. The rebels were also at the same time kind enough to state that they intended, in future, to fight on their original lines, and that their particular efforts would be directed to picking off the white officers, after which they did not expect to have much trouble in disposing of the native troops. On the 22nd, some five miles south of Ofesu, and twenty-five from Kumasi, the enemy were found in force, and, true enough, they had returned to their old "enveloping" tactics, and had no stockades. The hostile army was commanded by the turbulent and determined chief Kofia. This discovery had, however, been expected, as at 3 p.m. on the day before, after a distance of only nine miles had been covered, a number of Ashantis, who had at once retired when rushed, had been found in a village, and the Akim levies had later on succeeded in locating the hostile point of concentration, some five miles further on from thence. The S.L.F.P., scouting as carefully as ever, found the rebels, at about 9.30 a.m., near Danasi. This was one of the few times when the enemy were heard before they were aware of our approach, and when they were in a position awaiting us. They were completely surprised, and many were killed by the sudden fusillade of Maxims and rifles, which we had been able to get leisurely into position before we thought fit to disclose our presence.

The enemy were holding a strong position round a hill-top, and the jungle was as dense as ever. The hostile force, estimated at four thousand, then attacked our front and flanks, rushing up and firing, luckily high, at the shortest ranges. After some fifty minutes of this bombardment, to submit to which we had long ere this found to be a great mistake, Major Montanaro gave orders for a general forward move. F Company 1st Bn. W.A.F.F., and one company C.A.R. and the Sikhs, both again in the van, entered the bush on one flank, whilst on the other, Major Cobbe advanced in *échelon* with three companies W.A.F.F., and succeeded in forcing the enemy on to the path. They had scarcely been thus ousted, when they were fiercely charged by the W.A.F.F., under Major Melliss, who was again in command of the advance guard, and once more behaved with intrepid bravery, rushing well ahead of his men. Unfortunately he was again slightly wounded. It was then that Captain Stevenson, 1st Bn. W.A.F.F., who was close to Major Melliss, and cheering on his company, fell, shot through the chest. Such a sight is always unnerving to native troops, who depend so entirely upon their officers, and a momentary hesitation became apparent in their ranks. Then they dashed on, to avenge their loss, the flanking companies simultaneously emerging with a shout, and the whole rushing headlong up the hill. A charge once more did its work, and the enemy, many of whom were bayonetted, wavered for a moment, and then fled.

Thanks to the experience which had now been gained, our losses were not numerically large, whereas the enemy's were probably heavy ; many spots, particularly those in proximity to the village in rear of their position, were red with blood. But the death of any white man in this murderous pastime, which even in the open is ever a bloody game, made our casualties serious out of all proportion to their count. Captain Stevenson was a great loss to the Ashanti Field Force, and a sorrowful addition to the long list of casualties which his gallant regiment, the Manchester, suffered that year. It is a sad recollection to recall his delight when his company was chosen for this column instead of for the Kintampo one, where no fighting had been expected. It came about thus ; and, as it happened, the officer in command of the other rival company was Captain Wright, who was a brother officer of Captain Stevenson's, both in the Manchester Regiment and the W.A.F.F. The O.C., W.A.F.F., who of course had to detail the companies from these troops for both columns, was approached by the two of them, both asking to go with Major Montanaro. Both companies were Yorubas, and equally efficient, and there was no special reason why one should not go with the force any more than the other. Consequently, it was laughingly suggested that they should toss for it, and Captain Stevenson won ! In order to make certain that his body could not be subsequently dug up and decapitated by the enemy, Captain Stevenson was cremated.

After the fight, and a short halt for reorganisation, an advance was made to a village three miles beyond Ofesu, the intention being to attack again next morning. However, that evening a flag of truce, with an offer of surrender, came in ; and it was then learnt that the engagement had been fought with King Kofi Kofia, who had retired westwards. The envoy was sent back to inform the rebels that their offer would be accepted if made unconditionally, and between 5 and 6 p.m. the chief, a large number of prisoners, four hundred guns, and some sheep, arrived, with all of which the force subsequently returned to Kumasi. These prisoners gave information that Kofia was then holding Fufu, and would again give battle there.

After the arrival at the fort on the 26th, every one was shocked to hear that Dr. Langstaff had died. He was one of the most efficient and popular Medical Officers in the force, and I remember well, on my way out from England, a year and a half before, when he was in charge at Axim, that he was the first West African official who showed me that hospitality, which, in all these colonies, is so lavishly and generously extended to all comers.

Late on the 27th, some scouts who had been sent out brought in the alarming news that the rebel army had again concentrated, and was about four thousand strong, having been joined by a tribe called the Atchamas, who were very bitter enemies. The whole, under the command of King Kofia, were in a big war camp some twelve miles from Kumasi, along the Bantama-Berekum road. The last-named place, some one hundred and thirty miles to the north, was reported to be invested, and to have asked for help ; however, the piece of intelligence, just mentioned, made it impossible at the moment to send any troops to its assistance. The still turbulent Ashantis had heard, it appeared, of the proposed relief force for Berekum, and had gone where they were for the purpose of attacking it, knowing that such a force, encumbered as it would have been with a month's stores and baggage, would be very vulnerable. A column of twelve hundred strong, every available man in the garrison, with five guns, under the supreme command of the Commandant, was instantly formed, and moved out at 7 a.m. on the 29th, to give the enemy battle. In rear of the fighting portion of the force followed a supply column and the bulk of the carriers, and Captain Donald Stewart accompanied this expedition as political officer. Nobody was seen until the village of Adada was reached, nine miles from the capital. At this place there was a small Ashanti outpost, which forthwith retired. Here the Commandant halted for the night; and it was a wretched one indeed. The huts had been burnt by the rebels, so that again the troops had to sleep in the open, in a steady downpour of rain, while the Europeans essayed in vain to get a little rest, and keep dry, in some hastily constructed shelters roofed with banana leaves, which seemed only to collect water for a minute or two, until the weight depressed them sufficiently to admit of a drenching stream pouring down upon one. To add to our misfortunes, tornados blew away the majority of these fragile constructions, which are at best a very insufficient protection against the elements. The next day, Sunday (it is a curious fact that most of the fights in this campaign have occurred on this particular day), in wet clothes, and steady rain, an early forward move was made. Between 7 and 8 a.m. the rain ceased, and matters looked just a trifle more cheerful; when, almost at the same moment, the well-known b-o-o-m! like thunder, broke forth from every side, and rent the chill morning air. Then began the battle of Abiassu, the final crushing defeat the brave Ashanti was to have, and one of the fiercest encounters ever fought in West

African warfare. The enemy's, and our own tactics in this action were similar to those at Danasi. The advance guard, under Major Montanaro, with Major Melliss in command of the support, was as usual the first to become engaged, and with such determination did the enemy cling to their successive positions, and so stubbornly did they contest every foot of the ground, that reinforcements had to be called up. Two companies, one C.A.R. and one W.A.R., operated in the bush to our right, and eventually succeeded in getting the enemy on a retrograde movement, which continued all up the hillside in rear of their position, on the top of which, for the first time, and nobody knows why, the Ashantis had cut away the undergrowth, and decided to make their last stand ; and this time it was to be the very last of all the many they had so pluckily made against us. This turning movement developed quickest, and the village in the central rear of the hostile position was gallantly taken with cold steel. From this point of vantage the retreating rebels, who had by then been turned out of the jungle on our left flank, by companies moving through it in an extended line, were enfiladed with a galling fire, from which they turned only to be met by our frontal attack, which took the final character of a charge, led by Major Melliss, and headed by the Sikhs.

It is with regret that it has to be recorded that this brilliant performance was very costly to the plucky Sikhs, whose deeds of bravery have adorned some of the brightest annals of Indian military history. Major Melliss, himself of the I.S.C., was shot so severely through the foot, that he was subsequently compelled to be invalided home. On this particular occasion, Major Melliss, seeing that the position was critical, and that the enemy were more determined than ever, charged into the thick of them with the few men whom he could collect around him. One Ashanti fired at, but, fortunately, missed him, when Major Melliss at once put his sword through him, and they both rolled over together (*vide London Gazette*, January 15, 1901). Another rebel shot him through the foot, paralysing the limb. At that moment he was practically unarmed, inasmuch as he could neither use his sword nor his revolver, and might have been killed, had not another officer opportunely arrived, and shot the wounded Ashanti with whom he was wrestling on the ground. From start to finish of this campaign, in which he has been wounded four times, and repeatedly mentioned in despatches, Major Melliss' continuous and conspicuous bravery has been a theme of eulogy amongst all ranks; and one cannot but feel proud to have served in such intimate relations with him as it has been my privilege to do. Scarce a charge has taken place in any action at which he was present which has not been led by him, and it is marvellous how he has not been killed times and again. On these occasions he was invariably far ahead of his men, often engaging the enemy single-handed before his less fleet-footed followers could catch him up. Some few days later, the whole garrison in Kumasi turned out to do him honour, when he was carried down to the coast in a hammock, escorted by the company he had so bravely and efficiently commanded in so many fights. F (Hausa) Company, 1st Bn. W.A.F.F. has seen much hard service in this campaign; and their splendid record is due to the fact that they were always under the command of so experienced and dashing an officer as Major Melliss.[1]

[1] I am delighted to record that Major Melliss has since been accorded that most highly prized reward that any soldier can obtain—the Victoria Cross.

A forest fight, such as all these in Ashanti were, is always difficult to describe, inasmuch as so little can be seen by any one individual, and the enemy is often quite invisible. It is not until all is over that a correct conclusion can be arrived at; and even then the enemy's losses can never be accurately ascertained, as, of course, one does not spend time hunting about for such discoveries. On this occasion, the number of Ashanti corpses seen lying about the battlefield was a hundred and fifty, whilst over four hundred of them had been wounded. This list is longer than that of any previous encounter to our knowledge. Many parts of the path and scrub were constantly called to notice by the blood shed in the recent fighting. In one of the worst of all these spots was found the lifeless body of an Ashanti, and alongside of him a dead Sikh, who had years before, in Asia, been decorated with the special medal for distinguished conduct in the field. The defeat was a crushing one, and the smouldering fires of rebellion were finally trampled out. The most determined remnant, the flower of the Ashanti army, fled in panic and wildest confusion in every direction, so hopelessly demoralised that they never rallied again, and leaving behind them on the field some of their most anti-British chieftains. Our casualties were two officers severely, and three slightly wounded, and twenty-six rank and file killed and wounded. The smallness of these casualties is to be attributed to the excellent tactics of the Commandant, who had long ere this appreciated the hostile *mode de guerre*, and the best way to circumvent it. So, in the two principal actions of the war, namely, this one and the fight to relieve Kumasi, in both of which Colonel Sir James Willcocks directed the operations in person, the comparatively small number of killed and wounded was out of all proportion to the severity of the fighting and the results achieved.

When the wounded had been hastily dressed, and the scattered units re-collected, an advance was made on Issansu, where the wearied troops slept. The completeness of the rout was then unknown, and it was thought possible that the rebels might again fight, either on the banks of the unfordable river Offin, four miles ahead, or at Fufu, somewhat further on. In order to make certain of this fact, eight hundred men under Major Cobbe were sent forward on the following day, with orders to disperse any fresh body of the rebels who might have collected to oppose us. He was to go as far as he could, but was given a free hand, the only stipulation being that he was to return by the next evening. Marches in this country have already been described so frequently, that this one may be passed over, with merely two remarks: that it was one of the most trying, and that the latter part of it resembled the terrible night before the relief column reached Pekki, on its way to raise the siege. The river was some forty yards wide; however, the pioneers, though they had no technical equipment whatsoever, succeeded in making a rough bridge by the late afternoon. It was dusk before the last man got across. Major Cobbe was exceedingly anxious to reach Fufu, the furthermost point he was expected to gain. He was aided in this decision by the apparently truthful report of an old woman, who stated that throughout the previous night and day terrified rebels had been rushing through that place, unable to do more than call out in awestruck gasps: "The white man is coming." But, as is the case with many women in other quarters of the globe, her ideas of time and distance were erratic and misleading, and the guides were as useless as ever. The result was that the column, shortly after starting, found itself in the dark in this unknown region. The progress was necessarily slow, and the condition of the road was so shocking, that some of the officers lost the soles of their boots in the sticky mud, and had to complete the journey in their socks. It was ten o'clock before their destination was gained, and to the relief of all, it was found deserted. So the troops marched in, to the music of another howling, groaning, hissing tornado, and at once turned in.

The return journey next day was no better, through the now churned-up mud, the track being in many parts between two and three feet deep in water. The temporary bridge over the Offin, though submerged, had fortunately not been carried away, and the men were just able to cross. The force, in consequence, fulfilled its orders.

This flying column having returned, the next morning the Commandant with all the troops marched back to Kumasi, the levies triumphantly carrying on poles various relics of the Ashantis killed in the recent action. The skulls of victims taken in war are most precious trophies to all the native races of this part of the Dark Continent, for not only are fetish rites practised over them, but they are used as ornaments, particularly for their drums.

On arriving again at headquarters, it was found imperative to give the worn-out troops a prolonged rest. The condition of the elements demanded, in any case, a brief respite if possible, as the roads and rivers were next to impassable. The W.A.F.F. had been amongst the earliest arrivals in Ashanti, where the climate had not at all agreed with them. They had been continuously on active service for nine months, having been engaged in their own country before they left it; and all these weary months had been the sickly rainy season. Most of the original officers of the Ashanti Field Force had completed their year's service in West Africa before this campaign had begun, and were sorely tried by this prolongation of hardship, exposure, and anxiety. Just as a river increases from its source to its mouth, so had the steadily swelling stream of invalids been going to the coast, as time went on and the war progressed. The daily sick list had now reached an appalling length, nor was it possible, even then, to give the men a full peace-time ration, and the lack of fresh meat was keenly felt. As a black soldier always goes bare-footed, the state of their feet by this time was deplorable in the extreme. The congregation of such unwonted numbers not only caused great discomfort and difficulty, but freely engendered various diseases. Smallpox was rife, and only temporary measures could be taken to cope with it. In consequence, this lull was most welcome to all. The very dulness of these quieter times was their chief attraction, and that they were unproductive of incident worthy of record was not then regretted.

The Commandant now considered the time had arrived when it was possible to issue a proclamation, promising henceforward to spare the lives of all rebels who surrendered. He accordingly did so, and it achieved the desired result after their recent severe handlings from us. Hitherto, fear had kept many of them from this course, despite the fact that the majority of them were heartily sick of the war.

A rumour was at this time in circulation, that a mining engineer had reported at Accra that, on September 27th, another European had seen the famous Golden Stool and Prempeh's regalia, escorted by armed Ashantis, at chief Achampong's, in the village of

x

Yokoko, but that it had again been spirited away. Possibly this may have been a fact, but, as nobody seems to know what this particular throne looks like, it was the general opinion that it would never be obtained, and the less said about it the better.

October 6th was quite a gala day for such monotonous times. The Commandant and British Resident held a state levée, or palaver, as the term is in West Africa. It was attended by all the friendly and submitted kings, most of the former having been in the fort with the garrison during the siege, and come up from the coast with Captain Donald Stewart. Savage splendour and the gorgeous vulgarity of the native vied with each other under huge swaying umbrellas, and dancing to deafening drums and horns. Neither innate perjury nor demonstrations of insincerity were wanting in the speeches made by these sons of Ham. Refreshments for the assembled company being impossible, a little side show was organised to relieve any boredom ; and it took the form of target practice with the guns. Maxims riddled canvas dummies, and the millimètres demolished great stockades, constructed for their entertainment. The result was eminently successful in its object of impressing the guests, who exhibited keen competition in their requests for empty cases, which were taken away as souvenirs of their pleasant visit. Nor did Colonel Sir James Willcocks forget his troops. A few days later he presented a cup, and planned a little diversion for them in the shape of a rifle meeting, at which he himself was one of the competitors.

It was at this time that the sad news arrived of Major Cramer's death on the 19th, at Prahsu, from fever, after a very short illness ; and it is a pathetic coincidence that he also, like Captain Middlemist,

AN ASHANTI KING COMING IN STATE TO THE RECEPTION

had missed the happiness of seeing his first-born child. Death is no respecter of persons, and it is sorrowful to have to relate that all the combatant officers who died from disease during this campaign were married men, whose loss would be more acutely felt than that of others without family ties.

Almost daily, fresh capitulations came in, and on the 20th the chiefs of twelve Atchuma towns surrendered unconditionally. This was cheering, when one remembered that they had stirred up many to revolt, and fought so stubbornly in the very last encounter ; and a not unwelcome rumour was propagated that Ashanti envoys had been sent into French territory to implore intercession there. Five days later, however, one's hopes sank somewhat, when it was stated that Kwabina Cheri had got together a force at Bechim, and that a body of the rebels had collected a coupl of days' march westwards, with the intention of intercepting the friendly Juabin levies.

As the result of this information, Colonel Sir James Willcocks decided to send out forthwith two columns, which were more convenient than one very large one inasmuch as the villages were incapable of holding more than a limited number of people, and under these circumstances it was easier to feed the men. They were to clear out these hornets' nests by penetrating into and subduing all the rebel country in the extreme north-west, which had not yet had the mark of the white man's displeasure put upon it. Major Montanaro was to command one, composed of one 75-m/m gun, and seven hundred and fifty men of the W.A.F.F. and C.A.R. ; and Major Browne, one of the most recently arrived officers, and the second in command of the W.A.R., was to have charge of the other, which was composed of five hundred W.A.R., and the remaining men of the 3rd Bn. W.A.F.F. Their destination was to be Berekum, going through Adumasi, and they were to take rations for twenty-eight days. The dates of departure were the 1st and 2nd of November respectively. Their orders were to attack any remaining chieftains who might have taken refuge in that district compel their surrender, or drive them into the forest and to sternly suppress all disaffection. Such a very long outing, in the tired-out condition in which the troops were, was not wholly welcome, but the men were as keen as ever to go, after the tribute paid by the Commandant to the Ashanti Field Force, showing his appreciation of the services rendered by all ranks under him, in which he alluded to them as "the officers, N.C.O.'s, and men, who have already been called, time after time, to march and fight, in the worst season of the year, in this unhealthy climate." The particular months during which this campaign had been in progress were, as we know, no choice of the white man; in fact, until this time, expeditions had always been kept waiting until the rains were over, it having been the general opinion that operations were impossible at this season of the year. No doubt the same course would have been pursued in this case, had Kumasi fort never been besieged. The progress of the columns was eminently satisfactory, despite the fact that the late rains had not quite concluded, and in consequence increased the hardship, particularly at first. That they got no fighting was really a matter for congratulation instead of regret; for the flame of strength, in most of their constituent units, had burnt so low that a little more, and it might have gone out altogether. The kings of Techimaim and Inkwanta both surrendered on the 9th to Major Montanaro. At Bechim opposition had been expected, and in consequence the two columns had been previously concentrated. On arrival here, four columns, each two hundred strong, went out in all directions for a distance of about five miles, confiscating and collecting supplies. One of these parties, in the execution of its orders, went to Jemo, and captured a hundred guns; and Chief Adada gave himself up as a prisoner of war. Three hundred and fifty men, under Captain Gordon, C.A.R., were then left here as a garrison, in a redoubt about a hundred yards square, which had just been constructed by the troops with the assistance of their late enemies. The remainder of the men then continued on their march. On the 11th, Major Montanaro reached Adumasi, where he dropped three hundred men, and proceeded next day on his way to Berekum. This latter part of the march, from Inkwanta onwards, was extremely trying, owing to the heat of the sun. The forest had been left behind, and open country gained, which afforded no shade. Not only was no opposition met with, but the natives were delighted when they saw the troops, and were glad to surrender. The few isolated chiefs who wished to remain on the war-path were out of sympathy with the remainder of their people. In fact, at Adumasi, the Chief turned out in state to receive the column, offering presents in token of submission. Everywhere the same tale was told, namely, that the majority of the people had been forced, by fear of punishment, to join in the rebellion against the white man; and that the Kumasis were the real cause of the war, which we did not find difficult to believe from what we had noticed, and from the much more stubborn way in which they had fought. Major Browne, who had been left at Adumasi, at this time received secret information, from the daughter of a murdered friendly native, that Kwabina Cheri, then the Commander-in-Chief of the scattered Ashanti forces, was inthe neighbourhood. In consequence, a hundred men W.A.F.F., and two subalterns, were sent out to effect his capture. They surrounded his retreat with their men, and on entering the village, not only caught this rebel chief, but many of his followers, together with much loot. On top of this good news came that of Major Montanaro's safe arrival, with one hundred and thirty-five men, at Berekum, where several more chieftains had come in, and the country found to be equally friendly.

All the leaders of the rebellion of any account whatever were now prisoners, numbering between sixty and seventy, and nearly all at Kumasi, but King Kofi Kofia, who had been so often hemmed in, cornered, and outflanked, was still at large, having fled in terror to the extreme north-west. Some of the submitted rebels were sent to track him down, and duly brought him in, thus leaving only one name on the list of " wanted." This person was, however, the most important of all, and was none other than the Queen-mother Ya Ashantiwah, of Ejesu. However, she, too, was caught, and the campaign was finally concluded.

On November 23rd these two columns reached Kumasi, with all their surrendered chiefs, and nearly one hundred guns, but with over four hundred sick out of a total of two thousand, after this march of more than two hundred miles. Kwabina Cheri was tried by the military commission, and found guilty of having been an accessory after the fact to the bloody murder of eighty wretched rubber traders in April, at Adumasi ; and he was hanged outside the fort. He died as game as he had fought. He marched to the scaffold with the utmost *sang-froid*, with a look of contemptuous and undying hate upon his face ; in fact, his bearing was so manly that an involuntary murmur of admiration rose from the crowd of onlookers. It was on the 24th of November that the memorable and gratifying despatch, containing the words, " The campaign is at an end," reached the Secretary of State for the Colonies in London, from the Commandant of the Ashanti Field Force in Kumasi. A few days later Colonel Sir James Willcocks and the headquarter staff left for Cape Coast, through a two-mile avenue of troops and friendly chiefs, drawn up in state to render this last honour to the hero of Kumasi, and was afterwards met at Cape Coast in civic state, and presented with an address of thanks. In reply to it, he modestly refused to acknowledge his success as a personal matter, but extolled at the finish, as he had ever done, those under his command. What a contrast was this return to the march out! Now all the populace, white and black, had turned out to welcome the victor of Ashanti terrorism ; bands, triumphal arches, and gaily decorated streets, took the place of apathetic misgiving. With the exception of a strong garrison to be left in the fort, composed of the latest arrivals of the W.A.R. and C.A.R., under the command of Lieutenant-Colonel Burroughs, the troops moved down for transportation to their homes.

The good effects of this expedition are bound to be plentiful and far-reaching, particularly as delay will not be allowed to waste the opportunity. The most warlike race in West Africa has, for the first time in its history, been completely crushed, and has, moreover, owned to its inability to contend with the white man, and to its humiliation at his hands. It is not improbable that a small number of troops may be raised, as an experiment, from these fierce Ashantis (for the Gold Coast troops will undoubtedly have to be increased); and, judging by the manner in which they have fought, they ought to make excellent soldiers. There is every reason to expect that the previously projected light railway from Cape Coast to Kumasi will now be constructed, parts of which can to-day be seen lying at the roadside, silent testimony to a good but uncompleted scheme. Steam engines perhaps civilise more effectually than missionaries, and the railway will not only transport produce to the sea, but play its part in the abolition of human sacrifice and kindred savage customs. The direct trade route from the north is now opened up, and the Ashanti will probably soon be making the broad road for this purpose, which he promised to do twenty-seven years ago, but has hitherto never accomplished. The country, ere long, will be prospected, and it is impossible to forecast what this may mean if gold is ultimately found in the quantities in which it is believed to exist. In short, nobody can estimate the good that may come out of this recently stamped-out rebellion. It has been an expense; it has depressed West Africa to a certain extent, and the Gold Coast in particular; but just as the removal of some festering growth by a painful operation will lay a patient on his back awhile only that he may arise a healthier and stronger man, so assuredly will good come out of this; and the Gold Coast will benefit by far the most.

Thus then has ended the Ashanti War of 1900, a brilliant chapter in British history, another bright record of British pluck among the many which have occurred in Her Majesty's long reign of prosperity to her Empire. To Colonel Sir James Willcocks' ability and undaunted energy its success is chiefly due. No commander could have been asked to overcome greater difficulties, and to operate in a worse climate, or at a more unhealthy and almost impossible season of the year. Perforce ill supplied with troops, having an inadequate complement of British officers, with no regular staff, and at first only a small stock of war material, it is marvellous to see what he has achieved, and what his force, mostly composed of untried recruits, has accomplished under his direction. To them is all honour due. The absence, for the first time, of British soldiers, has made the cost of this campaign incomparably less than it would otherwise have been, and it has made it more expeditious.

Indeed, this fact has made operations possible in the wet season ; for white troops could not have stood the climate during the rains as the black soldiers did. In a certain sense, also, the decisive termination of the campaign is due to the same cause ; for it is quite probable that the resistance of the enemy might have melted away before Europeans, or at any rate have been much less stubborn than that which they offered to the native troops whom they expected so easily to overcome, without any conclusive results having been attained.

The casualties in action and cases of invaliding have, I believe, made a record, as will be seen from the accompanying statistics. The average strength of the Europeans was one hundred and fifty-two, and out of these were :

Killed in action (all officers)...	9
Died from disease	7
Wounded	52
Invalided from wounds and sickness...	54
Number of admissions to hospital	360

It will be seen that the whole force averaged between two and three visits to hospital.

The average strength of the native force was two thousand eight hundred and four, of which were:

Killed in action (also 1 Native officer) 113
Died from disease 102
Wounded (also 3 Native officers) 680
Missing 41
Admissions to hospital 4,963

Of the carriers, &c., the strength was fifteen thousand, which was thus reduced:

Killed in action 1
Died from disease 400
Admissions to hospital 5,000

Native Levies killed in action 50

To summarise, the composition of the Ashanti Field Force, the ranks of which were so sadly thinned, was as follows:

W.A.F.F., 1st and 2nd Bns. 8 companies
W.A.F.F., 3rd Bn. (Southern
   Nigeria) ... ... Detachment numerically
                               unequal to 2 companies
W.A.R. ... ... 1 weak battalion
C.A.R. ... ... 1 weak battalion
Lagos Hausa Force ... ... Less than 200 men
S.L.F.P. ... ... 50 rank and file
W.I.R. ... ... 1 gun detachment

Towards the conclusion, some of the Gold Coast Constabulary, originally of the besieged garrison, were enabled to assist in garrison duty on the lines of communication.

The Commandant's past distinguished record is attested sufficiently by his breast full of orders and

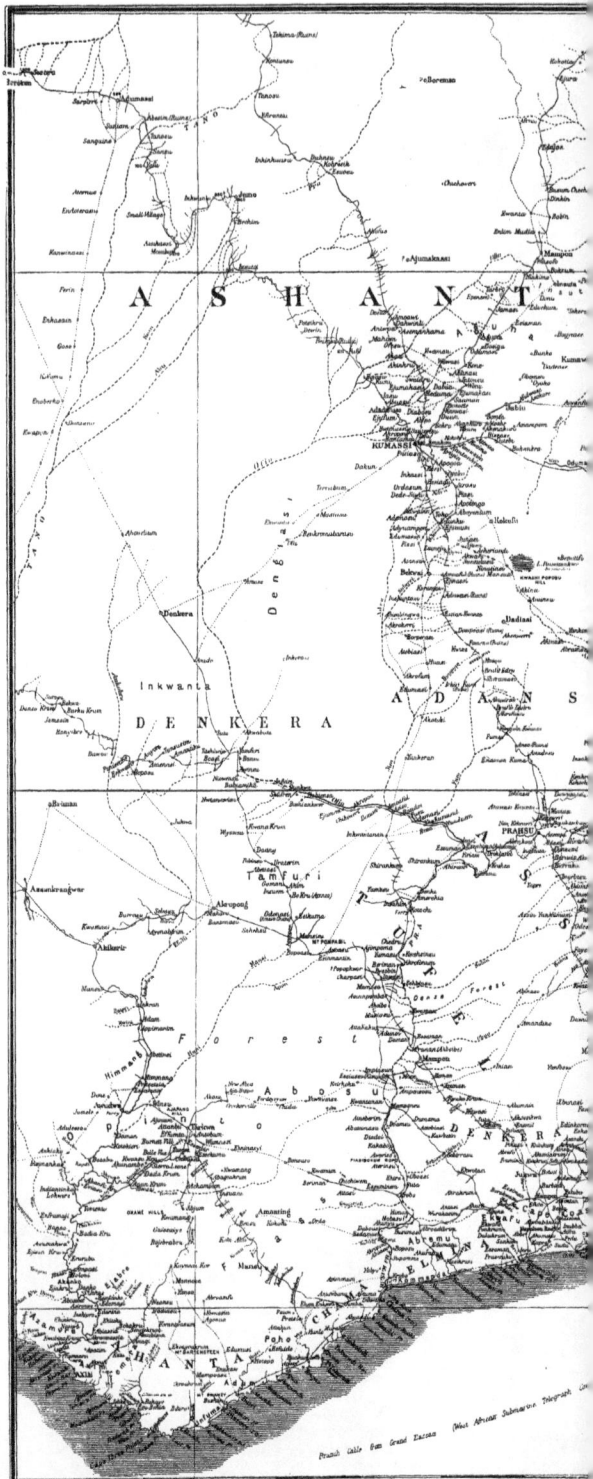

ASHANT

KUMASSI

DENKERA

Inkwanta

ADANS

PRAHSU

Tamfuri

Forest

Abou

DENKERA

Abenu

AHANTA

Dengira

Borumao

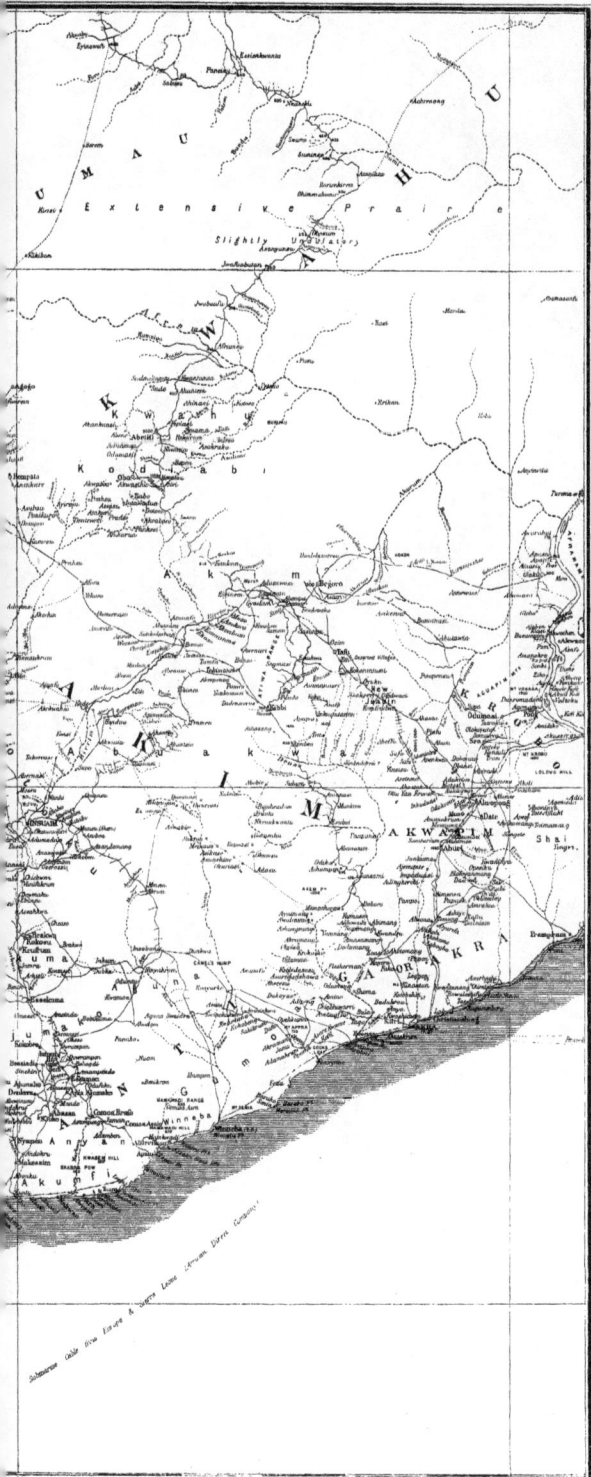

medals. Not only had he the complete confidence, but the highest personal esteem—I might almost say affection—of every officer and man in the Ashanti Field Force. There is not one of us who does not wish him every success in the future, who is not proud to have served under his command in this campaign, and who would not be glad to do so again; but next time, by preference, in a healthier climate, where physical fitness ought to enable all to do their duty even better.

www.ingramcontent.com/pod-product-compliance
Lightning Source LLC
Chambersburg PA
CBHW020806100426
42814CB00014B/354/J